Primary Commodities and Economic Development

Our post-industrialized global economy has achieved spectacular success and pushed back poverty to an extent previously thought impossible. This success is ultimately based on the continued supply of both renewable and non-renewable resources. Will this supply of primary commodities remain sufficient to support global economic growth? Why are the gains for countries specializing in commodity production often so limited? Can commodity-dependent countries diversify into other economic activities?

Primary Commodities and Economic Development addresses the changing position of primary commodities in the world economy and investigates their importance for commodity-exporting underdeveloped countries. The book commences with a review of the theoretical foundations for interdependence between commodity specialization and economic underdevelopment. Having related the role of commodity exports and the commodity terms of trade to growth models relevant to developing economies, the discussion shifts to an in-depth review of the statistical properties of the commodity terms of trade. The review of commodity price trends at the global level is then rounded off with a series of country case studies showing the concrete threats and opportunities surrounding commodity specialization.

This book will be essential reading for those with an interest in development economics and international economics, as well as for scholars of natural resources and agricultural economics.

Stephan Pfaffenzeller is a lecturer in economics at the University of Liverpool, UK. He has extensive research experience in the area of resource and development economics and has published on this subject in a number of peer-reviewed journals and book contributions.

Routledge Studies in Development Economics

Primary Commodities and Economic Development

Stephan Pfaffenzeller

Routledge
Taylor & Francis Group

LONDON AND NEW YORK

First published 2017 by Routledge

2 Park Square, Milton Park, Abingdon, Oxfordshire OX14 4RN
52 Vanderbilt Avenue, New York, NY 10017

Routledge is an imprint of the Taylor & Francis Group, an informa business

First issued in paperback 2019

British Library Cataloguing in Publication Data
A catalogue record for this book is available from the British Library

Library of Congress Cataloging in Publication Data
A catalog record for this book has been requested

ISBN: 978-1-138-01443-5 (hbk)
ISBN: 978-0-367-86959-5 (pbk)

Typeset in Times New Roman
by Sunrise Setting Ltd, Brixham, UK

Contents

Figures

Tables

1 Introduction

The production and extraction of agricultural products and other primary commodities is among the most basic of human economic activities. It has also long been linked to preoccupations about existential sustainability and future prosperity, so much so that concern with it traditionally lies at the heart of economics and of visions of economic development. In discussions of economics, concern with primary commodities has traditionally been linked to pessimistic visions of the future and, somewhat paradoxically, such pessimism has been rooted in predictions of commodity prices that are either rising or falling.

Economics has long focused on the constraints under which human production and human attempts to cope with scarcity must develop. It is the formulation of such a law of resource constraints that can be seen as one of the early contributions to what was to evolve into modern economics as a social science. It was Thomas Malthus who famously predicted that exponentially increasing human populations would eventually meet the limits imposed by a linearly increasing food supply. At this point food prices will rise as the higher population competes for increasingly scarce resources and the size of the population may eventually be checked by starvation. Rising commodity prices are thus seen as a sign of mounting resource scarcity and eventually of crisis. Modern predictions of resource exhaustion were made in the Club of Rome's *The Limits to Growth* study in more recent times.

Some years prior to the Club of Rome's pessimistic prognosis, another analysis of primary commodity markets anticipated the opposite. In what has become known as the Prebisch–Singer hypothesis, primary commodity prices, which had been falling for some time before the mid twentieth century were predicted to enter a period of permanent decline, thus trapping commodity-dependent developing countries in a position of low income and underdevelopment. While the Prebisch–Singer hypothesis directly opposes the predictions in a Malthusian tradition, they have one common element: a fundamentally pessimistic outlook. It is a peculiar characteristic of long run commodity market analysis that its predictions seem to range from the pessimistic to the apocalyptic regardless of the anticipated direction of change.

Of course, extreme price movements in either direction can have disruptive impacts on related markets or be manifest as symptoms of such disruptions. Economics should highlight mechanisms and development likely to lead to such disruptions and this was probably the objective in exploring the implications of either global resource exhaustion or sustained real commodity price decay. The present volume, however, will concentrate on the latter scenario and ask the empirical question to what extent the concerns originally voiced in the Prebisch–Singer hypothesis, and the more complex dependency theories inspired by it, have materialized.

Economic development can be measured in a number of ways, but one of the main criteria considered consistently has been the level of per capita income attained either in real terms or relative to richer economies. In other words, the conventional focus of economic development is either on per capita income growth in real terms or on convergence in relative terms. Chapter 2 places developing economies in this context and relates questions of growth and convergence to the condition of commodity export dependence. Following a review of the basics of neoclassical growth theory, the question of commodity dependence will be considered in the context of balance of payments constrained growth.

The notion of a tightening balance of payments constraint is itself intrinsically linked to the concept of a persistent net barter terms of trade decline for commodity export dependent economies. Chapter 3 is therefore dedicated to a study of long run trend movements in real commodity prices. This chapter will survey the past debate on empirical trend estimates and statistical trend measurements as well as commenting on the likely magnitude of any inferred trends. In addition to discussing the development of composite commodity price indices, the chapter will look at the evolution of individual, representative commodity price series.

Having covered the background scenario in terms of relevant growth concepts and commodity price trends, Chapter 4 reviews a number of country cases. In these case studies individual country growth and convergence experiences will be juxtaposed with their trade exposure and the evolution of commodity dependence over the years for which data are available. This discussion will draw on detailed trade data to track not only the size of the commodity sector as a whole but the distribution of commodity exports over sub-sectors. These trade data can then be placed in the context of general economic developments as well as the wider country background to assess the nature and persistence of commodity dependence as well as its qualitative change.

The choice of country cases for such a background discussion necessarily has to be selective given the overall reach of the present volume. However, an attempt has been made to present cases that are representative of the changing nature of trading relations for commodity-dependent developing and transition economies in recent years and over the preceding decades of the twentieth century.

The study of individual country cases, the evolution of commodity prices, and their interpretation against a background of balance of payments constrained growth can in their turn be interpreted in a unified setting, and to discuss the question of how the phenomenon of commodity export dependence in developing nations has evolved over time. The final chapter will therefore chart the changing incidence of commodity export dependence. The discussion will proceed to address the correlational pattern between developing country export earnings and economic growth and ask to what extent they are consistent with the notion of balance of payments constrained growth. Both the general evidence on commodity price trends and the country case studies can then be interpreted in this context.

Throughout, the empirical discussion concentrates on data from the twentieth century to the first decade of the twenty-first century. For estimates of long run commodity price trends, data are available going back to 1900, but for most of the subsequent empirical review, data were obtained from multilateral organizations, commonly extending back no further than 1960. At times, data availability is more limited than this. Limited data are a common problem in the study of developing economies, not least because data reporting can be preceded by policy or research interests. Detailed cross-national data on the net barter terms of trade were only included in the World Development Indicators from 1980, after policy interest in their role grew strongly from the 1950s onwards.

A further background fact to bear in mind throughout is the importance of the early twenty-first-century commodity price boom. This strong performance in a number of commodity prices took off in the first decade of the current century, experienced a brief interruption following the 2008 financial crisis, and may be coming to an end at the time of writing. This strong commodity price performance has been attributed to the influence of the Chinese economic take-off and is seen by some as the beginning of an upwards trend in commodity prices more generally.

The topic of primary commodity markets and economic development is likely to remain of interest for some time to come, even if the more extreme predictions in this area have consistently failed to materialize. This book[1] will survey the evidence on this topic to date and discuss it against the background of the recent commodity price boom. It aims to show that the focus of relevant research on development and convergence should increasingly be placed on the characteristics of individual country experiences in preference to the analysis of broad global constraints.

Note

1 I thank Dr. Gareth Liu-Evans for his help and advice as well as my family for their patience. All errors and omissions are naturally my own responsibility.

2   Developing country growth and the commodity terms of trade

2.1   Introduction

The evolution of primary commodity prices and commodity supplies can be seen as a constraint on industrial production and developing country growth, with price increases tending to constrain industrial production while tending to increase the unit value of developing country exports. The limits on the viability of industrial production produced by rising resource prices (and the contrary effect of falling prices) are intuitively plausible. The mechanism by which the economic transition of developing countries is constrained by primary commodity prices is less apparent and will be discussed in this chapter.

The chapter will commence by surveying developed and developing country specific growth models before focusing on the perspective offered by Thirlwall's balance of payments constrained growth model. The focus on the balance of payments constraint will enable an analysis of the role commodity-based export earnings can play in the transition towards a developed economy with a fully capitalized formal sector.

2.2   Modelling growth: the benchmark growth model

Among the various growth models present in the modern applied and theoretical literature, the Solow growth model continues to occupy a position as a benchmark model for empirical work as well as a conceptually simple framework for the introduction to growth theory more generally.[1] This chapter will start with a brief review of the model before discussing its drawbacks and limitations in the empirical study of developing country growth.

Some of the Solow model's core assumptions, such as the constant depreciation rate or the constant savings propensity, are non-trivial simplifications but do not seem to be especially problematic for any particular group of economies. Others appear to make it a priori unsuitable for the study of developing country growth. Among these is the assumption of a closed economy coupled with the assumption of full and efficient employment. The full and efficient employment assumption can be read as implying not only an allocatively efficient market economy, but also an internal market large enough to exhaust gains from specialization. The full employment assumption in turn assumes the existence of an economy which is sufficiently efficient to have absorbed surplus labour from more traditional sectors of the economy – a non-trivial simplifying assumption in the case of many developing economies, which are conventionally prone to exhibiting a dualist economic structure.

The formal model specification only considers three factors of production in its basic form: capital, labour, and technical efficiency. The production function for this model is often cast in Cobb–Douglas form, assuming linear homogeneity such that

$$Y = AK^\alpha L^{1-\alpha}, \quad 0 \leq \alpha \leq 1, \tag{2.1}$$

which can alternatively be expressed in per unit of labour terms as

$$y = Ak^\alpha, \quad 0 \leq \alpha \leq 1, \tag{2.2}$$

where $y = Y/L$ and $k = K/L$. It is easy to show that this production function has diminishing marginal returns to capital per unit of labour such that $\frac{\partial y}{\partial k} > 0$ and $\frac{\partial^2 y}{\partial k^2} < 0$, and that $y = 0$ for $k = 0$. A constant and exogenously given proportion s of this output is then assumed to be saved in each period, yielding total per unit of labour savings of $S = sy$. Since capital markets are assumed to clear at any point in time ($S^* = I$), this savings function also identifies actual investment per unit of labour at each level of capital intensity. Equilibrium in this model is produced by interaction with the break-even investment requirement, that is, the amount of investment required to keep the level of capital intensity constant.

In defining the break-even investment requirement, it is usually assumed that a constant proportion δ of the capital stock depreciates in each time period while a constant proportion (n) of the labour force is added to the existing labour force each period. The break-even investment constraint is then obtained as a function of these constant proportions and the measure of capital intensity as

$$BEI = (n + \delta)k. \tag{2.3}$$

This break-even investment requirement is intuitively plausible: if a given proportion of the capital stock wears out and is written off each period then a corresponding amount of investment is required to replace it and keep the capital stock from falling. If the capital labour ratio (that is, the level of capital intensity) is to be stabilized in addition, while population growth leads to regular additions to the labour force, then additional investment in capital is required to equip each generation of new workers as well as the previous one. This linear break-even investment requirement function will have a unique locus of intersection with the savings function so long as

$$\frac{\partial y}{\partial k} \lim_{k \to \infty} \to 0, \quad \frac{\partial y}{\partial k} \lim_{k \to 0} \to \infty, \tag{2.4}$$

which rules out that the break-even investment requirement function can be consistently positioned above or below the savings function. The equilibrium identified by this model is illustrated in Figure 2.1.

Both the break-even investment requirement function and the production and savings functions pass through the origin. The savings function, being a fixed proportion of the production function, lies under the production function while following its trajectory. A unique steady-state equilibrium is produced at the point where the break-even investment requirement line intersects the savings function. At this point, savings just cover the break-even investment requirement and stabilize the prevailing level of capital intensity.

At any point below the steady-state equilibrium, investment adds more to the capital stock than would be required to stabilize the capital to labour ratio. Capital intensity therefore increases and the build-up of capital adds to the total amount of output and output per unit of labour. As the capital intensity of the production process increases, the diminishing marginal returns property of the production function assures that the net additions to capital per unit of labour become progressively smaller, until they reach a zero value at the steady-state equilibrium. The system described in the Solow growth model will therefore converge to the steady-state equilibrium but will not expand beyond it, since additions to the capital stock beyond the steady-state equilibrium point do not produce sufficient extra savings to stabilize this new, higher level of capital intensity. At the steady-state point, then, output growth from capital accumulation is zero, and all further additions to national output arise from technical progress, *i.e.* that is, additions to A.[2]

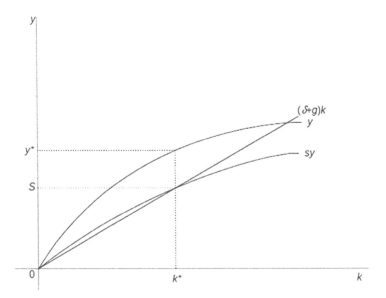

Figure 2.1 Steady-state equilibrium.

Note: y^*/k^*: equilibrium levels of income/capital per unit of labour.

The Solow growth model has attracted criticism for a number of reasons. One of its main weaknesses is its lack of explanatory power in accounting for long run growth performance: long run growth – in this framework – is a leftover, the Solow residual. In measurement, it is a by-product of the convergence process that is attributed to progress by mere assumption. More modern growth models have attempted to model growth based on intertemporal optimizing decisions or have attempted to model the innovation process directly – see Romer (2006, Chapters 2 and 3) for examples. This volume is primarily concerned with the importance of primary commodities for developing countries and will accordingly focus on growth models that are appropriate for commodity-dependent developing countries.

One of the Solow model's redeeming features is its relatively straightforward implementation in practical terms. One approach to doing so is to attempt to empirically estimate the explanatory power of the model per se; see, for example, Mankiw, Romer, and Weil (1992) for an extended version of the basic model, accounting for the role of human capital. More frequently, and more pertinently for the present subject, the drivers of steady-state convergence are empirically controlled to investigate the impact of other growth determinants – see Greenaway, Sapsford, and Pfaffenzeller (2007). A simple empirical model takes the form

$$\dot{y} = \alpha + \beta_1 pop + \beta_2 Iy + \varepsilon, \tag{2.5}$$

where $\dot{y}$ is the growth rate of income, for which data are available in levels and per capita terms for most countries; Iy is the growth rate of capital, which is commonly proxied by the gross fixed capital formation, a statistic conventionally available from national accounts; pop is the labour force growth rate and is normally proxied by the population growth rate; while ε is the model error. α, β_1, and β_2 are coefficients. The coefficient on the constant (α) does not have a counterpart in the theoretical basis for growth accounting but is usually included in regression-based estimating equations for technical reasons. With $\dot{y}$ as dependent variable, it should also capture residual trend growth after accounting for Iy and pop. The coefficient estimate $\hat{\beta}_1$ is expected to be positive, while $\hat{\beta}_2$ would be expected to be positive where the dependent variable relates to the level of gross domestic product (GDP). It would be expected to be negative for per capita GDP since an increase in the labour force tends to lower the capital to labour ratio, other things being equal.

When applied to mature, developed economies, empirical implementations of this model should identify a residual growth rate not attributable to factor accumulation. This Solow residual is conventionally interpreted as capturing growth attributable to technological progress as a driver of long run per capita income growth, although variant interpretations allowing for additional drivers can be found in the literature – see, for example, Mankiw, Romer, and Weil (1992) as discussed previously. Under the model's assumptions, including that of full employment, it therefore follows that increments in savings cannot drive economic growth in the long term. A higher savings propensity would initially increase

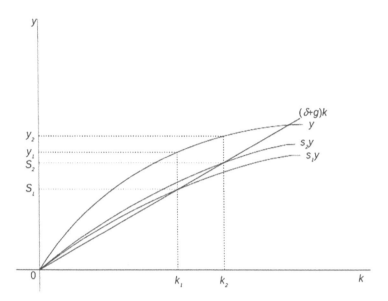

Figure 2.2 The impact of increased savings.

Note: y^*/k^* equilibrium levels of income/capital per unit of labour.

the amount saved at a given income level and thus make room for additional investment. Further additions to capital would also increase the amount of capital per worker in the production process leading to further diminishing marginal returns. Thus, while income growth would temporarily accelerate following such an increase in savings, this faster growth would be a temporary phenomenon which comes to an end when the induced marginal additions to income have fallen to a level where the extra savings generated are just sufficient to satisfy the higher break-even investment requirement. At this point, the level of income per unit of labour would indeed have increased to a permanently higher level. Its growth rate, however, has only accelerated temporarily during the process of convergence to the higher level of per capita income.

This process is illustrated in Figure 2.2: as a higher proportion of income is saved, the savings curve tilts upwards, intersecting the break-even investment requirement line at a higher level of capital intensity (k_2) with a correspondingly higher level of per capita income (y_2). This higher income level does mark a new steady state, however, so that long run growth performance cannot be explained by reference to capital accumulation alone.

Natural resources, including primary commodities, are something this model largely abstracts from. Some adaptation is possible though, and Romer (2006) presents a modified version of the basic model allowing for a tightening resource constraint. This modification would in principle allow for negative growth, but empirically the impact has been minor, yielding no more than a slightly reduced long term growth rate. The key role of primary commodity exports for developing countries is not addressed by this approach, since there are more fundamental deviations from the benchmark model that are of relevance here.

It is crucial to note that the above conclusion on steady-state convergence depends on the assumption of full and efficient factor employment. In an underdeveloped economy with a sustained availability of surplus labour, this convergence process would be by no means guaranteed. If the economy's labour force is not fully employed, so that an increase in the amount of capital available attracts new labour into the capital intensive production process, then K can increase while K/L, the measure of capital intensity, remains stable. In empirical studies relying on population growth as a proxy for labour force growth in the conventional way, this change would simply go undetected since full employment is assumed among the constituent premises of the model. The failure of capital intensity to increase during the accumulation process also implies that marginal returns to capital need not diminish, so that the expansion of output could well be sustained for longer, in which case the limiting factor could well be the availability of investable capital and the existence of viable mechanisms for its efficient allocation.

To discuss this possibility in more detail, a more formal analysis of the labour surplus economy and its long term convergence to full and efficient factor employment are needed. The transition from an underdeveloped economy to a mature one with fully employed resources is likely to occur in stages. The maturation process can be expected to involve the gradual absorption of underemployed labour resources into an expanding formal sector. In an open economy, integrating into global trade and investment relations, the materialization and speed of this process can at least in part depend on the availability of foreign exchange, which in turn will at least in part be a function of export earnings. It is to this subject that the remainder of this chapter is dedicated.

2.3 Stages of transition

The transition towards a mature economy with full and efficient allocation of production factors from a pre-industrial state is bound to be non-instantaneous. Rostow's analysis offers a traditional perspective on the sequence of structural transformations in this process of economic development in defining five discrete stages of growth. These stages were originally described in Rostow (1997) as follows:

i   Traditional society: this phase is characterized by traditional, pre-industrial modes of production and no or little innovation creating an intertemporally constant limit on output. This type of economic structure can be expected to coexist with a social structure based on this economic sub-stratum and directed to its preservation.

ii Preparation for take-off: This stage is typically characterized by the emergence of a modern, innovative sector which, at this point in development, coexists with the traditional sector.

iii   Take-off: at this stage, savings and investment rates rise and the innovative sector becomes a key driver of economic growth.

iv   Drive to mass consumption: savings and investment rise yet further and diminishing marginal returns set in in some industries.

v   Mass consumption: at this stage, the economy is structurally mature, and consumption moves beyond covering subsistence needs.

The subject context of commodity export dependence and economic development and convergence is clearly focused on stages i–iii, with the transition to take-off a particular point of interest. The movement towards establishing even the preconditions for take-off requires the traditional sector to generate a sufficient surplus to support an innovative formal sector and – in many cases – to establish access to foreign exchange earnings. Rostow (1997) notes further that these economic conditions are necessary but not sufficient for a stage transition.

These economic preconditions are seen as being further complemented by institutional changes that permit challenges to the social order that had until then complemented the premodern economic mode of production. Often, these institutional transformations will occur in the form of nationally unifying reform or in response to an external shock (cf. Rostow 1997, Chapter 3).

A necessary but not sufficient condition for take-off to eventually occur is the availability of sufficient surplus capital. For this surplus capital to stimulate the formal sector, there needs to be an appropriate economic infrastructure to transfer investable funds from the locus of their initial accumulation to their investment destination in the innovative sector. This latter point presupposes sufficient productive investment demand within the domestic economy and this latter factor is identified by Rostow (1997) as a frequently present bottleneck. This corollary requirement on domestic investment demand appears plausible, given the a priori possibility not only of attracting capital from abroad but also to direct domestic capital to foreign destinations: international capital flow channels should attract foreign investment if investment demand from sufficiently attractive domestic projects is present. Conversely, the absence of such domestic opportunities would see the leakage of successfully mobilized domestic investment capital to foreign destinations.

Rostow's analysis of the dynamics of economic transition differs in key respects from the approaches conventionally associated with a focus on commodity dependence. While Rostow (1997) focuses on the structure of domestic investment demand and the quality of domestic institutions, another perspective concentrates more narrowly on the transfer of resources from the informal to the formal sector and identifies the role of the traditional sector for economic development on this basis. It is this analysis of the interaction of two structurally distinct sub-sectors of the economy to which the present discussion turns next.

2.4 Dualist structure and the labour surplus economy

A stylized fact characterizing the structure of developing economies – those in the earlier stages of industrialization, at any rate – is the bifurcation of the economy into an advanced, formal sector and an underdeveloped informal sector. The formal sector can operate at the technological and organizational level of advanced economies, or can at least feed into their international supply chains. Its activities are therefore likely to be recorded in official statistics and its production process is likely to be relatively capital intensive.

The informal sector, by contrast, tends to be focused on subsistence production, which is often not recorded and tends to operate at a very low level of capital intensity. This latter focus is its pivotal characteristic, so much so that labour located in the informal sector is commonly considered to be underemployed or unemployed to a point where its marginal product is zero. The informal sector's excessive labour endowment therefore creates a *surplus labour reservoir*, which can provide labour resources to an expanding formal sector that offers a wage premium over the subsistence wage.

The presence of a dualist economic structure during the early stages of the development process is almost guaranteed by the simple fact that this transition is part of a multistage process in which the initially dominant traditional sector is gradually displaced by an expanding formal sector with which it initially coexists. As a basic stylized fact it is routinely noted in textbooks on the subject (see Smith and Todaro 2008 for an example), though the common reference point for its incorporation into development economics is Lewis (1954), who models the labour supply as unlimited. The background assumption of an unlimited labour supply is clearly confined to the early stages of the economic transition process and thus to a medium term horizon if the transition is in fact successful. As labour resources are gradually withdrawn from the informal sector, the surplus labour stock is progressively exhausted as the economy approaches full employment. At some point, the marginal product of labour in the informal sector will become positive and the wage premium offered in the formal sector will have to rise as the marginal product – and thus the opportunity cost of labour – in the informal sector is forced up. When this point is reached, the economy transitions away from the surplus labour scenario envisaged by Lewis (1954).

One factor of interest in this process is the relationship between capital accumulation and the rate of return on capital. The rate of return on capital is conventionally expected to decrease as capital intensity increases, that is, as the amount of capital in production increases relative to the amount of labour. The general law of diminishing marginal returns implies an analogous prediction for wages, that is, to factor payments to labour services, in a competitive labour market.

The characteristic property of a labour surplus economy is the stabilization of the capital to labour ratio during the early phases of capital accumulation as labour migration from the informal sector ensures that the quantity of labour employed increases in tandem with the added amount of capital in production so long as the constant wage premium remains available. A sustained period of capital accumulation can therefore coexist with a sustained period of high returns to capital. This high return on capital and investment can itself accelerate the convergence process by attracting foreign investment or through the reinvestment of retained domestic capital earnings, provided that the latter facilitate the acquisition of capital goods.

As will be discussed below, the question of whether this caveat will be met can depend crucially on the foreign exchange earnings mobilized by the formal sector.

Formally, and in general terms, the relationship between factor earnings is commonly expressed as

$$r = f'(k), \quad w = f'(k^{-1}), \quad f'(k) > 0, \quad f''(k) < 0, \tag{2.6}$$

where r is the rate of return on capital, w the wage rate, $k = K/L$ the capital to labour ratio, and $f()$ the production function. During the surplus labour stage, k will remain constant and r need not fall as L rises with K during the expansion of the formal sector. Diminishing marginal returns to capital will only set in as the surplus labour reservoir becomes exhausted. During this process, the rate of return on capital, r, will fall and w will rise. The reduction in r may come to an end because capital earnings converge on a feasibility or break-even constraint as in the Solow model discussed previously. Yet, even in the absence of such a constraint, the labour migration process from the subsistence sector to the formal sector is limited by the persistence of the wage gap between these two sectors.

One of the simplifying assumptions underlying Equation (2.6) is the abstraction from land rents. More problematic in the present case is the implied assumption of perfect competition driving factor earnings to their marginal products in a fully employed economy. The assumption that competitive pressure will drive fully employed capital resources to their most productive use and that they earn factor incomes close to their marginal products may be regarded as a defensible approximation even in a labour surplus economy. The same mechanism should not be expected to operate on labour earnings, however, precisely because labour initially has the status of a surplus resource and is therefore underemployed by definition.

During the surplus labour phase of the transition process, all that is required to attract further labour resources to match additional investment is a sufficiently high wage premium to motivate intersectoral migration. If the premium wage falls short of the marginal product of labour in the formal sector, there would simply be no market mechanism through which the wage would be driven up since there would be no competition for labour resources while the labour supply elasticity remains sufficiently high. The supply elasticity of labour is only predicted to fall once the surplus labour reservoir nears exhaustion.

While the wage rate is predicted to remain constant during the surplus labour phase discussed in Lewis (1954), wages can be expected to rise in both the formal and informal sectors as capital intensity increases in the formal sector as well as in the subsistence sector where labour is progressively withdrawn from a constant if rudimentary capital stock. The same general development would be observed if the capital stock in the subsistence sector does not remain constant but instead increases as agricultural mechanization takes place. In either case, labour intensity would tend to fall and the wages would tend to increase in both broad sectors. What cannot be predicted a priori based on the general discussion above is how the intersectoral wage gap will evolve during this process.

For the labour migration process to cease, industrial wage growth would have to slow down relative to subsistence sector wage growth at some point and continue to do so until the remaining wage gap is no longer sufficient to motivate relocation. More extensive modelling beyond the scope of the present volume would be required to address the dynamics of convergence. Experience from mature developed economies does, however, suggest that the major part of the labour force can be absorbed in the secondary and tertiary sectors while the primary sector ceases to operate at the subsistence level and accumulates capital in its turn.

One can observe then, that a dualist macroeconomic structure can persist, even as the unlimited labour supply approximation ceases to be an adequate characterization of the transition process. In this case, labour resources can continue to be attracted to the formal sector at an increasing premium as the formal sector expands and the economy matures. As importantly, the informal sector can reabsorb labour resources that become unemployed in an economic downturn – Griffith-Jones, Cailloux, and Pfaffenzeller (1999) discuss the operation of this process in the context of the 1998 Asian Currency Crisis. This role of the informal sector is set to diminish in importance as the economy matures and to the extent that the formal sector diversifies. It naturally remains strong, where a narrowly defined formal sector remains subject to substantial cyclical fluctuations.

With the completion of the convergence process, the economy should have reached a stage of maturity where its long term evolution can be adequately modelled by growth models such as the one proposed by Solow or more modern alternatives like the Ramsey–Kass–Koopmans model – again, the reader is referred to Romer (2006) for an introductory discussion. Labour absorption and capital deepening during the transition interval in turn require a sustained period of capital accumulation. The capital accumulation required to effect the transition in a contemporary context can be expected to rely on the importation of capital goods, and it is in this regard that the sustained availability of foreign exchange earnings can impose a constraint on the convergence process or enable its acceleration.

2.5 Thirlwall's law: economic growth and the balance of payments constraint

Given that the transfer of labour resources to the formal sector requires the accumulation of capital in the formal sector, the long term procurement and efficient investment of financial resources becomes a key concern for the transition process. If capital equipment is to be imported from abroad, the availability of financial resources in turn becomes a question of foreign exchange availability. To the extent that access to foreign currency for investment is limited, there will be a constraint on the domestic capitalization process imposed by the home economy's transactions with the rest of the world.

While this interpretation emphasizes the role of foreign exchange availability as a constraint on the supply side conditions for economic growth, a demand side interpretation is also possible. The preceding discussion of Rostow (1997) already placed investment demand in a key position in the economic transition process. The interpretation of the role of investment demand and of the related aspect of export demand in a small open economy is more complex than it may initially appear. Aside from the mainly quantitative effective demand aspect, the structural implications of well-developed investment demand and of a substantive export orientation matter. A strong export orientation in particular can be seen as a symptom of successful integration into the global economy. The effects of this integration can differ depending on the nature of the domestic economy's institutional infrastructure, and depending on the nature of its export specialization. The incidence of net export earnings is, however, frequently taken to define a constraint on sustainable growth.

A classic formal approach to modelling this constraint is the Thirlwall (1979) balance of payments constrained growth model (see also the discussion in McCombie and Thirlwall 1993). In this framework, export demand for a small open economy is assumed to be a negative function of the export price (relative to the price of imports) and a positive function of income in the rest of the world's economy, since more of the domestic economy's exports will be demanded abroad if foreign income rises. Likewise, the quantity of imports demanded varies inversely with the price of imports (relative to that of exports) while also increasing with domestic income.

Net export earnings are then represented by the trade balance, which can be expressed in domestic currency terms as

$$NX = P_X X - E P_M M, \tag{2.7}$$

where NX is the total value of net exports at a given point in time, P_X is the price of exports in domestic currency, P_M the price of imports in foreign currency, and X and M are the quantities traded of exports and imports respectively. E is the nominal exchange rate, defined as the domestic currency price of one unit of foreign currency. It should be noted that, with the exchange rate defined in this way, E increases in a depreciation (because the price of foreign currency increases) and falls in an appreciation (because the price of a unit of foreign currency falls in domestic currency terms).[3] In the absence of compensating financial flows, the amount of export earnings would then determine the amount of sustainable imports of foreign consumption goods or capital equipment.

While the concept of the trade balance is simple as well as familiar, it is worth spelling out how it is predicted to respond to a change in international relative prices. A decrease in export prices (P_X) tends to make exports internationally more competitive and thus unambiguously tends to drive up the quantity of exports. However, it will also reduce the amount of earnings received per unit of exports sold so that the impact of a price drop depends on the own price elasticity of export demand. If export demand is sufficiently price elastic, then the quantity increase should more than compensate the per unit earnings loss. A drop in sustainable export prices can then be seen primarily as an increase in competitiveness leading to higher export earnings. For price inelastic export demand, a drop in export prices would tend to lower export earnings since the dominant effect is that of lower per unit earnings which are at best ameliorated by a moderate traded quantity reaction. In that case, a drop in relative export prices is best conceptualized as a terms of trade deterioration lowering the foreign exchange earnings power of exports.

A similar analysis applies to *ceteris paribus* changes in the import price. If demand for imports is elastic, a rise in the price of imports will lead to an overall drop in the value of imports, because the induced fall in the import quantity more than compensates the increase in the price of remaining imports (and vice versa).

Fluctuations in the nominal exchange rate impact on the domestic currency value of imports and the foreign currency value of exports, for given values of product prices, thus directly impacting on the international prices of both trade flows. General predictions of the impact of exchange rate fluctuations under the *ceteris paribus* condition are usually taken to imply given product prices. This is conventionally the case for the derivation of the Marshall–Lerner condition as follows. Whether prices do, in fact, remain at their given levels will of course depend on circumstantial factors, such as the extent to which a given open economy is a price taker in international markets. Furthermore, the demand elasticities of traded goods demand will be central to the impact on net export earnings, with more price elastic demand tending to increase net export earnings following a devaluation while tending to lower them following an appreciation. This central role of demand elasticities has been formalized in the so-called Marshall–Lerner condition[4] as

$$|\eta_x| + |\eta_m| > 1, \tag{2.8}$$

that is, the absolute values of the own price elasticities of exports and imports with respect to the exchange rate have to sum to one or more, if a devaluation is to move an initially balanced trade balance into surplus. This rule applies equivalently to own price elasticities with the price expressed in the trade partner's currency, and can be modified for cases in which trade is not balanced initially – see Gandolfo (1994, Appendix C.1) for details. The consistent message in this discussion of net exports is that the consequences of international relative price variations crucially depend on the price elasticities of traded goods demand: the more elastic export and import demand, the more a relative price decline of domestic exports can help increase net export earnings; the less elastic demand is, the more a decline in relative export prices will mainly take the form of an international loss in earnings power.

These basic considerations are crucial for the interpretation of Thirlwall's model of balance of payments constrained growth. Thirlwall's growth model conceptualizes the sustainable growth rate of an open developing economy as a function of its foreign exchange earnings, and thus of its net export revenue. Thirlwall (1979) and McCombie and Thirlwall (1993) represent their model formally as follows:

$$y_{Bt} = \frac{(1+\eta+\psi)(p_{dt} - p_{ft} - e_t) + \varepsilon z_t}{\pi}, \tag{2.9}$$

where y_{Bt} is the balance of payments constrained growth rate of the domestic economy, z_t is the growth rate of world income, and ε the income elasticity of the rest of the world for the domestic economy's exports. η and ψ are the price elasticities of export and import demand respectively under the assumption that own and cross price elasticities coincide for both trade flows. p_{dt} is the contemporaneous domestic inflation rate, p_{ft} the contemporaneous foreign inflation rate, and e_t the contemporaneous rate of depreciation. Finally, π is the domestic income elasticity of import demand.

A detailed discussion of the model's derivation is presented in Thirlwall (1979), although it is worth noting the need to assume that domestic and foreign inflation rates closely approximate the growth rates of export and import prices respectively if this formulation is to be representative of the trade balance constraint. If this assumption is a good approximation and if the relative purchasing power parity condition holds in the long run then one should expect a long run equilibrium of $p_{dt} - p_{ft} - e_t = 0$ and a long term balance of payments constrained growth rate of

$$y_{Bt} = \frac{\varepsilon z_t}{\pi}, \tag{2.10}$$

which, in so far as $x_t = \varepsilon z_t$, implies that the long run balance of payments constrained growth rate is simply the growth rate of exports scaled by the domestic import elasticity: x_t / π. Based on the above model characteristics, price movements should mainly be of interest for short and medium term developments while the long term external constraint on the sustainable growth rate is based on longer term preferences or needs for traded products.

Thirlwall (1979) and Thirlwall and Hussain (1982) emphasize the quantitative over the structural aspects of the export demand constraint. From this perspective, export earnings drive growth to the extent that they facilitate access to foreign exchange. Under the criterion of foreign exchange procurement, the question of alternative sources for foreign currency clearly arises. Investment or other financial flows provide one such alternative source of foreign currency, and Thirlwall and Hussain (1982) modify the basic balance of payments constrained growth model to accommodate such flows. Their variant formulation of the model takes the form

$$y_{Bt} = \frac{(1 + \theta\eta + \psi)(p_{dt} - p_{ft} - e_t) + (1 - \theta)(f_t - p_{dt}) + \varepsilon z_t}{\pi}, \tag{2.11}$$

where θ is the proportion of import expenditure financed by export earnings, $f_t - p_{dt}$ is the amount of real financial inflows, and the remaining variables are as in Equation (2.9). Higher real investment flows can relax the balance of payments constraint in this specification. In principle, a permanently higher growth rate could then be sustained if repeated financial inflows, such as foreign aid, impact on the balance of payments constraint in a given period and are subsequently written off. In the more likely case where financial flows lead to future loan repayments or profit repatriations, the later financial outflow would of course tend to tighten the balance of payments constraint for a given level of export earnings. In theory, such an outflow might be compensated by increased export earnings which themselves could be based on previous successful foreign investment. Yet, the basic contention remains: from a quantitative, demand-based position, the loosening of the balance of payments constraint should be expected to have a temporary growth accelerating effect. In the long run, the role of export earnings should remain intact as discussed previously.

The primarily quantitative interpretation of the balance of payments constraint mechanism is implicitly limited with regards to its general explanatory power. As is observed by Thirlwall and Hussain (1982), it is not possible for all countries in the world to be simultaneously balance of payments constrained in this manner. If export participation is mainly interpreted as an indicator of international integration, this conclusion does not necessarily follow, of course: it is possible that all countries benefit from greater specialization, which in turn may correlate with a greater prominence of the comparative advantage driven export sector. With the focus on foreign exchange procurement and the limitation of a balance of payments constrained subset of national economies, the connection to developing and transition economies is easy to make. For developing countries with a dualist economic structure, the mobilization of capital to support the economic transition process would then clearly provide a relevant perspective.

It is worth considering the implications of this modelling framework for commodity-dependent developing economies in particular. A key concern for commodity-dependent developing economies are the elasticity characteristics of their export products. In Thirlwall's model, the balance of payments constraint on growth will tend to loosen, and accommodate a faster rate of growth, if export earnings increase.

If the price of commodity exports is in sustained decline relative to the price of imports, then the relative price term $p_{dt} - p_{ft} - e_t$ will be negative. The impact of this relative price decline on the sustainable growth rate is then determined by the magnitude of price elasticities. The price elasticities for traded goods (η, ψ) are assumed to be negative. If these elasticities sum to more than one in absolute value, that is, if traded goods demand is price elastic, then the product of the two negative terms $(p_{dt} - p_{ft} - e_t)$ and $(1 + \eta + \psi)$ will be positive so that increasingly competitive exports increase the amount of foreign exchange available and contribute to loosen the constraint on the domestic growth rate y_{Bt} (as in the discussion of the trade balance above).

The opposite conclusion holds if traded goods demand is price inelastic (if $|\eta| + |\psi| < 1$). In this case, the product of the negative term $(p_{dt} - p_{ft} - e_t)$ and the positive term $(1 + \eta + \psi)$ will be negative. The main effect of the relative price decline will then be a reduction in foreign exchange earnings, leading to a tightening of the balance of payments constraint on domestic income growth. This price effect shows the impact of a terms of trade deterioration considered in the original debate surrounding the Prebisch–Singer hypothesis, although the growth model under consideration is sufficiently flexible to incorporate the alternative high elasticity scenario.

The balance of payments constrained growth model is also consistent with another aspect of the Prebisch–Singer debate. Singer (1950) argued that commodity price fluctuations would bias domestic investment efforts towards the dominant commodity sectors when these were experiencing temporarily high prices, as it was during such boom periods that investment funds were available. To the extent that foreign investments are likewise biased towards the comparative advantage commodity sector, one can further predict that the relative importance of the export dominant sector should tend to increase over time. The balance of payments constrained growth model likewise predicts that resources available for domestic investment will increase during booms in the dominant commodity sector, but does not in itself imply predictions about the investment destination.

A final observation on the relative price term in the balance of payments constrained growth model relates to the realism of the relative purchasing power parity assumption. The theoretical foundation of purchasing power parity is the law of one price: arbitrage trade will eliminate local price differences due to market specific supply concentrations in the absence of trade impediments. Strictly speaking, such price convergence should only be expected for identical commodities traded in and between different markets. In a case where a developing country is specialized in commodity exports and its developed trading partners are specialized in the production and export of manufactured goods and capital equipment, the basis for price arbitrage is not given: in the absence of identical or near identical traded goods the basis for price convergence underlying the law of one price can no longer be assumed. Such a situation implies that the relative price term in the balance of payments constrained growth model may have a permanent presence. Secular price trends would then be predicted to be an intertemporally sustained determinant of the growth constraint.

If the relative purchasing power parity condition holds, and the economy converges to the long run equilibrium growth rate x_t/π, there remain structural reasons why commodity dependence and commodity specialization can be expected to condition long run growth performance. Demand for primary commodities is generally income inelastic on the basis of what is known as Engel's law: as per capita income increases, household demand for food rises proportionately less than household demand for non-food items. This original observation on food has been extrapolated to primary commodities in general. Ingersent and Rayner (1999) are among many authors documenting the decline in the relative importance of the agricultural sector growing economies, while Radetzki (2010) shows a similar pattern for primary commodities more generally.

In the context of Thirlwall's law on long term growth constraints, this stylized fact implies that $0 < \varepsilon < 1$ in the case of a commodity dependent developing economy, that is, global demand for commodities should be expected to grow relatively less than the global economy overall. In other words: the very fact of commodity dependence implies the presence of a structural growth constraint for commodity dependent developing economies. To the extent that this structural constraint persists over time, it will tend to slow down or prevent global convergence of per capita income levels.

2.6   Concluding reflections: export diversification and internal resource flows

The discussion so far has been dependent on two assumptions: (i) the assumed homogeneity of commodity price movements to a point where commodities can be realistically modelled as a single earnings constraint in the trade balance, and (ii) the assumption that the external earnings constraint is crucial, so that available financial resources facilitate the capitalization of the formal sector once they are available internally.

The interpretation of commodity exports as showing strong common pattern in their evolution over time extends beyond the core hypothesis of a shared downwards price trend towards correlated shorter term movements – a pattern commonly described as excess comovement. Commodity prices are often held to be strongly driven by demand in markets for industrial inputs (Radetzki 2010, pp. 64ff.) or influenced by commodities in other categories – see Baffes (2007) for a discussion of oil and non-oil commodities. The extent of comovement as well as the presence of shared long term trends have been the subject of an extensive empirical debate (see Cashin, McDermott, and Scott 1999; Cuddington 1992; Newbold, Pfaffenzeller, and Rayner 2005, among others). In the present volume, the empirical basis for the assumption of shared price movements between commodities will be further discussed in Chapter 3.

At this point it is worth bearing in mind that heterogeneous price movements redefine the commodity dependence problem to the extent that volatility exposure is transformed from a characteristic of primary sector dependence to one of narrow specialization within the primary sector: the less short and medium term price movements are correlated between commodities, the more commodity export earnings volatility will be reduced by diversifying across different commodity sub-sectors. If not all commodities share the same downwards trend in real prices, then a tightening of the growth constraint may be avoided or mitigated by diversifying away from rapidly declining commodity sectors.

Assumption (ii) regarding the pivotal position of the external earnings constraint has been extensively discussed in the literature. This topic is closely linked to the aid effectiveness debate in so far as institutional impediments to internal resource transfers are concerned. Where the main recipients of commodity export earnings are commercial private sector operations, the investment destination should largely be a function of prospective earnings in different sectors and destination economies, as well as legal and institutional restrictions on foreign investment. It is further important to distinguish regular commercial entities from illegal non-governmental agencies such as insurgent forces contesting the existing national power structure. Export earnings clearly can counteract the development of the formal sector depending on whether they accrue to private sector agents with a preference for expansion in the formal sector or with an interest in destabilizing the existing institutional structure – see, for example, Collier (2010) for the potential role of commodity earnings in financing conflict.

Where the state is the main recipient or a major beneficiary of commodity export earnings, key concerns familiar from the aid and development debate will become relevant. The effectiveness with which centrally administered commodity export receipts feed into the development process will depend on the policy and institutional variables which have become the conventional focus of this debate; see Burnside and Dollar (2000) and Collier (2008) for an overview and a seminal contribution to this field.

What is of general relevance is the potential presence of the internal transfer problem within the transition economies receiving export earnings. This problem identifies Thirlwall's balance of payments based growth constraint as a necessary but not sufficient condition for a foreign exchange based economic transition: while economies cannot expand beyond their constrained growth rate in the long run, they can perform within it, not growing at the highest rate compatible with export earnings (cf. Thirlwall 1979). It thus defines a *caveat* which deserves attention when evaluating the role of foreign exchange earnings against a background of a developing economy's growth and transition performance. Sufficient and stable export earnings in a transitional comparative advantage sector can provide an opportunity for economic development. Its materialization crucially depends on domestic institutions and infrastructure.

Notes

1 The discussion of the Solow growth model provided here is intentionally brief, aimed primarily at recapitulation of the material, since this model is widely known. For a more extensive discussion, see Romer (2006, Chapter 1).
2 The basic characteristics of the Solow growth model remain unaltered in its variant formulation in effective labour terms and based on the assumption of labour augmenting technological progress. The intensive form would yield $y = Y/AL$ and $k = K/AL$ in this case and the steady-state growth rate would be zero. Yet, even in this variant of the model an equilibrium long run growth rate of $g = dA/dt$ would be implied for income per unit of physical labour.
3 This is known as *price quotation* of the exchange rate. The opposite definition (specifying the amount of foreign currency that can be bought for one unit of domestic currency) is known as *volume quotation*. See Gandolfo (1994, Chapter 2) for a detailed discussion of alternative exchange rate definitions.
4 If the export elasticity is formulated explicitly with respect to the domestic exchange rate in price quotation, the value of this elasticity term is of course predicted to be positive. Own price elasticities more generally are, however, predicted to take negative values for non-Giffen goods.

References

Baffes, J. (2007). 'Oil spills on other commodities'. *Resources Policy* 32.3, 126–34. Available at: www.sciencedirect.com/science/article/B6VBM-4PT2FV9-1/2/a49dfeac 77c22e3c9c18c3529d3a9f7e (accessed on 15th March 2010).
Burnside, C. and D. Dollar (2000). 'Aid, policies, and growth'. *American Economic Review* 90.4, 847–68.

Cashin, P., J. McDermott, and A. Scott (1999). *The Myth of Comoving Commodity Prices*. Working Paper WP/99/169. Washington, DC: International Monetary Fund.

Collier, P. (2008). *The Bottom Billion: Why the Poorest Countries are Failing and What Can Be Done About It*. New York: Oxford University Press.

Collier, P. (2010). *Wars, Guns and Votes: Democracy in Dangerous Places*. 1st edn. New York: Vintage.

Cuddington, J. (1992). 'Long-run trends in 26 primary commodity prices'. *Journal of Development Economics* 39.2, 207–27.

Gandolfo, G. (1994). *International Economics*. Vol. 1. Berlin: Springer Verlag.

Greenaway, D., D. Sapsford, and S. Pfaffenzeller (2007). 'Foreign direct investment, economic performance and trade liberalisation'. *The World Economy* 30.2, 197–210.

Griffith-Jones, S., J. Cailloux, and S. Pfaffenzeller (1999). 'Changes in the financial architecture required to prevent and manage better crisis in emerging markets'. *Revue du Financier* 118–19, 57–79.

Ingersent, K. and A. Rayner (1999). *Agricultural Policy in Western Europe and the United States*. Cheltenham: Edward Elgar Publishing.

Lewis W. (1954). 'Economic development with unlimited supplies of labour'. *The Manchester School* 22.2, 139–91.

Mankiw, N. G., D. Romer, and D. N. Weil (1992). 'A contribution to the empirics of economic growth'. *The Quarterly Journal of Economics* 107.2, 407–37. Available at: http://qje.oxfordjournals.org/content/107/2/407 (accessed on 28th November 2014).

McCombie, J. and A. Thirlwall (1993). *Economic Growth and the Balance of Payments Constraint*. New York: Palgrave Macmillan.

Newbold, P., S. Pfaffenzeller, and A. Rayner (2005). 'How well are long-run commodity price series characterized by trend components?' *Journal of International Development* 17.4, 479–94.

Radetzki, M. (2010). *A Handbook of Primary Commodities in the Global Economy*. Cambridge: Cambridge University Press.

Romer, D. (2006). *Advanced Macroeconomics*. 3rd edn. New York: McGraw-Hill Higher Education.

Rostow, W. (1997). *The Stages of Economic Growth: A Non-Communist Manifesto*. Cambridge: Cambridge University Press.

Singer, H. (1950). 'U.S. foreign investment in underdeveloped areas – the distribution of gains between investing and borrowing countries'. *American Economic Review* 40.2, 473–85.

Smith, S. C., and M. Todaro (2008). *Economic Development*. 10 edn. Harlow: Addison Wesley.

Thirlwall, A. (1979). 'The balance of payments constraint as an explanation of international growth rate differences'. *Banca Nazionale del Lavoro Quarterly Review* 32.128, 45–53.

Thirlwall, A. and N. Hussain. 'The balance of payments constraint, capital flows and growth rate differences between developing countries'. *Oxford Economic Papers* 34.3, 498–510.

3 The statistical properties of commodity prices

3.1 Introduction

As economies develop from their agricultural basic infrastructure to a manufacturing base and beyond, the primary sector declines in relative economic importance. In many ways, this is a mathematical necessity. Its economic implications have been documented from a number of perspectives – observations on the declining share of agricultural and raw material producing sector participation feature routinely in texts on agricultural economics or primary commodities; see Ingersent and Rayner (1999) and Radetzki (2010) for examples. It was also observed early on that food expenditure accounts for a declining proportion of rising incomes in what has become known as Engel's law (Zimmerman 1932). Such a shift in the relative magnitude of an economy's constituent sectors can be expected to coincide with a shift in relative prices and factor incomes, guiding resources from the contracting to the expanding part of the economy.

An exception to this general pattern can be expected in raw material producing sectors providing pivotal inputs into the expanding secondary and tertiary sectors and being limited in their capacity to expand supply. Such a scenario could constrain the expansion of commodity-dependent derivative activity and would be expected to result in rising prices for the primary sub-sector concerned. This tendency has arguably been observed in the case of oil for most of the 1973 to 2014 interval – though likely for political and commercial rather than economic reasons in the strict sense of physical resource scarcity. Until very recently, the Organization of the Petroleum Exporting Countries (OPEC) cartel successfully regulated the overall supply of oil and was able to maintain an inflated price. This price setting scenario is currently under potential threat from the development of non-conventional oil resources in the US (Baffes and Cosic 2014).

Such an upward drift is not generally expected for non-fuel commodity prices, although Baffes (2007) has shown that there is some impact of oil price movements on other commodity prices. At the other extreme is the prediction of a sustained price decline in the tradition of the Prebisch–Singer hypothesis, which anticipates a strong and sustained decline in primary commodity prices from a combination of demand characteristics and market structure. Some real price decline in most commodity sectors would moreover have to be expected if there is to be a sustained resource migration to manufacturing and service sectors. The conflicting influences of high prices in some sectors and expanding resource demand and manufacturing production in emerging and developed markets leave commodity price developments subject to a number of potentially antagonistic influences.

The following discussion will focus on the empirical development of the 24 non-fuel commodity price series studied by Grilli and Yang (1988) throughout the twentieth century and up to the early twenty-first century primary commodity price boom. The discussion will consider alternative assumptions regarding the stationarity characteristics of the series and will place the conclusions on the significance and size of the trend measurements obtained in the context of the shorter term volatility observed. In addressing the time series characteristics of composite commodity indices as well as that of individual price series in different commodity groups, a stylized picture of long run commodity price trends will emerge, albeit one that is not simple enough to be reduced to the summary measure of a common trend.

3.2 Long run trends in composite commodity price indices

The discussion of secular trends in commodity prices has long centred on the choice of data period and, to some extent, the quality of the data sources employed. In a seminal article on the topic, Spraos (1980) discussed a number of aspects of Prebisch and Singer's original findings. Among the qualitative aspects of the data series discussed is the correspondence between British terms of trade data with developed versus developing country terms of trade as well as possible biases arising from systematic failure to account for transport costs in terms of trade computations. The extent to which these factors distort conclusions on the intertemporal evolution of the barter terms of trade does of course depend on the degree and the direction in which such distortions vary over time. Where the statistical error introduced at the data recording stage is itself time invariant, inferences on the time series properties of the series need not be affected.

The pivotal argument of Spraos (1980) focuses on the data period considered by Prebisch and Singer. The early period in Prebisch and Singer's (cf. Toye and Toye (2003)) data set covers 1876–1938 (Spraos 1980), that is, from a period with relatively high commodity prices during the late nineteenth century to the great depression and the eve of the Second World War. Spraos (1980) contends that the pronounced decline in primary commodity prices can mainly be confirmed for this period, but is not robust to an extension of the data set covering the 1970s. This conclusion is contested by Sapsford (1985), who maintains that the continued presence of a downward trend can be confirmed when structural breaks are accounted for.

A key development in the literature on secular commodity price trends came with the data set presented by Grilli and Yang (1988) covering a weighted average of 24 primary commodity price series from 1900–1986. The 24 non-fuel commodity price series in this index are weighted by their 1977–1979 average weights in world trade; the composite index is in turn indexed to its 1977–1979 arithmetic mean. The series is commonly deflated by a version of the Manufacturing Unit Value (MUV) index representing the unit value of leading developed economy exports to developing countries.[1]

One concern raised with regard to the suitability of the Grilli and Yang data set was the continuity of the commodity price series (see Pfaffenzeller, Newbold, and Rayner 2007) as well as the suitability of the weighted averaging method used for the composite index. Cuddington and Wei (1992) discuss the original Grilli and Yang index and argue that the arithmetic weighting procedure used in constructing it does not in fact guarantee that the incidence of individual commodity price series over time will remain constant according to the base period weight. Cuddington and Wei propose a geometric weighting method instead, and find that evidence for a decline in the value of the composite index is less pronounced in this case.

Grilli and Yang (1988) estimated linear trends for their overall commodity index (GYCPI) and a number of sub-indices covering food (GYCPIF), metals (GYCPIM), non-food commodities (GYCPINF), and tropical beverages (GYCP-BEV). Trend estimates were obtained for the series in real terms, deflated alternatively by the MUV or the USMPI, expressing the series in natural logarithms; with the logarithmic transformation providing a basis for linear trend estimates. Over the sample period 1900–1986, the trend estimates obtained are mostly negative with coefficient estimates implying annual rates of decline of between 0.4 and 0.8 per cent. The one exception to this general finding is the real price index for tropical beverages for which the reported trend estimate is 0.006, indicating an annual rate of increase of around 0.6 per cent (Grilli and Yang 1988).

The trend estimates of Grilli and Yang (1988) generally appear statistically significant for commodity price series deflated by the MUV. The problem here is an implicit assumption of stationarity of the data series. While Grilli and Yang test and correct for first-order serial correlation, they do not test for unit roots, and thus for the long term stationarity characteristics of their series. This issue is addressed by Cuddington and Urzua (1989) for composite commodity price indices and by Cuddington (1992) for individual price series. These texts apply unit root tests to the Grilli and Yang data and allow for structural breaks in the series.

The stationarity problem can be illustrated with the simple case of a model error following a first-order autoregressive process. A trend stationary econometric model for a real price series can be defined as

$$p_t = \alpha + \beta t + u_t, u_t = \phi u_{t-1} + \varepsilon_t, \tag{3.1}$$

where p_t is the real price series in logarithms, α and β are coefficients, and t is a trend vector with $t = 1, 2, \ldots, T$. The model error u_t is considered stationary so long as $|\phi| < 1$. In this case, serial correlation can be corrected for through appropriate maximum likelihood based estimation techniques. This approach is not sufficient if the autoregressive coefficient ϕ takes a value of 1.

In a purely first-order autoregressive time series (y_t), it is possible to test for the presence of a unit root through a simple Dickey–Fuller test of the form

$$y_t = \rho^* y_{t-1} + \varepsilon_t, \rho^* = \rho - 1, \tag{3.2}$$

where ρ is the unobserved true autoregressive parameter, and the testing equation can be used to test if the coefficient estimate for ρ^* is significantly different from 0 (and hence ρ is significantly different from 1). In applying this test, the test statistic τ on $\hat{\rho}^*$ has non-standard critical values which were computed by Dickey and Fuller for their original test and have since been updated and extended by MacKinnon (1996) for different variants of the unit root test.[2]

More general specifications of unit root tests allow for a constant or trend and constant under the alternative hypothesis and include a number of lagged differenced terms. For a potentially trending real price series as above, the augmented Dickey–Fuller (ADF) test equation would take the general form

$$\Delta p_t = \alpha + \beta t + \rho p_{t-1} + \sum_{i=1}^{q} \psi_i \Delta p_{t-i} + \varepsilon_t, \tag{3.3}$$

for which the critical values are as in MacKinnon (1996). Other variants of unit root tests, such as the one by Perron (1989), allow for structural breaks in the data-generating process. Where the unit root null hypothesis for a real commodity price series cannot be rejected it is still possible that the series is stationary in first differences – a further hypothesis which can be tested by applying the appropriate unit root test to the differenced series. What matters to the study of commodity price trends is that the linear trend can in principle be represented in differenced form.

Where a commodity price series is represented as in Equation (3.1), its equivalent differenced presentation would simply be $\Delta p_t = \beta + \varepsilon_t$, where it is assumed that the model error for the undifferenced model is $u_t = u_{t-1} + \varepsilon_t$ and the trend is simply represented by a constant capturing the average rate of change of the differenced series in natural logarithms. That this is so can be simply and formally demonstrated by subtracting the lagged value of a trend vector ($t - 1 = 0, 1, 2, \ldots, T - 1$) from the contemporaneous level values of the trend vector ($t = 1, 2, 3, \ldots, T$) to obtain a vector of ones of length $T - 1$ for the differenced model, while the first difference of the constant obviously reduces to zero.

A practical reason why the trend and difference stationary representations of commodity price trends matter is the familiar phenomenon of spurious correlation, leading to the possible acceptance of de facto insignificant price trends if trend stationary models are fitted to non-stationary real price series – see Newbold and Granger (1974) for an early discussion of this phenomenon. An added problem in the application to commodity price and price index series is the fact that the series are often highly correlated as well as being highly volatile, a combination of properties that often makes it difficult to obtain robust and unambiguous conclusions on the presence of unit roots or structural breaks.

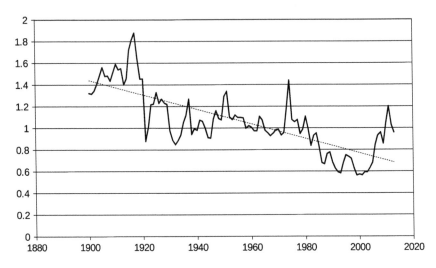

Figure 3.1 Grilli and Yang index relative to MUV.

Note: GYVPI/MUV 1900–2013, 1977–1979 = 1.

The Grilli and Yang data have been updated to 2003 in Pfaffenzeller, Newbold, and Rayner (2007) and are here extended further up to 2013 following the same methodology. The updated Grilli and Yang Commodity Price Index deflated by the Manufacturing Unit Value Index is shown in Figure 3.1. The graph shows a period of volatile, but relatively high, prices in the early twentieth century, followed by a sustained gradual decline leading up to the commodity price boom from 1999 onwards. It is remarkable how stable this sustained upwards pressure on real commodity prices was compared to previous price booms and in the face of the 2008 financial crisis, which led to a moderate dip in prices followed by a renewed and sustained increase before the downturn of 2012–2013.

A linear trend line fitted to the real term index series clearly seems to illustrate an overall tendency towards declining real prices that has only recently been reversed. The most dramatic contrast is with the very elevated index value in the earlier sub-period and the lower values towards the late twentieth century, with a pronounced sharp drop in the index around 1920/21. It is this localized drop that has been attributed to a structural break by Cuddington and Urzua (1989) and Cuddington (1992), who account for its impact through dummy variables. Sapsford, Sarkar, and Singer (1992) by contrast supply extraneous evidence for a sustained real commodity price decline by interpolating data for the period surrounding the structural break from an inversion of the Schlote (1938) terms of trade index for Britain to find support for a sustained and continuous decline in the series.

A more fundamental concern relates to the adequacy of broad composite indices per se and, in this case, the weighting method used. Figure 3.2 plots the overall

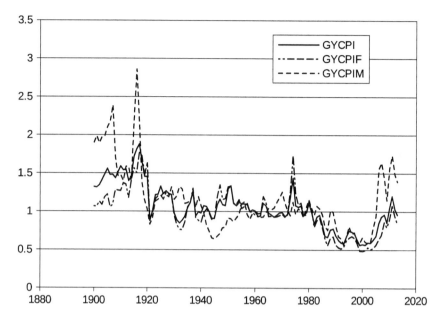

Figure 3.2 Grilli and Yang index and metal and food sub-indices.
Note: GYVPI, GYCPIM, GYCPIF/MUV 1900–2013, 1977–1979 = 1.

Grilli and Yang index against the metal sub-index (GYCPIM) and the food sub-index (GYCPIF). Both series are again deflated by the MUV. It is readily apparent that the metal sub-index is substantially more volatile than either the food sub-index or the overall Grilli and Yang index: pronounced deviations from the overall GYCPI are readily discernible throughout the period covered. The GYCPIF by contrast takes values below the overall GYCPI – and substantially below the metal sub-index – while barely being visually discernible from the overall commodity index for the remainder of the time period covered. If extreme values in a subset of the commodity price series included are crucial to the inference of a long term downwards trend, this could raise questions about the adequacy of the broad composite index in question as a summary measure for the commodity terms of trade.

A similar discrepancy arises if the arithmetically weighted GYCPI is compared to the geometrically weighted index compiled by Cuddington and Wei (1992), as shown in Figure 3.3. This time, early-period values of the conventionally (arith-metically) weighted Grilli and Yang Index lie above the index series following the geometrically weighted alternative composition introduced by Cuddington and Wei (1992). Again, both series comove much more closely in the later part of the sample. A detailed discussion of index properties likely to be responsible for this effect is beyond the scope of the present discussion. One should note, though, that both index composition method and discrepancies in intertemporal commodity

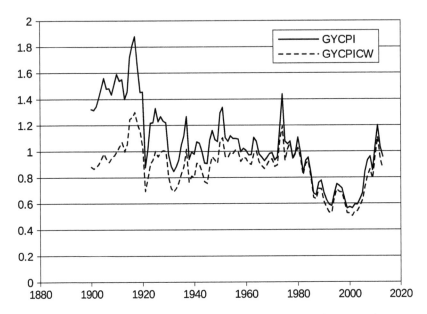

Figure 3.3 Real Grilli and Yang index: arithmetic versus geometric aggregation.

Note: GYVPI, GYCPICW/MUV 1900–2013, 1977–1979 = 1.

price trajectories can make the use of composite price indices problematic. A more detailed discussion of individual price series behaviour will be taken up in the second part of this chapter, following a review of trend estimates for composite indices.

To formally assess the magnitude of the average annual decline in composite commodity price indices, linear trends have traditionally been estimated for long run index series. A generalized decline in the commodity terms of trade should then be captured in a negative trend coefficient estimate. More recently, these trend estimates have commonly been preceded by unit root tests (as discussed above) to decide if the average decline in the index value should be modelled as a linear trend, as in Equation (3.1), or as a stochastic trend that can be captured by the coefficient estimate on a constant in the index series.

The first column in Table 3.1 reports test statistic values for an augmented Dickey–Fuller test allowing for trend and constant under the alternative hypothesis. Among the arithmetically weighted index series, only the sub-index for metals (GYCPIM) is not identified as stationary in levels. Among the geometrically weighted index series, this is only the case for the non-food commodities sub-index. All index series are identified as stationary in first differences, however.

The conventional approach to unit root testing would rely on identification of the order of integration of the series through unit root pretests: where the unit root null hypothesis is rejected for the series in levels, it would be concluded that the

Table 3.1 Trend estimates for composite price indices*

Series	ADF-τ	Trend	u_t	Trend	v_t
GYCPI	-3.445 $_{-8.702}$	-0.006 $_{-3.919}$	$u_t - \underset{-14.940}{0.814}u_{t-1} = \varepsilon_t$	-0.003 $_{-0.351}$	$v_t = \varepsilon_t + \underset{0.121}{0.011}\varepsilon_{t-1} - \underset{-2.701}{0.262}\varepsilon_{t-2}$
GYCPIM	-3.267 $_{-7.937}$	-0.005 $_{-2.052}$	$u_t - \underset{-13.217}{0.813}u_{t-1} = \varepsilon_t + \underset{3.345}{0.322}\varepsilon_{t-1}$	-0.003 $_{-0.166}$	$v_t = \varepsilon_t + \underset{2.459}{0.244}\varepsilon_{t-1}$
GYCPINF	-4.351 $_{-9.363}$	-0.007 $_{-5.618}$	$u_t - \underset{-11.654}{0.736}u_{t-1} = \varepsilon_t$	-0.004 $_{-0.706}$	$v_t = \varepsilon_t - \underset{-0.975}{0.088}\varepsilon_{t-1} - \underset{-3.973}{0.373}\varepsilon_{t-2}$
GYCPIF	-3.434 $_{-8.654}$	-0.006 $_{-3.104}$	$u_t - \underset{-15.082}{0.814}u_{t-1} = \varepsilon_t$	-0.002 $_{-0.223}$	$v_t = \varepsilon_t - \underset{-0.011}{0.001}\varepsilon_{t-1} - \underset{-2.988}{0.283}\varepsilon_{t-2}$
GYCPI-CW	-2.473 $_{-8.571}$	-0.003 $_{-2.047}$	$u_t - \underset{-10.511}{0.754}u_{t-1} = \varepsilon_t + \underset{2.919}{0.325}\varepsilon_{t-1}$	0.000 $_{0.034}$	$v_t - \underset{-1.429}{0.130}v_{t-1} + \underset{-2.884}{0.263}v_{t-2} = \varepsilon_t$
GYCPIM-CW	-3.106 $_{-7.397}$	-0.003 $_{-1.211}$	$u_t - \underset{-13.980}{0.826}u_{t-1} = \varepsilon_t + \underset{2.614}{0.249}\varepsilon_{t-1}$	-0.001 $_{-0.058}$	$v_t = \varepsilon_t + \underset{1.846}{0.178}\varepsilon_{t-1}$
GYCPINF-CW	-3.393 $_{-9.370}$	-0.001 $_{-0.933}$	$u_t - \underset{-12.800}{0.768}u_{t-1} = \varepsilon_t$	0.001 $_{0.256}$	$v_t = \varepsilon_t - \underset{-0.546}{0.050}\varepsilon_{t-1} - \underset{-3.803}{0.373}\varepsilon_{t-2}$
GYCPIF-CW	-2.336 $_{-8.832}$	-0.003 $_{-2.138}$	$u_t - \underset{-10.540}{0.761}u_{t-1} = \varepsilon_t + \underset{2.674}{0.327}\varepsilon_{t-1}$	-0.000 $_{-0.031}$	$v_t - \underset{-1.064}{0.096}v_{t-1} + \underset{3.177}{0.287}v_{t-2} = \varepsilon_t$

* All estimates are for index series in real terms and in natural logarithms. Critical values for ADF tests in levels, allowing for trend and constant, are -3.99, -3.43, and -3.13 at the 1%, 5%, and 10% level respectively. The corresponding values for ADF tests allowing for a constant only are -3.46, -2.88, and -2.57.

series is stationary in levels, and the coefficient for a trend vector would be estimated for the undifferenced series. If, on the contrary, the unit root null hypothesis can only be rejected after first differencing, the stochastic trend model would be applied and the trend would be measured by the constant in the regression model, whose coefficient estimate captures the average rate of change of the series over time. Where the unit root null hypothesis cannot be rejected after differencing, conventional methods for assessing the significance of trend estimates cannot be applied.

Simple reliance on unit root pretesting has problems of its own, however. Dickey–Fuller type tests are known to lack reliability or power in the presence of strong serial correlation – see Agiakloglou and Newbold (1996, 1992) for a discussion of size–power trade-offs and related reliability issues. Another approach therefore relies on basing inference on results for both deterministic and stochastic trend based models. This approach is taken by Kim *et al.* (2003) and Newbold, Pfaffenzeller, and Rayner (2005), and is adopted here in presenting deterministic and stochastic trend estimates in parallel. The second and fourth columns in Table 3.1 show the deterministic and stochastic trend estimates respectively, together with the *t*-ratios obtained. In contrast to earlier studies like Grilli and Yang (1988), the above trend estimates have been obtained allowing for more general correlation pattern than a simple first-order autoregressive process. As in Cuddington (1992) and Newbold, Pfaffenzeller, and Rayner (2005), among others, the error processes are modelled allowing for a combination of autoregressive and moving average components.[3] The third and fifth columns show the autoregressive–moving-average (ARMA) models for the model error, obtained using maximum likelihood estimation. The ARMA parameterizations shown were obtained using the Schwarz–Bayesian criterion (SBC) to find an optimum trade-off between model parsimony and goodness of fit. The SBC, also known as the Bayes information criterion (BIC), can be defined as

$$\mathrm{BIC} = -2\log L(\tilde{\psi}) + n\log T, \tag{3.4}$$

where $L(\tilde{\psi})$ is the maximized value of the likelihood function, n the number of parameters in the ARMA model, and T the length of the time series (Harvey 1993, pp. 79–80). The estimates reported in Table 3.1 show consistently significant deterministic trend estimates for the arithmetic composite indices ranging in value from -0.005 to -0.007. The overall GYCPI has a trend coefficient point estimate of -0.006, which corresponds to the one for the food sub-index (GYCPIF) but lies below the estimated trend for the metals sub-index (-0.005 for the GYCPIM) and above the one for the non-food commodities index (-0.007). The stochastic trend (or *drift*) estimates presented in the fourth column, in contrast, are higher in value, ranging from -0.002 to -0.004, and thus imply a lower average rate of decline for the real commodity price indices: the stochastic trend estimate for the overall GYCPI is -0.003 and this value is shared with the metal sub-index. The non-food commodity price sub-index (GYCPINF) continues to take a somewhat lower value of −0.004 while the food sub-index now has a marginally higher point estimate of −0.002. These estimates are also consistently insignificant.

The results discussed above have been obtained without explicitly considering a possible structural break in 1921, though, and addressing this can be shown to be relevant to the conclusions obtained. A potential structural break in 1920–1921 was discussed soon after the publication of Grilli and Yang (1988), leading Cuddington and Urzua (1989) to conclude that most of the decay in primary commodity prices over the twentieth century can be accounted for by a single drop in the composite price index after 1920. Other authors, like Newbold, Rayner, and Kellard (2000), caution against the attribution of pronounced changes in volatile series to structural breaks. The hypothesized break is clearly discernible as a sharp drop after 1920 and is followed by a pronounced recovery in the index, which is not sufficiently strong to restore the pre-break value. There is room for discussion, then, as to whether this discontinuity should be interpreted as an outlier, which could be modelled by a single year dummy, or as a level shift dummy as in Cuddington and Urzua (1989). Given the precedent set in the literature, the following discussion will focus on the interpretation adopted by Cuddington and Urzua (1989).

Likelihood ratio tests for simple trend based models and alternative model specifications including a level shift dummy reject the null hypothesis of no structural break for all of the four index series. The likelihood ratio test statistic for the overall GYCPI is $\chi^2(1) = 20.2$, with values of $\chi^2(1) = 4.98$, 14.58, and 16.8 for the metal, non-food, and food sub-indices respectively; the 5 per cent critical value is 3.84. For the overall Grilli and Yang Index, the model including a level shift dummy variable no longer indicates the presence of a significant trend term:

$$\text{GYCPI} = \underset{4.250}{0.490} - \underset{-4.439}{0.445 D_{1921}} - \underset{-0.985}{0.002t} + u_t, \ u_t - \underset{16.436}{0.855 u_{t-1}} = \varepsilon_t,$$

where D_{1921} is the level shift dummy, which now seems to account for most of the recorded decline in the index value. Similar results are obtained for the metal sub-index ($\hat{\beta}_M = -0.003$, $t = -1.252$ and $\hat{\beta}_{D1921} = -0.290$, $t = -2.300$) and for the food commodities sub-index ($\hat{\beta}_F = -0.000$, $t = -0.143$ and $\hat{\beta}_{D1921} = -5.419$, $t = -4.186$). A significant trend estimate remains for the case of the non-food commodities sub-index:

$$\text{GYCPINF} = \underset{8.242}{0.593} - \underset{-3.904}{0.350 D_{1921}} - \underset{-3.208}{0.004t} + u_t, \ u_t - \underset{10.058}{0.697 u_{t-1}} = \varepsilon_t,$$

where the trend estimate does not appear substantially affected with respect to either its magnitude or its inferred significance. The decline in the non-food sub-index during the early twentieth century has, if anything, been more pronounced than that in the overall Grilli and Yang index. The series does also show a number of sustained increases in value throughout the earliest years of the twentieth century, though, and their magnitude seems to dominate the impact of the 1920–1921 price decline.

These results are also consistent with those obtained for the difference stationary model alternative. The impact of a dummy capturing a larger than average
decline in a specific period is not relevant to the stochastic trend estimates in
models identified by SBC, since these are insignificant to begin with.

For arithmetically aggregated indices, evidence for secular trends can be
detected conditional on underlying conclusions regarding stationarity characteristics. Even then, the observed decline is often attributed to a potential structural
break in 1920–1921. When considering trend and drift estimates for the geometrically weighted index series, the evidence for secular trends is weakened.
Significant trend coefficient estimates are obtained for the overall GYCPI-CW
index and the food commodities sub-index in levels only, while stochastic trend
estimates are consistently insignificant. For the geometrically weighted indices,
too, the point estimates for stochastic trends tend to be somewhat higher than those
for deterministic trend vectors and would therefore suggest a slower rate of price
decay, if these coefficient estimates could be taken to be statistically significant.
However, this is clearly not the case when significant estimates are expected for
both stochastic and deterministic trend terms. The more conventional approach,
based on unit root pretesting, would likewise fail to identify trend terms for the
geometrically weighted indices as statistically significant, since only the metal
and non-food indices are classed as stationary among the geometrically weighted
index alternatives, and no significant deterministic trend estimates are obtained
for these.

A further property of the models presented for the trend estimates is
the substantive serial correlation in the ARMA processes identified by SBC.
Kim *et al.* (2003) and Newbold, Pfaffenzeller, and Rayner (2005) suggest selecting ARMA parameterizations for difference stationary model alternatives through
the AIC, which, like the SBC, aims to trade off model parsimony against goodness
of fit. Formally, it differs from the SBC by substituting $2n$ for $n \log T$ in Equation (3.4). The SBC generally tends to be preferred over the AIC on the grounds
that the AIC tends to select overparameterized model alternatives and thus fails to
optimally trade off parsimony and fit – see again Harvey (1993) for details.

In the present case this generally disadvantageous property of the Akaike criterion can be used productively to avoid the selection of underparameterized ARMA
specifications for the model error in the differenced model alternative. An overdif-
ferenced stationary process can be identified by the presence of a unit moving
average root in the estimate of the ARMA process for the differenced model estimate. It can be shown that the successful identification of unit moving average
roots is less likely in underparameterized ARMA models (Kim *et al.* 2003) and
that the t-test on the trend coefficient estimate tends to lack power in such a scenario. In comparing deterministic and stochastic trend estimates, identification of
significant trend terms can therefore be facilitated by considering AIC-selected
ARMA specifications for the difference stationary alternative where these provide evidence for the presence of a unit moving average root, and to assess the
significance of the stochastic trend coefficient estimate on this basis (Newbold,
Pfaffenzeller, and Rayner 2005).

When difference stationary models are reselected using the Akaike criterion, the estimated stochastic trend coefficients obtained are similar in size to those obtained in trend stationary models, as well as being statistically significant for most series. Moreover, the estimated moving average coefficients are indicative of unit moving average roots, so that these results are consistent with the scenario expected for underparameterized models fitted to differenced trend stationary series (see Kim *et al.* 2003 and Newbold, Pfaffenzeller, and Rayner 2005). Significant coefficient estimates in models selected by AIC are obtained for the GYCPI ($\hat{\beta} = -0.006$, $t = -3.412$), GYCPINF ($\hat{\beta} = -0.007$, $t = -4.700$), and GYCPIF ($\hat{\beta} = -0.005$, $t = -2.588$) indices. For the metal sub-index, a moving average unit root is identified, but the drift coefficient estimate continues to appear statistically insignificant (GYCPIM $\hat{\beta} = -0.005$, $t = -1.848$). Among the geometrically weighted index series, evidence of a unit moving average root is confined to the metal sub-index, when identifying ARMA processes by AIC. The drift coefficient estimate remains statistically insignificant in this case too (GYCPIM-CW $\hat{\beta} = -0.003$, $t = -1.075$).

For difference stationary model alternatives identified by the Akaike information criterion (AIC), the question of whether the decline in 1920–1921 does have a pivotal influence on the estimate obtained for the drift term does arise and can be addressed by including a differenced version of the level shift dummy discussed previously. The results obtained again mirror those for the trend stationary case with insignificant drift coefficient estimates for all index series other than the non-food sub-index.

The model for the overall GYCPI identified by AIC does exhibit a unit moving average root and a significant stochastic trend coefficient estimate ($\hat{\beta} = -0.006$, $t = -3.412$) when the structural break dummy is omitted. When accounting for a structural break, this estimate appears insignificant ($\hat{\beta} = 0.003$, $t = 0.333$ and $\hat{\beta}_{D1921} = -0.561$, $t = -6.070$). The food sub-index (GYCPIF) likewise registers a stochastic trend estimate of ($\hat{\beta} = -0.005$, $t = -2.588$) without a structural break dummy compared to ($\hat{\beta} = 0.004$, $t = 0.462$ and $\hat{\beta}_{D1921} = -0.652$, $t = -6.067$) once the 1921 break point is taken into account. Reselection by AIC does not identify a significant stochastic trend estimate for the metals sub-index (GYCPIM), while the estimate for the non-food sub-index (GYCPINF) is robust to the inclusion of a structural break dummy: the drift estimate obtained without the structural break dummy is ($\hat{\beta} = -0.007$, $t = -4.700$), while the estimate allowing for a structural break in 1920–1921 is ($\hat{\beta} = -0.004$, $t = -3.432$ and $\hat{\beta}_{D1921} = -0.341$, $t = -3.945$), indicating a slower rate of decline when part of the price index development is attributed to a one-off drop in the level value of the series.

Univariate estimates for composite commodity index series do provide evidence of some tendency towards long term decline if the conventional, arithmetically aggregated index series are used. Such evidence is consistently absent for the geometrically indexed series and is not consistently robust to adjustments for structural instability. It is also worth noting that the discrepancy apparent in the visual inspection of the overall GYCPI compared to sub-indices such as the GYCPIM is not similarly mirrored in strong and consistent discrepancies in the conclusions reached on the significance and size of a time trend. The presence and influence of heterogeneous intertemporal trajectories for different commodity aggregates, as well as the different conclusions reached from variant weighting methods, justify some caution in the interpretation of trend measurements for composite index series. One should therefore proceed to ask to what extent a composite commodity index is apt to provide a representative measure of long term real commodity price movements of potentially heterogeneous individual price series. To explore this question, the remainder of the chapter will turn to the characteristics of individual real commodity price series.

3.3   Long run trends in individual real price series

A general justification for the use of a composite commodity price index constructed from broad commodity aggregates is the background assumption of largely homogeneous long term commodity price movements. At first hand, such a fundamental assumption seems consistent with the observed long term decline in the relative importance of primary commodities in overall national income against a background of sustained income growth. A declining relative price for primary sector output could be part of a market-based resource allocation process that channels investment from the primary sector into the secondary and tertiary sectors. The acceptance of a sustained decline in the real price of primary commodities and therefore in the terms of trade of commodity-dependent economies is furthermore a constituent assumption of the Prebisch–Singer Hypothesis discussed previously.

On the other hand, the above discussion of trend estimates for a number of composite indices obtained from the Grilli and Yang data set has given rise to some doubts on the representative potential of these composite indices. In the particular case of the Grilli and Yang data set, the existence of substantive differences in the magnitude and direction of secular trend components in individual real commodity price series has already been noted by Cuddington (1992) and Newbold, Pfaffenzeller, and Rayner (2005), among others. Other authors, drawing on variant data sources, reach similar conclusions for a variety of time windows – see Cashin, McDermott, and Scott (1999) and Harvey *et al.* (2011) for two studies looking at very different time intervals and periodicities. It is this concern which motivates a shift in focus towards the study of individual real commodity price series for the remainder of this chapter. The individual price series will be grouped in subcategories, such as cereals, tropical beverages, metals, miscellaneous food prices, and miscellaneous non-fuel commodity prices, where some common economic influences and hence some comovement may be expected a priori. Along with the trend estimates, evidence for a post-1920 structural break will be discussed where appropriate.

3.3.1   Trends in cereal prices

The three cereal price series included in the Grilli and Yang data set are rice, wheat, and maize. These commodities have some potential to act as substitutes for

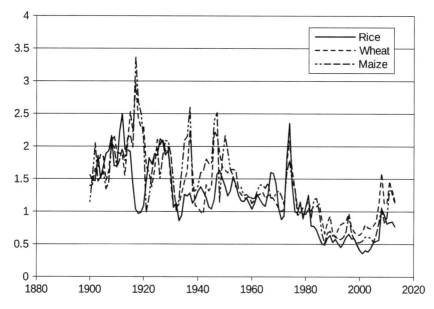

Figure 3.4 Real cereal price indices.

Note: Average annual price indices deflated by MUV, 1900–2013, 1977–1979 = 1.

each other while also being located in notably differentiated markets. Figure 3.4 shows the intertemporal trajectories of the three commodities. Visual inspection gives the impression of a shared gradual decline in the real price accompanied by substantial and sustained volatility around the trend locus. The three series seem to comove broadly, but prices for rice (indicated by the solid line) appear much less susceptible to the short-lived price spikes to which wheat and maize are susceptible (a pattern that is particularly pronounced during the early twentieth century part of the series).

All three series experience a period of real price depression during the last two decades of the twentieth century before experiencing a pronounced recovery during the early twenty-first century commodity boom. In this latter episode, the price increase observed for rice again falls short of that observed for wheat and maize.

Formal trend estimates for the three cereal price series are presented in Table 3.2. Augmented Dickey–Fuller tests allowing for trend and constant fail to reject the unit root null hypothesis for rice and wheat, but not for maize. ADF tests including a constant performed on the first differenced price series reject in all three cases, suggesting that the series are at least difference stationary. However, considering the general discussion of unit root pretesting above, the subsequent analysis will consider estimates for both deterministic and stochastic trend coefficients as in Newbold, Pfaffenzeller, and Rayner (2005), identifying the parameterization of the ARMA process as previously discussed.

Table 3.2 Trend estimates for cereal prices*

Series	ADF-τ	Trend	u_t, v_t
Rice	−3.091	−0.010 −5.557	$u_t - 0.661u_{t-1} = \varepsilon_t + 0.450\varepsilon_{t-1}$ $\quad\quad\;\,^{-7.855}\quad\quad\quad\quad\;\,^{4.071}$
$(1-L)^{**}$	−4.997	−0.010 −5.273	$v_t - 0.679v_{t-1} = \varepsilon_t - 0.557\varepsilon_{t-1} - 0.443\varepsilon_{t-2}$ $\quad\quad^{-7.931}\quad\quad\quad\;^{-4.818}\quad\quad\;\,^{-3.944}$
Wheat	−3.078	−0.007 −4.723	$u_t - 0.230u_{t-1} - 0.292u_{t-2} = \varepsilon_t + 0.814\varepsilon_{t-1}$ $\quad\quad^{-1.732}\quad\quad\;\,^{-2.302}\quad\quad\quad\quad^{9.576}$
$(1-L)$	−6.515	−0.002 −0.254	$v_t = \varepsilon_t + 0.103\varepsilon_{t-1} - 0.501\varepsilon_{t-2}$ $\quad\quad\quad\quad^{1.070}\quad\quad\;\,^{-4.829}$
Maize	−4.218	−0.009 −4.119	$u_t - 0.736u_{t-1} = \varepsilon_t$ $\quad\quad\;\,^{-11.059}$
$(1-L)$	−7.551	−0.003 −0.298	$v_t = \varepsilon_t - 0.159\varepsilon_{t-1} - 0.393\varepsilon_{t-2}$ $\quad\quad\quad\quad^{-1.820}\quad\quad\;\,^{-4.447}$

* All estimates are for index series in real terms and in natural logarithms. Critical values for ADF tests in levels, allowing for trend and constant, are −3.99, −3.43, and −3.13 at the 1%, 5%, and 10% level respectively. The corresponding values for ADF tests allowing for a constant only are −3.46, −2.88, and −2.57.
** $(1-L)$: First difference of series.

Estimated coefficients for the trend based model take values between −0.007 and −0.010, suggesting a trend rate of real price decline up to 1 per cent per year; the slowest rate of decline (−0.007) is estimated for the wheat price index, while the most pronounced downwards trend among the three cereal series (−0.010) is estimated for rice. The real price index for maize takes an intermediate value of −0.009. All three trend coefficient estimates appear statistically significant at standard critical values. This is not generally true for coefficient estimates on the stochastic trend terms in the difference stationary model alternative. The point estimate for rice takes a value of −0.010, corresponding to the trend estimate under the trend stationary model alternative. The drift coefficient estimates for wheat and maize take markedly lower absolute values of −0.002 and −0.003 respectively, and appear statistically insignificant at standard critical values.

When the Akaike information criterion is considered as an alternative approach towards model selection for the difference stationary model alternative, a unit moving average root can be identified for wheat, and the estimated drift coefficient takes a value of −0.008 ($t = -5.546$), which is close to the trend stationary estimate of −0.007 and appears statistically significant.

No such evidence is found for the series on maize prices, where the AIC reselects the minimum SBC autoregressive integrated moving average (ARIMA) parameterization. If the differenced equivalent of the trend stationary ARMA parameterization is imposed for maize,[4] the point estimate for the drift coefficient falls to −0.008, implying a more similar magnitude of annual price decline to that of the trend stationary estimate. This drift coefficient estimate does appear significant and the estimated coefficient for the MA(1) term is on the invertibility boundary. This result is as expected if the true data-generating process is trend stationary and produces a first-order autoregressive model error. In this case, differencing would produce a unit moving average root by construction. However, since this particular differenced model was not identified independently by the information criterion adopted, imposing it is tantamount to relying on the pretest result supporting the trend stationary AR(1) specification.

It further turns out that support for a significant negative trend term in the real price series for maize not only depends on rejecting the unit root null hypothesis but also on the a priori assumption of structural stability. A likelihood ratio test for the putative 1920–1921 break point date in the general GYCPI rejects the null hypothesis of structural stability ($\chi^2(1) = 5.22$). The coefficient on the level shift dummy included in the trend stationary model for maize is significant and the trend coefficient estimate now takes a higher value, close to the stochastic trend estimate, and no longer appears statistically significant:

$$\text{Maize}: p_t = \underset{3.730}{0.832} - \underset{-2.229}{0.538D_{1921}} - \underset{-0.737}{0.003t} + u_t, \ u_t - \underset{12.557}{0.845u_{t-1}} = \varepsilon_t.$$

Some room for discussion remains in interpreting this evidence for a structural break. Maize prices take very high values before 1920 and experience a pronounced fall thereafter – a pattern that is qualitatively similar to the one observed for wheat but with a more pronounced magnitude. The short-lived nature of the price movements concerned again lends some plausibility to an interpretation in terms of outliers attributable to short term idiosyncratic price movements, rather than sustained structural change to be modelled by a level shift. An attempt to address this question would have to address the history of cereal prices in more detail than is appropriate here. One should note for the purpose of the present discussion, though, that empirical support for a negative trend in maize prices is dependent on a number of corollary assumptions, of which structural stability of the market process over time is one.

For rice, the Akaike criterion reselects the model previously identified by SBC. It can be confirmed from Table 3.2 that this model also has a unit moving average component in the ARMA process and returns a statistically significant estimate for the stochastic trend coefficient.

The observed results in the trend coefficient estimates obtained are plausibly attributable to the difference in estimation technique. A large short term price swing, like that observed towards the end of the sample period, can be interpreted as a temporary deviation from the long term trend line in the case of the trend stationary model, and may largely be captured by a more extensive parameterization of the ARMA process. In the case of more parsimoniously parameterized econometric models, a large upswing, such as the early twenty-first century commodity boom, can have a larger impact on the recorded average decline of the series. This impression is further confirmed if the ARIMA models identified by minimum SBC for the three cereal series are fitted to a truncated time sample ending in 2000. As the aforementioned commodity price boom is omitted from the series, the estimated drift coefficients are -0.012, -0.008, and -0.010 for rice, wheat, and maize respectively. Of these, only the estimate for rice appears statistically significant, but the sizes of the point estimates now suggest annual rates of decline closer to those implied by the trend stationary models. This scenario of similar point estimates but divergent conclusions on statistical significance between trend and difference stationary modelling approaches is typical of situations where spurious rejections of the null hypothesis in time series are driven by unit root processes; it was commonly observed in applied studies of real commodity price trends over the twentieth century – see Newbold, Rayner, and Kellard (2000) and Newbold, Pfaffenzeller, and Rayner (2005) for examples.

Cereal prices, then, have declined at a somewhat faster rate than the overall Grilli and Yang commodity price index over the course of the twentieth century. This is merely a summary statement of historic price developments, though. A more relevant concern relates to future projection, and in this respect support for extrapolating the historic tendency towards declining prices is modest at best. A price projection in this direction would need to draw on more than just a historic record of statistical regularity, in particular in view of the recent price boom.

3.3.2   *Trends in tropical beverage prices*

The one composite price index for which Grilli and Yang (1988) found a positive real price trend is the tropical beverages index, which is composed of the price series for coffee, cocoa, and tea. The trajectories of the three constituent series for this index are shown in Figure 3.5, revealing a sustained and pronounced decline in the price of tea, while coffee and cocoa appear approximately stable but highly volatile.

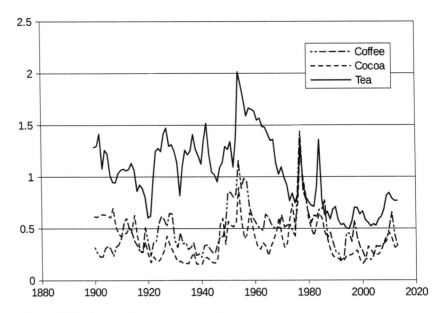

Figure 3.5 Real tropical beverage price indices.

Note: Average annual price indices deflated by MUV, 1900–2013, 1977–1979 = 1.

The series for tea, which appears to show a pronounced decline during the second half of the twentieth century, enters the tropical beverages index with a relatively low weight of around 11 per cent, while the more stable series for coffee (71 per cent) and cocoa (18 per cent) have a much larger combined impact on the composite index figure.[5] Grilli and Yang's trend estimate of $\beta = 0.0063$ is not robust to re-estimating their econometric model over the present 1900–2013 horizon, as this would yield $p_t = -0.660 - 0.001t + u_t$ with a model error following the ARMA process of $u_t - 0.846u_{t-1} = \varepsilon_t$, where the t-ratio on the trend coefficient takes a value of -0.377. This suggests an insignificant trend estimate while the estimate for the 1900–1986 sub-sample appears clearly significant. These results seem consistent with a combination of time series of which at most one (coffee) shows a positive trend and dominates the composite index due to the high weight it is accorded.

These general impressions are also consistent with the trend estimates obtained for individual commodity price series over the full sample range. Augmented Dickey–Fuller tests do not reject the unit root null hypothesis for any of the series in levels, lending support to the notion of difference stationary processes under the conventional pretest approach (see Table 3.3). However, even among the trend estimates for undifferenced price series, there is little support for deterministic trends. The only trend coefficient estimate which appears significant in this commodity group is the one for tea, which would imply a real price decline of 0.5 per cent per annum. Trend estimates for coffee and cocoa are not significant, and even here only the point estimate for coffee is positive.

Stochastic trend estimates appear clearly non-significant for all three commodities, with only the point estimate for the rate of change of real coffee prices taking a positive value. This result is robust to reselecting the real price series concerned through the Akaike criterion.

Table 3.3 Trend estimates for tropical beverage prices*

Series	ADF-τ	Trend	u_t, v_t
Coffee	−2.973	0.001 $\scriptstyle 0.376$	$u_t - 0.824u_{t-1} = \varepsilon_t$ $\scriptstyle -15.992$
$(1-L)^{**}$	−8.500	0.002 $\scriptstyle 0.136$	$v_t = \varepsilon_t + 0.017\varepsilon_{t-1} - 0.267\varepsilon_{t-2}$ $\scriptstyle 0.177 \qquad -2.603$
Cocoa	−2.424	−0.003 $\scriptstyle -0.565$	$u_t - 1.060u_{t-1} + 0.456u_{t-2} - 0.278u_{t-3} = \varepsilon_t$ $\scriptstyle -11.855 \qquad 3.596 \qquad -3.105$
$(1-L)$	−9.569	−0.005 $\scriptstyle -0.282$	$v_t - 0.128v_{t-1} + 0.342v_{t-2} = \varepsilon_t$ $\scriptstyle -1.451 \qquad 3.895$
Tea	−2.356	−0.005 $\scriptstyle -2.273$	$u_t - 0.850u_{t-1} = \varepsilon_t$ $\scriptstyle -18.023$
$(1-L)$	−9.156	−0.005 $\scriptstyle -0.543$	$v_t = \varepsilon_t - 0.013\varepsilon_{t-1} - 0.355\varepsilon_{t-2}$ $\scriptstyle -0.143 \qquad -3.495$

* All estimates are for index series in real terms and in natural logarithms. Critical values for ADF tests in levels, allowing for trend and constant, are −3.99, −3.43, and −3.13 at the 1%, 5%, and 10% level respectively. The corresponding values for ADF tests allowing for a constant only are −3.46, −2.88, and −2.57.
** $(1-L)$: First difference of series.

It thus appears that the positive trend estimate registered by Grilli and Yang can be attributed to the a priori assumption of stationarity as well as the incidence of trade-based index weights. The more pronounced downward trajectory of tea prices may simply have taken time to manifest itself in the composite index. For the individual price series there is no strong evidence of either stochastic or deterministic trends. Cuddington (1992) reached this conclusion when investigating individual real price series over the initial 1900–1986 sample period: the increase in coffee prices is mainly attributed to a structural break, leaving no evidence for a significant upwards trend; stochastic trend estimates for tea and cocoa are negative and insignificant over this period too.

One further point worth considering in this context is the increasing diversification of some primary commodities in the agricultural sector. Kaplinsky (2006) gives one example of this when discussing the differentiated market placement of different coffee varieties, with some, such as Jamaican Blue Mountain, being classed as a premium product. Such product differentiation adds to the extent by which reference to a single benchmark product (such as Arabica coffee in the present case) simplifies price developments in actual product markets and may accordingly fail to capture all their relevant aspects.

3.3.3   Trends in miscellaneous food prices

In addition to the cereal and tropical beverage series discussed above, the Grilli and Yang data set includes series for a further five food commodities: sugar, beef, lamb, bananas, and palm oil. Visual inspection does not give the impression of a common intertemporal pattern among these commodities. Most of the commodities in this category show highly volatile real price trajectories over time, but no pronounced pattern of increase or decline. Two commodity series where a common pattern is apparent are the price series for beef and lamb shown in Figure 3.6.

Both series show short term volatility without any obvious trending behaviour in the early part of the twentieth century, before experiencing a sharp real price increase in the late 1950s. The trajectory thereafter continues to be highly volatile, though it does not seem clear, from visual inspection, whether the long term development would be appropriately characterized by a rising trend. The time series graph can plausibly be interpreted as that of upwards trending price series that experienced a period of temporarily low values in the decade following the Second World War, or as an illustration of price series experiencing a structural shift around this time.

Table 3.4 shows formal stationarity test results and trend estimates for the series under discussion. Among the five real food price series, the unit root null hypothesis can be rejected for sugar and lamb prices before differencing. The remaining series are identified as stationary in first differences. Sugar prices seem to follow a strong downward trend with significant estimates for both the deterministic and stochastic trend terms. Moreover, the selected ARIMA(1,1,2) specification for the model error of the difference stationary model alternative directly corresponds

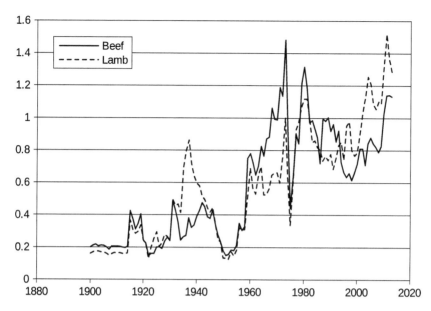

Figure 3.6 Beef and lamb price indices.

Note: Average annual price indices deflated by MUV, 1900–2013, 1977–1979 = 1.

Table 3.4 Trend estimates for miscellaneous food prices*

Series	ADF-τ	Trend	$u_t,\ v_t$
Sugar	−3.470	−0.009 -4.467	$u_t - 0.440u_{t-1} = \varepsilon_t + 0.411\varepsilon_{t-1}$ $\quad\ \ $ -3.613 $\qquad\qquad\qquad\quad$ 3.139
$(1-L)$**	−7.114	−0.009 -4.331	$v_t - 0.459v_{t-1} = \varepsilon_t - 0.597\varepsilon_{t-1} - 0.403\varepsilon_{t-2}$ $\quad\ \ $ -3.710 $\qquad\qquad$ -4.379 $\qquad\quad$ -2.998
Beef	−3.019	0.016 5.254	$u_t - 0.836u_{t-1} = \varepsilon_t$ $\quad\ \ $ -16.980
$(1-L)$	−7.943	0.015 0.760	$v_t = \varepsilon_t + 0.003\varepsilon_{t-1}$ $\qquad\qquad\quad$ 0.032
Lamb	−3.665	0.018 5.741	$u_t - 0.828u_{t-1} = \varepsilon_t$ $\quad\ \ $ -16.437
$(1-L)$	−4.578	0.018*** 0.840	$v_t + 0.332v_{t-1} = \varepsilon_t + 0.386\varepsilon_{t-1}$ $\quad\ \ $ 0.839 $\qquad\qquad\qquad\quad$ 1.023
Bananas	−1.896	0.001 0.469	$u_t - 0.945u_{t-1} + 0.321u_{t-2} - 0.287u_{t-3} = \varepsilon_t$ $\quad\ \ $ -10.561 $\qquad$ 2.620 $\qquad\quad$ -3.192
$(1-L)$	−9.968	0.004 0.579	$v_t + 0.010v_{t-1} + 0.329v_{t-2} = \varepsilon_t$ $\quad\ \ $ 0.117 $\qquad\quad$ 3.735
Palmoil	−3.123	−0.010 -5.168	$u_t - 0.600u_{t-1} = \varepsilon_t + 0.398\varepsilon_{t-1}$ $\quad\ \ $ -6.540 $\qquad\qquad\qquad$ 3.857
$(1-L)$	−9.819	−0.004 -0.271	$v_t - 0.076v_{t-1} + 0.357v_{t-2} = \varepsilon_t$ $\quad\ \ $ -0.869 $\qquad\quad$ 4.104

* All estimates are for index series in real terms and in natural logarithms. Critical values for ADF tests in levels, allowing for trend and constant, are −3.99, −3.43, and −3.13 at the 1%, 5%, and 10% level respectively. The corresponding values for ADF tests allowing for a constant only are −3.46, −2.88, and −2.57.
** $(1-L)$: First difference of series.
*** Differenced equivalent of minimum SBC stationary model.

to the first difference of the ARMA process identified for the trend stationary model alternative, while showing evidence of a unit moving average root. All these aspects of the two econometric model alternatives correspond to what one would expect when trend and difference stationary models are fitted to a trend stationary data generating process.

The price series for sugar is one case where the null hypothesis of structural stability around the putative 1920–1921 break point can be rejected ($\chi^2(1) = 11.9$). Including a level shift dummy in the estimating equation yields the familiar result of a significant coefficient estimate for the level shift dummy combined with an insignificant trend estimate:

$$\text{Sugar}: p_t = \underset{5.990}{0.964} - \underset{-3.184}{0.723D_{1921}} - \underset{-1.253}{0.003t} + u_t,$$

$$u_t - \underset{3.860}{0.468u_{t-1}} = \varepsilon_t + \underset{3.761}{0.441\varepsilon_{t-1}}.$$

In the cases of the remaining four commodity price series, we encounter the familiar pattern of statistically significant deterministic trend coefficient estimates and statistically insignificant drift terms. The one exception to this pattern is found for the price index for bananas, where no significant estimates for a price trend are obtained in either the differenced or undifferenced model alternatives: the estimated magnitude of the coefficient is small in both cases with $\hat{\beta} = 0.001, t = 0.469$ for the deterministic trend and $\hat{\beta} = 0.004$, $t = 0.579$ for the drift term. For palm oil, there is no evidence of a significant trend that holds across stationarity scenarios, and this conclusion is robust to model reselection by AIC for the differenced series.

In the cases of beef and lamb, the case for positive trend estimates is stronger. When ARIMA models for the model error are identified through the SBC, trend estimates for beef prices are significant for the deterministic trend but not for the stochastic trend coefficient. The latter estimate does appear statistically significant, though, if the ARIMA model is identified by AIC ($\hat{\beta} = 0.016, t = 5.153$) and there is evidence for a unit moving average root in this case. In the case of lamb, the evidence is somewhat weaker: the trend stationary model is supported by the unit root pretest and the trend coefficient obtained is significant. This is not the case for the difference stationary model alternative, though. The ARIMA(3,1,1) model identified by SBC returns autoregressive coefficient estimates summing to more than one, suggesting an increasingly destabilized series. While the price series for lamb is volatile, this characterization seems hardly plausible. Reselecting the model by AIC yields more plausible ARMA coefficient estimates, but no evidence of overdifferencing.[6] In Table 3.4 the differenced version of the minimum SBC ARMA model is therefore reported; this, too, yields a statistically insignificant drift coefficient estimate.

An alternative interpretation of the time series trajectories of beef and lamb prices is that of volatile series with a structural break. The putative break date can be located at 1956 from visual inspection of Figure 3.6. The likelihood ratio test rejects with $\chi^2_{\text{Beef}}(1) = 5.83$, $\chi^2_{\text{Lamb}}(1) = 9.14$ for a hypothesized break point date of 1956. The stationary models reported in Table 3.4 were then re-estimated including a dummy variable D_{1956} which takes a value of zero before the break date and a value of one thereafter, to yield:

$$\text{Beef: } p_t = \underset{-9.948}{-1.589} + \underset{3.207}{0.610} D_{1956} + \underset{2.683}{0.009} t + u_t, \ u_t - \underset{13.130}{0.778} u_{t-1} = \varepsilon_t$$

and

$$\text{Lamb: } p_t = \underset{-7.701}{-1.713} + \underset{2.419}{0.503} D_{1956} + \underset{2.902}{0.012} t + u_t, \ u_t - \underset{16.900}{0.839} u_{t-1} = \varepsilon_t,$$

with t-ratios reported below their respective coefficient estimates. The coefficient estimates for the structural shift dummy appear significant in both cases, while the trend coefficient estimates continue to appear statistically significant but now take smaller, arguably more plausible, values. Thus, while there appears to be some support for the view of a structural shift around the middle of the twentieth century in both real price series, this structural shift cannot account for the observed real price increase to such an extent that the trend component in the stationary model specification becomes obsolete.

Among the miscellaneous food prices there is no obvious common trend in terms of magnitude, size, or even statistical significance. In contrast to sub-categories like tropical beverages or cereals, there is of course less of a reason to expect such common elements in a miscellaneous category whose constituent commodities do not share common production constraints or target markets. Any such expectation should therefore result from the generalized thesis of broad commodity price comovement. Its relevance for developing countries arises from food commodities' prevalence in the export profiles of some developing countries relying on earnings from cash crops. The lack of a pronounced common intertemporal trajectory, while not surprising, is therefore worth noting with a view to the study of individual country export profiles.

3.3.4 Trends in metal prices

Price series for metals show a pattern of pronounced volatility without a clearly discernible pattern of common trends from visual inspection, though there appear to be shared experiences of commodity price booms among commodities like lead, zinc, and tin. Very pronounced spikes in copper and zinc prices can be seen in the early twentieth century, during the First World War, and again in the early twenty-first-century commodity price boom against the background of China's nascent industrialization (see Figure 3.7). Given the fundamental role of derived demand from industrial activity in creating short term price pressure for metals, this pattern is not surprising in itself.

Other metal price series like those for tin and silver show no clear pattern of comovement or common trend. In the case of aluminium, the series does appear to trend downwards from relatively high values in the early twentieth century.

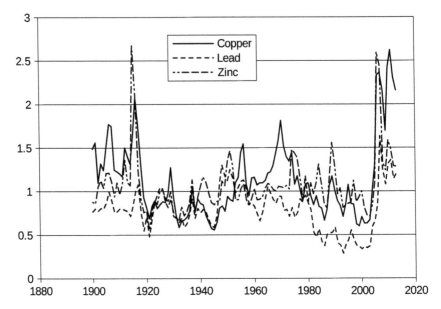

Figure 3.7 Price indices for copper, lead, and zinc.

Note: Average annual price indices deflated by MUV, 1900–2013, 1977–1979 = 1.

These informal impressions of time series characteristics are largely mirrored in formal estimates of commodity price trends.

Among real price series for metals, the time series for aluminium and zinc are identified as trend stationary by ADF tests, with the remaining series identified as stationary in first differences (see the first column in Table 3.5). Few of the commodities show significant evidence for the presence of trends.

The trend coefficient estimates for four of the six metal price series are in fact positive, though estimated trends for five of the six series (copper, tin, lead, silver, and zinc) are not statistically significant for either deterministic or stochastic trends.

The one exception to this overall pattern is aluminium, where a pronounced negative trend, suggesting an average annual price decline of 1.5 per cent, is noted for both the deterministic and the stochastic trend specification. Moreover, the stochastic trend based model shows evidence of a unit moving average root in the ARIMA process identified by either BIC or AIC, supporting the interpretation of this estimate as relating to a differenced trend stationary series. The series takes high values in the early twentieth century and experiences a rapid decline towards the hypothesized 1920–1921 break point date. The above trend estimate is robust to the inclusion of a level shift dummy for the post-1921 period. The likelihood ratio test fails to reject in this case ($\chi^2(1) = 2.72$) and the trend coefficient remains

Table 3.5 Trend estimates for metal prices*

Series	ADF-τ	Trend	u_t, v_t
Copper	−2.969	0.001 (0.383)	$u_t - 0.887u_{t-1} = \varepsilon_t$ (−20.084)
$(1 - L)^{**}$	−7.153	0.003 (0.183)	$v_t = \varepsilon_t + 0.105\varepsilon_{t-1}$ (1.094)
Aluminium	−3.618	−0.015 (−6.616)	$u_t - 0.766u_{t-1} = \varepsilon_t + 0.309\varepsilon_{t-1}$ (−11.325) (3.016)
$(1 - L)$	−7.991	−0.015 (−6.180)	$v_t - 0.784v_{t-1} = \varepsilon_t - 0.698\varepsilon_{t-1} - 0.302\varepsilon_{t-2}$ (−11.295) (−6.244) (−2.907)
Tin	−2.572	0.005 (1.316)	$u_t - 0.876u_{t-1} = \varepsilon_t$ (−20.143)
$(1 - L)$	−7.252	0.008 (0.420)	$v_t = \varepsilon_t + 0.063\varepsilon_{t-1}$ (0.567)
Silver	−1.726	0.007 (1.381)	$u_t - 0.915u_{t-1} = \varepsilon_t$ (−24.031)
$(1 - L)$	−8.553	0.009 (0.634)	$v_t - 0.096v_{t-1} + 0.249v_{t-2} = \varepsilon_t$ (−1.053) (2.731)
Lead	−2.519	−0.001 (−0.291)	$u_t - 0.863u_{t-1} = \varepsilon_t$ (−18.180)
$(1 - L)$	−7.161	0.004 (0.233)	$v_t = \varepsilon_t$
Zinc	−5.514	0.001 (1.149)	$u_t - 0.427u_{t-1} = \varepsilon_t + 0.386\varepsilon_{t-1}$ (−3.638) (3.271)
$(1 - L)$	−6.439	0.001 (1.120)	$v_t - 0.445v_{t-1} = \varepsilon_t - 0.621\varepsilon_{t-1} - 0.379\varepsilon_{t-2}$ (−3.754) (−5.095) (−3.178)

* All estimates are for index series in real terms and in natural logarithms. Critical values for ADF tests in levels, allowing for trend and constant, are −3.99, −3.43, and −3.13 at the 1%, 5%, and 10% level respectively. The corresponding values for ADF tests allowing for a constant only are −3.46, −2.88, and −2.57.
** $(1 - L)$: First difference of series.

significant with its approximate size unaltered:

$$\text{Aluminium: } p_t = \underset{9.521}{1.314} - \underset{-1.692}{0.241}D_{1921} - \underset{-5.670}{0.013}t + u_t,$$

$$u_t - \underset{-9.915}{0.734}u_{t-1} = \varepsilon_t + \underset{2.904}{0.294}\varepsilon_{t-1}.$$

Two metal price series for which the likelihood ratio test does reject the null hypothesis of no structural break in 1920–1921 are silver ($\chi^2(1) = 4.26$) and zinc ($\chi^2(1) = 8.50$). In both cases, re-estimating the trend stationary model with a level shift dummy at the putative break date yields a statistically significant positive trend coefficient estimate. For silver, the trend estimate now emerges in the following re-estimated equation:

$$\text{Silver: } p_t = \underset{-2.993}{-0.836} - \underset{-2.093}{0.389}D_{1921} + \underset{2.269}{0.010}t + u_t, \quad u_t - \underset{-20.673}{0.894}u_{t-1} = \varepsilon_t,$$

which suggests that real silver prices follow a strong upwards trend once a sharp one-off decline after 1920 has been discounted. One should note, though, that silver prices remain volatile at later dates, with pronounced price swings in both directions, and that this result is not replicated for a stochastic trend if the equivalent dummy variable is introduced.

For the less volatile zinc price series, the re-estimated equation now yields the following result:

$$\text{Zinc: } p_t = \underset{0.837}{0.070} - \underset{-3.035}{0.343D_{1921}} + \underset{2.914}{0.004t} + u_t,$$

$$u_t - \underset{-2.921}{0.350u_{t-1}} = \varepsilon_t + \underset{4.028}{0.434\varepsilon_{t-1}},$$

where discounting the post-1920 drop in real prices now produces a modestly positive trend. This result is reproduced for the stochastic trend, which now takes a value of $\hat{\beta} = 0.004$, $t = 2.859$ if a dummy variable for the 1920–1921 drop is included. In spite of the apparent robustness of the result, some caution is in order in its interpretation: the positive trend estimate may, at least in part, be driven by the early twenty-first-century commodity price boom. This may be appropriate if the upwards pressure on prices continues, but whether this will be the case will be revealed by further developments of the data series. For now, the end point of the data series does in fact show a pronounced metal price boom, but its duration to date is not unprecedented.

Evidence for a secular real price trend as a general characteristic is clearly absent for this commodity group. The price of aluminium, the one commodity that does show clear signs of a negative deterministic trend, does, however, conform to the hypothesis of a pronounced secular real price decline. Moreover, the price of metals is likely to be largely dependent on natural endowments on the one hand and fluctuations in industrial demand on the other. In this sense, the basic centre–periphery structure in the international division of labour appears to apply here, where some countries specialize in metal exports.

3.3.5 Trends in miscellaneous non-fuel commodity prices

Among the remaining seven miscellaneous commodities (cotton, jute, wool, hides, tobacco, rubber, and timber) there appears no obvious common trend or readily apparent comovement pattern. The series for timber seems to be trending upwards, while prices for hides and rubber seem to be consistently falling, although in the case of rubber this impression may be partly attributable to relatively high prices in the early part of the sample. The series for cotton, jute, and wool take relatively low values towards the end of the sample period (see Figure 3.8), but a pattern of consistent decay over the sample as a whole is less clear. Tobacco prices finally appear relatively stable following a period of low values in the early part of the sample.

When formally testing for unit roots, only the series for hides, rubber, and timber are identified as stationary in levels, while the unit root null hypothesis is rejected for all price series in first differences (see the first column of Table 3.6). Trend estimates for this set of commodity price series repeat the frequently

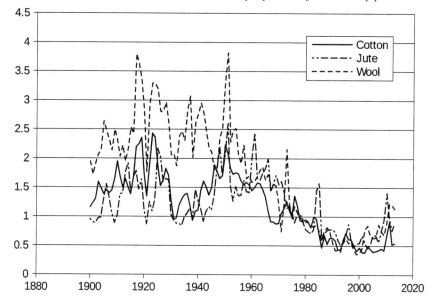

Figure 3.8 Price indices for cotton, jute, and wool.

Note: Average annual price indices deflated by MUV, 1900–2013, 1977–1979 = 1.

observed scenario of significant deterministic trend estimates and statistically insignificant estimates for stochastic trend coefficients.

Six of the seven miscellaneous non-food commodity price series have deterministic trend coefficient estimates that appear statistically significant; four of them are negative. By contrast, only one of the seven stochastic trend estimates in the difference stationary models selected by SBC appears to be statistically significant: the estimated drift coefficient for hides. This coefficient estimate is negative, and it is worth noting that the ARIMA process identified for this series shows evidence of overdifferencing in the form of a unit moving average root.

The real price series for hides is one of the cases where the likelihood ratio test for a structural break in 1920–1921 rejects ($\chi^2(1) = 9.08$). The finding of a statistically significant trend coefficient is robust to the inclusion of a level shift dummy in the estimating equation, although the inferred rate of decline is now noticeably slower:

$$\text{Hides: } p_t = \underset{5.690}{0.615} - \underset{-2.964}{0.444D_{1921}} - \underset{-2.038}{0.004t} + u_t, \ u_t - \underset{-7.430}{0.588u_{t-1}} = \varepsilon_t.$$

This slower rate of decline results as part of the overall drop in the index value over the sample period is captured by the level shift dummy, which has a significant coefficient estimate and shares the negative sign of the coefficient estimate on the trend vector.

When reselecting ARIMA models based on the AIC, two further price series (rubber and timber) show evidence of unit moving average roots combined with

Table 3.6 Trend estimates for miscellaneous non-food prices*

Series	ADF-τ	Trend	u_t, v_t
Cotton	−2.650	−0.010 $\underset{-3.127}{}$	$u_t - \underset{-11.224}{1.004}u_{t-1} + \underset{3.337}{0.424}u_{t-2} - \underset{-3.203}{0.303}u_{t-3} = \varepsilon_t$
$(1-L)^{**}$	−9.776	−0.007 $\underset{-0.755}{}$	$v_t = \varepsilon_t - \underset{-0.389}{0.034}\,\varepsilon_{t-1} - \underset{-4.538}{0.370}\varepsilon_{t-2}$
Jute	−2.610	−0.004 $\underset{-1.208}{}$	$u_t - \underset{-15.604}{0.913}u_{t-1} = \varepsilon_t + \underset{0.040}{0.004}\varepsilon_{t-1} - \underset{-3.665}{0.392}\varepsilon_{t-2}$
$(1-L)$	−10.811	−0.001 $\underset{-0.105}{}$	$v_t = \varepsilon_t - \underset{-0.708}{0.060}\varepsilon_{t-1} - \underset{-5.260}{0.450}\varepsilon_{t-2}$
Wool	−1.808	−0.010 $\underset{-2.112}{}$	$u_t - \underset{-26.418}{0.952}u_{t-1} = \varepsilon_t - \underset{-0.174}{0.017}\varepsilon_{t-1} - \underset{-4.395}{0.407}\varepsilon_{t-2}$
$(1-L)$	−7.344	−0.006 $\underset{-0.633}{}$	$v_t = \varepsilon_t - \underset{-0.506}{0.043}\varepsilon_{t-1} - \underset{-5.116}{0.429}\varepsilon_{t-2}$
Hides	−3.792	−0.007 $\underset{-4.739}{}$	$u_t - \underset{-8.143}{0.605}u_{t-1} = \varepsilon_t$
$(1-L)$	−6.218	−0.007 $\underset{-4.548}{}$	$v_t - \underset{-8.149}{0.619}v_{t-1} = (1-L)\varepsilon_t$
Tobacco	−3.000	0.009 $\underset{2.977}{}$	$u_t - \underset{-25.887}{0.925}u_{t-1} = \varepsilon_t$
$(1-L)$	−7.785	0.011 $\underset{1.634}{}$	$v_t - \underset{-1.019}{0.090}v_{t-1} + \underset{0.396}{0.035}v_{t-2} + \underset{1.462}{0.128}v_{t-3} + \underset{3.826}{0.334}v_{t-4} = \varepsilon_t$
Rubber	−3.898	−0.020 $\underset{-4.290}{}$	$u_t - \underset{-18.233}{0.862}u_{t-1} = \varepsilon_t$
$(1-L)$	−7.524	−0.017 $\underset{-0.606}{}$	$v_t = \varepsilon_t + \underset{0.655}{0.068}\varepsilon_{t-1}$
Timber	−4.628	0.009 $\underset{6.459}{}$	$u_t - \underset{-13.284}{0.774}u_{t-1} = \varepsilon_t$
$(1-L)$	−8.579	0.009 $\underset{0.993}{}$	$v_t = \varepsilon_t + \underset{0.157}{0.015}\varepsilon_{t-1} - \underset{-2.255}{0.233}\varepsilon_{t-2}$

* All estimates are for index series in real terms and in natural logarithms. Critical values for ADF tests in levels, allowing for trend and constant, are −3.99, −3.43, and −3.13 at the 1%, 5%, and 10% level respectively. The corresponding values for ADF tests allowing for a constant only are −3.46, −2.88, and −2.57.
** $(1-L)$: First difference of series.

significant stochastic trend estimates.[7] As in the deterministic trend based estimates, the estimated trend coefficient is positive for timber prices and negative
for the rubber price series. The series for rubber also experiences relatively high
price level values prior to the putative break point in 1921, and the likelihood ratio
test ($\chi^2(1) = 12.7$) clearly rejects the null hypothesis in this case. Re-estimating
the trend stationary model with a level shift dummy for the post-1921 sub-sample
yields the following result:

$$\text{Rubber: } p_t = \underset{8.837}{2.030} - \underset{-3.878}{0.912}D_{1921} - \underset{-3.637}{0.013}t + u_t, \; u_t - \underset{-13.796}{0.794}u_{t-1} = \varepsilon_t,$$

which shows that that the trend coefficient estimate remains significant, with only
a modest effect on the value of the point estimate. In contrast to the case of
aluminium, the dummy variable now appears statistically significant and takes
a negative sign as expected.

Given the heterogeneous nature of the seven miscellaneous commodities selected, the observed discrepancy in time series characteristics need not be seen as surprising. The most closely related commodity price series are those for the textile inputs cotton, jute, and wool, while prices for hides will also be strongly influenced by conditions in related food sectors. The one scenario under which a common trend should be expected for such a set of commodity price series is the clustering of commodity-dependent exporters in a declining primary sector of the global economy as envisaged in the Prebisch–Singer hypothesis. The absence of this predominant common trend characteristic is demonstrated for these non-homogeneous primary commodities as for other commodity groups previously.

3.4 Concluding reflections: commodity prices and trends

The results presented in this chapter show decidedly mixed results regarding the presence of secular trends in primary commodity prices. Only three of the eight compound indices and eight of the 24 individual commodity price series considered show any reliably significant trends at all, by the criteria adopted in this chapter. All compound index series show evidence of a structural break after 1921, but this is only true of six individual commodity price series. If inference on trends had been based simply on the result of the ADF unit root test and subsequently fitted trend or difference stationary models, the overall number of identified trending price series remains unaltered, although different conclusions would be reached for some commodities: no significant trend would be inferred for rice and wheat, while significant trends would be inferred for maize and lamb prices. It is further worth noting that some of the more robust conclusions on the presence of trends relate to positive secular trends (for beef and timber) and that a further upwards trend would be inferred for lamb under the pretest method.

The observation of non-homogeneous trend movements between commodities, and reference to it in opposition to the Prebisch–Singer hypothesis, is not in itself new. Kindleberger (1958) made this general point in the context of the original debate, and – like Singer – without the benefit of hindsight, of advanced statistical methods and computational resources, or of long run continuous data series. The general observation of non-homogeneous long run trajectories is borne out by observations based on higher quality data and over longer run time horizons, though: the pretest method as well as the approach of establishing evidence for the presence of a trend across stationarity alternatives point to the incidence of a statistically significant trend component in about a third of cases. The inferred trends differ in magnitude and, at times, in direction. This general result is also similar to the one obtained by Cuddington (1992) based on unit root pretesting, although with more in-depth discussion of structural breaks in a data set which included two fuel price series. Cuddington (1992) infers the presence of trend terms for 10 out of 26 real commodity price series considered over a shorter 1900–1983 sample period; five of these price series have positive trends.

One important conclusion to draw from this result is that broadly defined composite commodity indices like the Grilli and Yang index are likely to obscure relevant details about the time series characteristics of their constituent series. The implications of this conclusion are highly policy relevant: a key motivating factor in the discussion of the commodity terms of trade was the assumption that these would drive developing country terms of trade more generally, acting as a uniform constraint on developing country growth through their deterioration. The intertemporal correlation between the commodity terms of trade and country-specific net barter terms of trade series has therefore received some attention in the context of the empirical debate surrounding the Prebisch–Singer hypothesis and the Grilli and Yang index – see Leon and Soto (1995) and Lutz (1999) for examples. If broad composite commodity indices do not consistently represent the mean evolution of their constituent elements over time then any correlation between such indices and individual country terms of trade should be seen as a statistical curiosity rather than an empirical test of generalized trade based resource constraints.

Another aspect that dominated the earlier part of the debate was the choice of time interval (see the introductory discussion to this chapter). One hypothesized reason for Singer's early result was the data period used, extending from the late nineteenth century to 1938. If the stochastic trend for the Grilli and Yang index is estimated for the 1900–1940 interval (again selecting by SBC, for $p+q \leq 5$), the following estimate is obtained:

$$\text{GYCPI}: (1-L)p_t = \underset{-2.378}{-0.011} + v_t, \quad v_t - \underset{-5.909}{0.724}v_{t-1} = (1-L)\varepsilon_t.$$

A significant stochastic trend estimate is also obtained for GYCPIM for this sub-period ($\hat{\beta}_M = 0.0169$, $t = -3.443$), but not for the overall food and non-food sub-indices.[8] There is also no indication that trend movements were more pronounced for individual commodities during this interval, with significant negative stochastic trends recorded for cocoa, aluminium, and silver, while a positive drift term would be inferred for lamb prices. In all these sub-sample estimates, the presence of a significant trend coefficient estimate coincides with a unit moving average root in the ARIMA process. Thus, the overall link between the presence of a trend and an assumption of stationarity appears to be evident in the earlier sub-sample period as well.

The statistical significance of a trend is mainly of interest for the extrapolation of measured price trajectories to future periods. The historic price decline over most of the twentieth century for a number of primary commodities can at most draw on trend estimates as descriptive summary measures. What is relevant over this past period and with regards to the Prebisch–Singer hypothesis is the question of economic significance, that is, the magnitude of the average rate of decline. In those cases where the presence of a stable trend component can be inferred with sufficient confidence, this magnitude can also be of relevance for forecasting. A small trend component in a volatile and serially correlated data series may simply not have sufficient impact on the future values of the series over short forecast horizons. Its inclusion may therefore not improve forecast performance even if it is known to be part of the data series.

This phenomenon is discussed with regards to commodity price forecasts in Newbold, Pfaffenzeller, and Rayner (2005) against the background of more general simulation results. To assess the magnitude of trend coefficient estimates compared to the volatility of their price series, Newbold, Pfaffenzeller, and Rayner (2005) divide the value of the point estimate of the trend coefficient by the standard error of the ARMA model. This normalized coefficient value then allows a tentative comparison with the simulation results in which the prediction errors from forecast models with and without trend were compared when the data-generating process to which these models were fitted contained a trend. Some caution is needed when comparing empirical coefficient estimates to these results, since the general simulations were undertaken for simple AR(1) and MA(1) data-generating processes rather than the more complex parameterizations observed for some commodity price models.

The normalized coefficients here are consistently above the value of $\tilde{\beta} = 0.2 - 0.3$ that the simulation results indicate as necessary for a forecast improvement over a ten-year horizon when the autoregressive series are highly correlated ($\phi = 0.8 - 0.9$), while being below the absolute value required for improved forecasts from the inclusion of stochastic trend terms (see Newbold, Pfaffenzeller, and Rayner 2005, p. 491). A tentative assessment of empirical trend estimates against this simulation evidence therefore supports the view that commodity price trends are best interpreted within the context of a deterministic trend based model. Where a stochastic trend is more appropriate, the information added by a moderately sized drift estimate is also likely to be less useful in practical terms.

The long run characteristics of commodity price series are more prominently captured by a stylized fact of pronounced volatility than a shared negative trend. The above results in terms of a 'signal to noise' ratio interpretation of price trends are broadly consistent with the results of Newbold, Pfaffenzeller, and Rayner (2005), which are based on a shorter sample. They are also qualitatively similar to the conclusion reached by Cashin and McDermott (2001), who based their study of commodity price cycles on *The Economist*'s commodity price index in real terms and note that estimated trends are commonly too small to be considered economically significant.

This central observation of price volatility contrasts markedly with the historical assumption of a sustained and pronounced real price decline across different primary commodity categories. Significant trends are only identified for a sub-sample of the 24 non-fuel commodities considered, and these differ in magnitude or even in sign. This absence of pronounced and secular trend movements implies a lack of support for one of the key postulates of the Prebisch–Singer hypothesis. It does not imply, however, that a strong primary sector orientation in developing countries is unproblematic. The extent to which price volatility translates into export earnings volatility will itself depend on a number of factors, including the degree of product diversification within the overall primary sector. Other factors include the scope for increasing the amount of value added within the local economy or the ability to capture rents from premium products. An increase in locally added value is a particularly attractive prospect with a view to wider economic development objectives, if it is linked to more extensive skill acquisition.

In addition to the question of the stability and potential decline of commodity export earnings, the preceding discussion highlights the importance of a domestic institutional infrastructure to channel these earnings into productive investment opportunities. It is at this point that the balance of payments constrained growth perspective and the stage transitions envisaged in the previous chapter combine with the stylized facts characterizing the intertemporal evolution of developing country export earnings at the pre-industrial and industrializing stages. This topic focus aligns closely with Rostow's view of generating sufficient and appropriately structured investment demand as well as with Thirlwall's focus on the balance of payments constraint in this context.

The possible role of declining barter terms of trade in tightening the balance of payments constraint is easy to conceptualize within the overall topic of developing country transition. Commodity price volatility, on the other hand, is likely to have an impact mainly through export earnings uncertainty. This topic is in turn closely linked to country-specific institutions geared towards managing export earnings and earnings fluctuations, as well as to track records of fiscal discipline. It will, therefore, need to be informed by country-specific data.

In view of the fact that commodity price movements are not well captured by common stylized facts such as common trends or excess comovement, it should come as no surprise that individual country experiences are no less diverse. The following chapter will therefore direct the focus to a more general account of individual country experiences for a selection of developing countries with differing degrees of commodity export dependence, different degrees of sectoral concentrations, and differing experiences in moving towards a structural transition.

Notes

1 Grilli and Yang (1988) also discussed the US Manufacturing Price Index (USMPI) as an alternative deflator series, but the MUV has been more frequently adopted in the literature – see Cuddington (1992), Newbold, Pfaffenzeller, and Rayner (2005), and Pfaffenzeller, Newbold, and Rayner (2007).

2 For a general introductory discussion of stationarity and unit root testing, see Enders (1995, Chapters 2 and 4).

3 For a general discussion of ARMA models see Enders (1995, Chapter 2) or Harvey (1993, Chapters 2 and 3).

4 The differenced equivalent to a stationary ARMA(1,0,0) process is an ARIMA(1,1,1) process.

5 See Pfaffenzeller, Newbold, and Rayner (2007) for the computation of sub-index weights; the figures given here are rounded to whole digits.

6 The minimum SBC ARIMA model yields a coefficient estimate of $\hat{\beta} = 0.019$, $t = 1.175$ and a model error parameterization of $v_t + 0.829v_{t-1} + 0.198v_{t-2} + 0.317v_{t-3} = \varepsilon_t + 0.877\varepsilon_{t-1}$ with $\sum \hat{\phi} = -1.344$, while the analogous AIC-selected ARIMA process would imply $\sum \hat{\phi} = -0.821$.

7 The estimates obtained are $\hat{\beta} = -0.021$, $t = -4.318$ for rubber and $\hat{\beta} = 0.009$, $t = 7.246$ for timber.
8 These estimates are: $\hat{\beta}_F = -0.005$, $t = -0.257$ and $\hat{\beta}_{NF} = -0.006$, $t = -0.234$ for GYCPIF and GYCPINF respectively, with ARIMA models identified by SBC.

References

Agiakloglou, C. and P. Newbold (1992). 'Empirical evidence on Dickey–Fuller type tests'. *Journal of Time Series Analysis* 13.6, 471–83.

Agiakloglou, C. and P. Newbold (1996). 'The balance between size and power in Dickey–Fuller tests with data dependent rules for the choice of truncation lag'. *Economics Letters* 52.3, 229–34.

Baffes, J. (2007). 'Oil spills on other commodities'. *Resources Policy* 32.3, 126–34. Available at: www.sciencedirect.com/science/article/B6VBM-4PT2FV9-1/2/a49dfeac77c22e3c9c18c3529d3a9f7e (accessed on 15th March 2010).

Baffes, J. and D. Cosic (2014). *Commodity Markets Outlook – April 2014*. Technical report. Washington, DC: The World Bank. Available at: www.worldbank.org/content/dam/Worldbank/GEP/GEPcommodities/Commodity-Markets_Outlooks_April_2014.pdf (accessed on 6th March 2015).

Cashin, P. and J. McDermott (2001). *The Long-Run Behavior of Commodity Prices: Small Trends and Big Variability*. Working Paper WP/01/68. Washington, DC: International Monetary Fund.

Cashin, P., J. McDermott, and A. Scott (1999). *The Myth of Comoving Commodity Prices* Working Paper WP/99/169. Washington, DC: International Monetary Fund.

Cuddington, J. (1992). 'Long-run trends in 26 primary commodity prices'. *Journal of Development Economics* 39.2, 207–27.

Cuddington, J. and C. Urzua (1989). 'Trends and cycles in the net barter terms of trade: a new approach'. *The Economic Journal* 99.396, 426–42.

Cuddington J. and H. Wei (1992). 'An empirical analysis of real commodity Price trends: aggregation, model selection and implications'. *Estudios Económicos* 7.2, 159–79.

Enders, W. (1995). *Applied Econometric Time Series*. Wiley Series in Probability and Mathematical Statistics. New York: John Wiley & Sons, Inc.

Grilli, E. and M. C. Yang (1988). 'Primary commodity prices, manufactured goods prices, and the terms of trade of developing countries: what the long run shows'. *The World Bank Economic Review* 2.1, 1–47.

Harvey, A. (1993). *Time Series Models*. London: Harvester Wheatsheaf.

Harvey, D. I. et al. (2011). 'The Prebisch–Singer hypothesis: four centuries of evidence'. *Review of Economics and Statistics* 92.2, 367–377. Available at: http://dx.doi.org/10.1162/rest.2010.12184 (accessed on 4th August 2011).

Ingersent, K. and A. Rayner (1999). *Agricultural Policy in Western Europe and the United States*. Cheltenham: Edward Elgar Publishing.

Kaplinsky, R. (2006). 'Revisiting the revisited terms of trade: will China make a difference?' *World Development* 34.6, 981–95.

Kim, T.-H., S. Pfaffenzeller, A. Rayner, and P. Newbold (2003). 'Testing for linear trend with application to relative primary commodity prices'. *Journal of Time Series Analysis* 24.5, 505–629.

Kindleberger, C. (1958). 'The terms of trade and economic development'. *Review of Economics and Statistics* 40.1, 72–85.

Leon, J. and R. Soto (1995). 'Términos de intercambio en La América Latina, una cuantificación de La hipótesis de Prebisch y Singer'. *El Trimestre Economico* 62.2, 171–99.

Lutz, M. (1999). 'Commodity terms of trade and individual countries' net barter terms of trade: is there an empirical relationship?' *Journal of International Development* 11.6, 859–70.

MacKinnon, J. G. (1996). 'Numerical distribution functions for unit root and cointegration tests'. *Journal of Applied Econometrics* 11.6, 601–18. Avaliable at: http://onlinelibrary.wiley.com/doi/10.1002/(SICI)1099-1255(199611)11:6%3C601::AID-JAE417%3E3.02CO; %202-T/abstract (accessed on 26th August 2011).

Newbold, P. and C. Granger (1974). 'Spurious regressions in econometrics'. *Journal of Econometrics* 2.2, 111–20.

Newbold, P., S. Pfaffenzeller, and A. Rayner (2005). 'How well are long-run commodity price series characterized by trend components?' *Journal of International Development* 17.4, 479–94.

Newbold, P., A. Rayner, and N. Kellard (2000). 'Long-run drift, co-movement and persistence in real wheat and maize prices'. *Journal of Agricultural Economics* 51.1, 106–21.

Perron, P. (1989). 'The great crash, the oil price shock and the unit root hypothesis'. *Econometrica* 57.6, 1361–401.

Pfaffenzeller, S., P. Newbold, and A. Rayner (2007). 'A short note on updating the Grilli and Yang commodity price index'. *The World Bank Economic Review* 21.1, 1–13.

Radetzki, M. (2010). *A Handbook of Primary Commodities in the Global Economy.* Cambridge: Cambridge University Press.

Sapsford, D. (1985). 'The statistical debate on the net barter terms of trade between primary commodities and manufactures: a comment and some additional evidence'. *The Economic Journal* 95.379, 781–8.

Sapsford, D., P. Sarkar, and H. Singer (1992). 'The Prebisch–Singer terms of trade controversy revisited'. *Journal of International Development* 4.3, 315–32.

Schlote, W. (1938). *Entwicklung und Strukturwandlungen des englischen Außenhandels.* Probleme der Weltwirtschaft. Kiel: Institut für Weltwirtschaft and der Universität Kiel.

Spraos, J. (1980). 'The statistical debate on the net barter terms of trade between primary commodities and manufactures'. *The Economic Journal* 90.9, 107–28.

Toye, J. and R. Toye (2003). 'The origins and interpretation of the Prebisch–Singer thesis'. *History of Political Economy* 35.3, 437–67.

Zimmerman, C. (1932). 'Ernst Engel's law of expenditures for food'. *The Quarterly Journal of Economics* 47.1, 78–101.

4 Country case studies
Primary commodities and economic development

4.1 Introduction

The preceding chapter discussed the intertemporal behaviour of real primary commodity prices at some length. One key assumption underlying the study of primary commodities as a determinant of economic development prospects is their predominant role in the position of underdeveloped economies. This situation has been traditionally assumed to translate into commodity dependence on the side of export earnings. While the intertemporal developments of real commodity prices have been shown not to be as homogeneous as previously assumed, the current discussion has yet to focus on the general economic properties of developing countries and on the extent and role of their commodity dependence in particular.

For a first, somewhat informal, impression of commodity dependence among developing countries we can turn to Table 4.1, which shows the share of manufacturing exports for selected developing economies from 1965 onwards in ten-year intervals up to the crisis year of 2008. An implicit assumption underlying the focus on the share of manufactured commodities in overall merchandise exports is that of a complementary incidence of primary sector exports: if developing countries export manufactured goods, agricultural products, raw materials, and mining products but have no significant presence in trading services (such as in the information technology sector) then the primary commodity export share should correspond to the difference between the export share of manufactured goods and the total.

This assumption is likely to be most realistic for the early part of the sample period considered (that is, for the years 1965 and 1975 in Table 4.1). In later years, service sector exports are likely to become increasingly important in at least some of the countries (for example China or India) simply because an ongoing and to some extent successful development process can open up possibilities for services trade and international interaction, for example in information and communications technologies. A further problem arises due to limited data availability. The World Development Indicators report data on the manufacturing sector's export share from 1962. A number of developing countries did not systematically report data until 1985 or later, though. In a number of cases (for example Nigeria and Zambia), data from adjacent years have been included instead of the selected years in Table 4.1 and are identified as such. In other cases, data for early or

Table 4.1 Selected developing countries: manufacturing export shares

Country	1965	1975	1985	1995	2005	2008
Argentina	5.61	24.38	21.35	33.86	30.80	31.17
Bangladesh	–	–	65.80	85.15	91.19	91.92
Botswana	–	–	–	–	85.35	76.29
Brazil	7.74	25.29	43.74	53.53	52.96	44.85
Cameroon	4.96	10.57	–	7.92	3.13	23.38
Chile	3.92	10.03	6.87	13.48	15.09	15.96
China	–	–	26.43	84.13	91.88	92.99
India	48.24	44.86	58.11	73.55	71.07	62.78
Nicaragua	5.30	16.88	6.31	20.72	10.52	35.26
Nigeria	1.12	0.17	0.04	1.11[1]	1.34[2]	5.46
Vietnam	–	–	–	–	50.19	55.17
Zambia	0.15[3]	0.67	–	6.95	8.76	6.70

Source: World Development Indicators. [1]1996, [2]2006, [3]1966.

intermittent time periods are simply not available and had to be omitted. This lack of continuous data availability is a frequent problem in the study of developing and emerging economies, yielding incomplete and potentially biased data records. The potential for bias should be considered for cases where data reporting correlates with the presence of a stable institutional structure, which in its turn can be linked to transformative investment and sustained growth. While the extent and magnitude of any such bias are naturally difficult to quantify, one should bear in mind that periods of low growth and inadequate economic infrastructure are particularly likely to coincide with gaps in the data record: when reviewing Africa's lost decade, Meredith (2013, Chapter 22) notes that statistical offices are among the first victims of tightening fiscal constraints.

With these caveats in mind, one can note that a large number of those developing countries which did supply data for the earlier periods did indeed have very low manufacturing export shares in 1965, and often in 1975 as well. One exception to this rule is India,[1] which ran a strongly protectionist trade regime prior to 1990, as well as Argentina and Brazil, where the manufacturing export share increased between 1965 and 1975. On the other hand, it does not appear to be the case that those countries which started off with low manufacturing export shares also consistently remained in this condition. With the exception of Cameroon, Chile, and Nigeria, all countries in the sample for whom a comparison with early period data is possible appear to have significantly and consistently increased their shares of manufactured goods exports, even though the underlying economic development processes for the individual countries concerned can differ markedly.

In the case of Chile, manufactured product exports remain at a rather modest level, although the country remained macroeconomically stable and has experienced healthy income growth rates. Nigeria and Cameroon have both retained very low levels of manufacturing export participation, with different economic consequences. In the case of Nigeria, the underlying driver of this development is the large amount of oil export revenue accruing at the national level. The export profile for Cameroon has been more diversified after depending mainly on agricultural exports in earlier periods, with a non-trivial role for oil exports in more recent years (see UN trade data and World Bank 2014a). On the other hand, Bangladesh, a persistently low income country, has experienced a substantial increase in manufacturing sector export participation to a very high level of 91.92 per cent by 2008. Yet, in that same year, the purchasing power parity adjusted level of per capita GDP for Bangladesh had reached a mere 3.58 per cent of the equivalent figure for the USA. This compares to 31.80 per cent for Chile, 5.08 per cent for Cameroon, 5.51 per cent for Nigeria, and 4.74 per cent for Zambia.[2]

This informal contemplation of the evolution and comparative prevalence of commodity exports casts some doubt on the view of a consistent correlation between manufacturing export participation and economic growth (and ultimately convergence to high levels of GDP per capita). It also calls into question the a priori assumption that an initial condition of commodity export dependence is generally self-perpetuating. Examples of successful export diversification from the primary to the secondary sectors are not a universal characteristic of developing economy trajectories, but they are not rarities either. If there is one message arising from this informal discussion of selected trade data it is the need to consider the nature of individual country experiences in some detail, and to consider a number of additional indicator variables.

The preceding discussion has been intentionally eclectic in its attempt to illustrate the empirical background with a set of suitably diverse examples. The following discussion of country cases will be even more narrowly focused before a wider view is taken in the concluding chapter. The subsequent discussion in this chapter will turn to a number of country case studies from Latin America, Africa, and Asia. In all three regions, developing countries have experienced different developments of commodity dependence and real export growth. While this book is not a study of convergence as such, the individual country studies will address the issue of evolving commodity export dependence against the background of other contextual macroeconomic variables.

The level of real GDP and purchasing power parity adjusted real GDP, as well as the evolution of income growth rates, are clearly relevant indicator variables in this context. Data for these variables are available from the World Bank's World Development Indicators, normally from 1960 onward, although purchasing power parity adjusted series have been obtained from the Penn World Tables since they were often unavailable for earlier years in the World Development Indicators. GDP per capita figures are of course limited in scope in so far as they do not take account of distributional characteristics and drivers of wellbeing that are not captured by monetary income measures of any kind. This problem is well recognized in development economics and has given rise to alternative indicators such as the Human Development Index. Detailed consideration of alternative measures of development success is, however, beyond the scope of the present volume, which will content itself with looking to per capita income figures and growth rates as an approximate measure of development and convergence.

Another variable that can be seen as an indicator of labour market formalization and hence of modernization is female labour market employment participation outside the agricultural sector. Employed labour is likely to impact on recorded participation rates when entering the formal sector, and this is more likely to be the case as developing country agricultural sites, and subsistence plots in particular, are left behind for employment in a nascent industrial sector. This gender role division is well documented and literally a textbook topic – see Smith and Todaro (2008, pp. 450–3) on the role of women in subsistence agriculture and economic development; Young (1995) comments on the impact of increasing female labour force participation on recorded participation rates in newly industrializing countries. Overall parity in formal labour force participation is reached at around 50 per cent female labour force participation outside the agricultural sector. Data series on this indicator are often incomplete, yet the World Development Indicators attempt to provide a comprehensive international data set. Data on non-agricultural female labour force participation will be reported where available, although data gaps are frequent. (This is true at the aggregate level for the World Development Indicators and more so in the disaggregated manufacturing sector data published in the UNIDO Industrial Statistics database, where this data series is listed in principle.)

While other peripheral variables like inflation rates and exchange rate movements may be of interest in some cases and periods, the main focus in country case studies is naturally on the role of commodity exports in the overall export profile and its development over time. The analysis of commodity trade profiles is based on individual country trade data with the rest of the world from the UN Comtrade database. Data series were retrieved for all commodities at the one- and two-digit SITC (Standard International Trade Classification) levels, although not all data series listed in the Comtrade database are complete.

SITC classifications identify categories of economic activity but are not intended, nor necessarily suited, for mirroring economic aggregates corresponding to particular aspects of economic theory. Radetzki (2010, p. 24) proposes a further aggregation of commodity data into broader categories. To obtain a measure of food trade in a broad sense, the one-digit SITC categories 0, 1, and 4 and the sub-category 22 can be added (where higher-digit SITC classifications correspond to finer disaggregations of economic activity). Agricultural raw materials are defined as the difference between SITC category 2 and sub-categories 22, 27, and 28.[3] Minerals and metals are given by the aggregate of SITC sub-classifications 27, 28, 67, and 68,[4] while mineral fuels are represented by the one-digit SITC classification 3.

The sum total of the total export value over these broad categories then captures the overall value of commodity exports and can be expressed as a percentage of total exports (the aggregate of export values over all SITC categories). Likewise, percentage shares of each of the four broad commodity aggregates and their evolution over time can give some indication of the extent to which an economy depends on a narrowly defined export niche and to what extent it diversified over the sample period covered. Similar computations are possible for import values, of course.

In spite of the fact that SITC classifications do not readily map onto economic theoretical concepts, the development of concentrations of trading activity across classification categories can indicate how narrowly commodity export dependence is focused and to what extent such a dependency characteristic strengthens or weakens over time. One conventionally used concentration measure is the Hirschman–Herfindahl concentration index. A common definition (Rhoades 1993) for this index takes the form

$$\text{HHI} = \sum_{i=1}^{N} \left(\frac{x_i}{X}\right)^2,$$

(4.1)

where x_i is sector i's export value and X is the total value of exports across all SITC classes at the relevant level of disaggregation. In other words, the Hirschman–Herfindahl index simply takes the sum of squared market shares as a measure of concentration, although Hirschman (1964) points out that the Herfindahl variant of the index is expressed as $\sqrt{\text{HHI}}$.

By using squared trade shares, industrial categories with larger trade participation are given disproportionately larger weights. This property is deemed desirable in the assessment of market concentration as well as in the study of commodity dependence since in either case the importance of concentration increases as individual component shares come to dominate the underlying market or trading process. The Hirschman–Herfindahl index tends to a maximum value of one for the highest possible concentration measure; in the present case, this would correspond to a scenario where only commodities in one product category are exported or imported. At the other extreme, the lowest possible concentration occurs when all products have equal trade shares of $1/N$ for N different product classes. To obtain an index measure that is bounded between zero and one, the Hirschman–Herfindahl index can be normalized to yield[5]

$$\text{NHHI} = \frac{\text{HHI} - \frac{1}{N}}{1 - \frac{1}{N}}, \quad N > 1,$$

(4.2)

which clearly takes a value of one where the non-normalized HHI does, and converges on zero for a uniform participation share of $1/N$. In theory, the non-normalized Hirschman–Herfindahl index likewise approaches a lower bound of zero for a uniform distribution of market share and a very large number N of competitors or categories. In the particular case of high-level SITC categories, the number of one-digit categories is 10 and the number of two-digit categories is 61. The lower bound of the non-normalized concentration index therefore remains recognizably above a zero lower value in both cases.

In contrast to its usage in the study of competitive market structure, there are no conventionally defined threshold values for the Hirschman–Herfindahl index, nor would it be obvious how such values would be defined with regards to a number of discrete, administratively and ultimately arbitrarily defined activity classifications. What can, however, be judged relatively unambiguously is the intertemporal trajectory of concentration measures and, to some extent, their close proximity to extreme values. An economy dependent on a single commodity export (a so called monoeconomy; Radetzki 2010) should be expected to have a very high concentration measure. The traditional predictions based on the theoretical framework of Prebisch and Singer would be for an intertemporal persistence of this high export concentration coupled with a protracted stagnation of real national income. Successful diversification into other commodity sectors would accordingly surface in an intertemporal decline in export concentration values.

This prediction motivates inclusion of rates of decay for Hirschman–Herfindahl index values, although it is vital to bear in mind that these indicators are somewhat crude and limited in their scope. An increase in export concentration, in particular at the two-digit level, could well be indicative of an increased focus on a country's area of comparative advantage. It thus need not be a sign of economically undesirable developments, although there is an inherent aspect of vulnerability linked to strong dependence on a single, narrowly focused export sector. With a view to recent developments it is also worth noting that a protracted commodity price boom is likely to be reflected in increased export concentration values, simply because the value of exports in an existing comparative advantage sector has experienced a price driven increase. Such an episode would give the appearance of an increasingly narrowed export profile, but need not be indicative of lasting structural changes.

A comparison of concentration indices at one- and two-digit SITC levels can play a similar role in identifying developments consistent with ongoing intra-industry diversification. In such a situation, a country's export profile may remain consistently dominated by one commodity category at a high (one-digit) level of aggregation, while diversification into related further processing is identifiable in a more disaggregated trade profile. Where such a situation occurs, one would expect the Hirschman–Herfindahl index at the one-digit aggregation level to show a consistently high level of trade concentration while the two-digit trade profile becomes more diversified over time. In the following discussion, the ratio of the Hirschman–Herfindahl index at the two-digit SITC level relative to the index at the one-digit level will be considered as a summary measure of relative trade activity concentration at different aggregation levels. If this ratio falls in value, the concentration of trading activity is becoming relatively lower at the higher disaggregation level. The absolute concentration level should, of course, be expected to be weakly lower at the higher trade activity disaggregation by definition. What is of interest here is the comparative pattern of movement indicative of relative speeds of decline or increase.[6] The above caveats for the interpretation of concentration measures apply here too; index measures of trade concentration can often be produced by more than one structural process and are susceptible to large and protracted price booms. They should therefore be interpreted with care, against a background analysis of the relevant country's economic profile and on the understanding that such index measures provide at best circumstantial evidence in the broader context of a more detailed analysis of a country's economic profile.

Alongside the general macroeconomic profile data discussed above, the sectoral composition of the domestic manufacturing sector can provide additional insights into the ongoing development and transformation of an emerging economy. The UNIDO Industrial Statistics database provides sectorally disaggregated data on output, value added, and investment (as captured by the gross fixed capital formation). While even an informal discussion of such disaggregated manufacturing activity profiles can be highly informative, access to these profiles themselves depends on data availability, and this is where the data series supplied tend to fall short for many developing countries. Data on the distribution of industrial activity[7] will therefore be considered in so far as they are available as part of a general discussion of the country's economic profile.

The remainder of this chapter will provide case study examples of individual developing countries in a number of regional contexts. In each case, the role of commodity trade will be highlighted and interpreted against the background of a broader analysis of the country's economic profile. Data on general macroeconomic indicators and female labour force participation outside the agricultural sector have been taken from the World Bank's World Development Indicators (WDI). While the choice of indicators has been discussed above, it is worth reiterating that the series obtained from the WDI were the average annual inflation rate (based on the GDP deflator) and exchange rates with depreciation rates computed as the rate of change of the average annual exchange rate vis à vis the US dollar. The manufacturing sector share in exports and GDP (as well as the service sector share in the latter) along with the net barter terms of trade and real GDP per capita were also obtained from the WDI. Purchasing power parity real per capita income data have been obtained from the Penn World Tables 8.1[8] since the equivalent WDI data series frequently do not cover earlier sample years. On the basis of these data, country-specific data on income convergence can be obtained by computing per capita GDP as a percentage of the US equivalent level – implicitly focusing on the United States as a benchmark case. The GDP per capita series used is the one obtained from the World Development Indicators and does not incorporate any purchasing power parity adjustment. This measure seems appropriate in a trade-related discussion. Purchasing power parity adjusted series are clearly the superior measure if the primary focus is on the convergence of living standards. For a population size adjusted measure of the local concentration of internationally articulatable purchasing power a simple GDP per capita series is the more adequate variable.

Sectorally disaggregated trade data were obtained from the United Nations Comtrade database; the incidence of commodity trade flows in different primary commodity categories, as well as concentration indices, were computed on this basis. Disaggregated data on value added and investment in different manufacturing sectors were obtained from the UNIDO Industrial Statistics database where available and are discussed against the background of recorded international trade activity.[9] The case studies presented in this chapter are selected from a number of regions and countries. The first examples are taken from Latin America and focus on three southern cone economies (Argentina, Brazil, and Chile). These economies are of interest not least because among them is the region of origin of post-war import substitution strategies, in the cases of Argentina and Brazil, as well as a sustained exception to this rule under otherwise similar circumstances in the case of Chile. The three economies in this region experienced strong commodity based growth around the turn of the twentieth century and experienced some degree of disruption to international trade links during the two World Wars. The theme of stagnating commodity export earnings, the objective of industrialization, and the historic backdrop of the international debt crisis during the 1980s is a common experience in the region and has determined the experience of these economies to differing extents. Later case studies will draw on examples from sub-Saharan Africa and Asia, but for now we will turn to the case of the Argentinian economy in the discussion of Latin American examples of commodity dependent developing countries.

4.2   Argentina

Argentina has in the past prospered while trading on its comparative advantage sectors in agriculture. From 1930 onwards, the country's economy increasingly diversified into manufacturing production. Initially, this development was a reaction to disruptions in international trade, complicating access to imports from a world market in the shadow of the Second World War. Following the end of the war, this orientation towards the domestic manufacturing sector was intentionally promoted to further economic development through a process of accelerated industrialization and an anticipated clustering of high value added activities within the domestic economy. In fact, this import substitution based industrialization strategy is closely associated with the Argentinian economist Raul Prebisch, and was widely adopted throughout Latin America (Reyes and Sawyer 2011).

Based on aggregate data, Argentina's economy is no longer dominated by the primary sector. Argentina's policy regime has been subject to repeated changes in fundamental orientation. The country's economy has a significant industrial sector, increasing manufacturing export participation, and a significant service sector. Argentina's population is highly urbanized (91.45 per cent in 2013) and female labour force participation in the non-agricultural sector is high, reaching 44.00 per cent in 2012, the latest year for which data are available.

As of 2013, the industrial sector accounted for 28 per cent of GDP, agriculture for 7 per cent, and services 65 per cent.[10] Manufacturing value added as a percentage of GDP fell at an average rate of 2.09 p.a. per cent per annum from 41.18 per cent in 1965 to 15.27 per cent in 2013. The evolution of domestic manufacturing sector participation differs from its importance in international trade, though: the performance of manufactured products in merchandise exports was relatively better than in the economy overall from the mid 1980s onwards. From 1987, manufactured product exports accounted for between 26 and 35 per cent of total merchandise exports, while the percentage of GDP accounted for by manufacturing value added continued to fall. These developments in manufacturing sector production and trade appear consistent with a consolidation of the country's manufacturing sector in an area of competitive advantage. It does not mark a fundamental shift from agriculture to manufacturing production or manufacturing dominated export specialization since manufacturing exports appear to stagnate at levels of around 30 per cent of merchandise exports.

The prolonged decline in the manufacturing sector share of domestic value added as well as the sustained increase and eventual consolidation of the manufacturing export share for Argentina are illustrated in Figure 4.1, which shows the evolution of both aggregate series over the sample period covered.

The evolution of the manufacturing sector took place against a background of turbulent macroeconomic conditions. Argentina's GDP growth rate has shown substantial volatility and frequent recessions over the course of the sample period. The sample period itself contains not only the oil price shocks of 1973 and 1979 but also the 1982 debt crisis, which led to what is commonly known as a lost decade in much of Latin America. Growth performance has improved in recent years, though, against the background of the early twenty-first century commodity boom.

The 1980s saw a period of hyperinflation, with inflation rates peaking at 625.80 per cent in 1985, with an average annual depreciation rate of 218.56 per cent. After declining to a somewhat lower level of 74.46 per cent in 1986, annual inflation accelerated once more, peaking at 3057.63 per cent

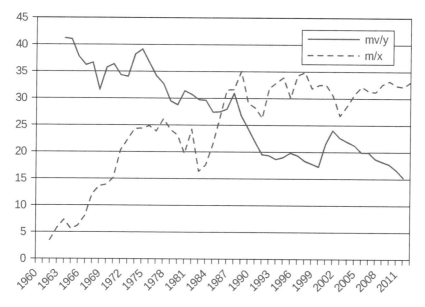

Figure 4.1 Argentina manufacturing share in national value added and exports.

Note: mv/y: manufacturing sector share in value added; m/x: manufacturing export share.

Table 4.2 Argentina: export shares and concentrations

Year	Food	Raw Mat.	Minerals	Fuel	Total	NHHI
1965	81.64	11.82	0.69	0.62	94.77	0.54
1975	68.87	5.92	1.05	0.49	76.34	0.38
1982	62.51	4.48	5.96	7.19	80.14	0.21
1990	56.26	4.31	8.79	7.80	77.16	0.13
2000	43.78	1.73	5.36	17.74	68.61	0.09
2011	54.10	1.27	5.16	6.04	66.57	0.11

Shares are in per cent. Raw Mat.: agricultural raw materials; Minerals: minerals and metals; Fuel: mineral fuels; Total: total commodity exports; NHHI: normalized Hirschman–Herfindahl index.

in 1989 with a depreciation rate of 387.88 per cent. Subsequent reforms achieved some monetary and economic stability against a background of economic liberalization, and the introduction of a currency board. Inflation dropped to 11.92 per cent per year by 1992 and further to near zero levels while the currency board remained in operation until 2001. In the 2001–2002 currency crisis, the Argentinian peso depreciated 112.00 per cent against the US dollar and inflation accelerated from −1.10 per cent to 30.56 per cent. There was no return to hyperinflation during subsequent years, though.

In spite of the changing macroeconomic policy regimes and the apparent external consolidation of the manufacturing sector, Argentina's export orientation remained focused on the primary sector. Commodity exports continued to account for the majority of merchandise exports throughout the sample period, although their incidence gradually fell from 96.54 per cent of total exports in 1962 to 64.97 per cent in 2013. Food exports remained the most important category, accounting for 71.52 per cent of total exports in 1962, although this percentage fell to 43.78 per cent in 2000, while mineral fuel exports at this time had increased their relative importance from 1.08 per cent in 1962 to 17.74 per cent in 2000 (see Table 4.2). The relative export participation of food products subsequently recovered somewhat, reaching a value of 55.22 per cent in 2013, while the incidence of mineral fuel exports fell to 4.72 per cent of total merchandise exports as oil prices fell in the wake of the 2008 crisis.

Mineral and metal exports have consistently played a minor role, reaching a peak value of 12.34 per cent in 1989 and accounting for less than 5 per cent of total exports in most years. Agricultural raw material exports made up 23.09 per cent of total merchandise exports in 1962 but then fell rapidly to 7.14 per cent by 1971, while only accounting for 0.92 per cent in 2013. The degree of diversification between broad commodity categories thus seems modest. However, considering the concentration of exports at a higher level of disaggregation, the normalized Hirschman–Herfindahl index for exports has fallen at an average rate of 1.99 per cent per annum. It took relatively high values of up to 0.54 during the 1960s when food exports were strongly dominant before eventually falling to 0.08 in 2002–2004. The concentration index subsequently rose again, reaching a value of

Table 4.3 Argentina: import shares and concentrations

Year	Food	Raw Mat.	Minerals	Fuel	Total	NHHI
1965	6.51	12.60	23.23	9.66	51.99	0.11
1975	4.56	6.54	27.16	13.23	51.49	0.10
1982	4.41	4.76	10.28	12.77	32.23	0.13
1990	4.03	3.96	9.40	8.07	25.45	0.13
2000	5.01	1.48	3.94	3.76	14.19	0.18
2011	2.40	1.03	5.80	12.68	21.91	0.19

Shares are in per cent. Raw Mat.: agricultural raw materials; Minerals: minerals and metals; Fuel: mineral fuels; Total: total commodity imports; NHHI: normalized Hirschman–Herfindahl index.

0.11 in 2011 and 0.14 in 2013 against the background of the early twenty-first century commodity boom.

Imports were dominated by minerals and metals in the early part of the sample period, with Table 4.3 showing import shares of 23.23 per cent and 27.16 per cent for 1965 and 1975 respectively. During the 1980s, mineral and metal imports remained at levels close to 10 per cent of total imports before dropping to shares of around 5 per cent in the twenty-first century. Fuel imports, by contrast, remained important, with an overall import share fluctuation of between 5 and 15 per cent in the early part of the sample up to the late 1980s. Their incidence fell to levels of around 5 per cent of total imports during much of the 1990s and the first decade of the twenty-first century, with import shares rising notably from 2011.

Agricultural raw material imports decreased from 12.60 in 1965 to 1.03 per cent in 2011, and further to 0.88 per cent 2013. The incidence of food imports remained low at rates around 5 per cent throughout the sample period. Commodity imports, then, were not strongly concentrated among the four categories defined here. The participation of overall commodity imports in total imports fell from over 50 per cent in 1965 and 1975 (see Table 4.3) to 14.19 per cent in 2000. The commodity import share recovered somewhat in the early twenty-first century commodity boom, rising to 21.91 per cent in 2011.

Considering import concentrations across all SITC categories, concentration levels show no continuously increasing or decreasing tendencies, but do show an apparent difference in value range between the earlier and the later part of the sample. During the earlier sample period, normalized Hirschman–Herfindahl index values fluctuate mostly in the range 0.1–0.15 after dropping perceptibly from a value of 0.27 in 1962. The observed value range then increases to approximately 0.15–0.25 after 1992, marking a modest increase in the recorded concentration of import activity as well as of its volatility.

Hirschman–Herfindahl index ratios do not show any clear trend for imports and mostly fluctuate in the 0.25–0.35 interval for exports between 1960 and 1983. Export concentrations rose notably in 1983, mainly due to an increase in the dominant agricultural export category (food and live animals: SITC 0) leading to some rise in the concentration index ratio around 1983–1984. Following a subsequent decline in the concentration index ratio, the ratio between SITC 2 and SITC 1 Hirschman–Herfindahl indices began to recover gradually from 1986 onwards, indicating that the differentiation of export activity within the two-digit category developed more slowly than the decline in one-digit SITC export concentrations, although export concentration indices dropped for both levels of aggregation. Contemplation of aggregate index figures on their own is insufficient to interpret their relationship with underlying structural developments, but the observed trajectory does appear consistent with a consolidation of activity in various export sectors, as export activity gradually diversifies into the non-primary sector.

While Argentina has seen some strengthening of its manufacturing exports, its export profile remains dominated by primary commodities, with a strong presence of the food sector. Imports, on the other hand, remain diversified across product categories. In spite of this continued commodity sector orientation, the net barter terms of trade have not experienced a pronounced decline, but have risen gradually at an average rate of 0.66 per cent per year over the 1980–2013 period for which data are available.

Disaggregated manufacturing value added data are available from 1984–2002, with a gap in 1991–1992 from the UNIDO Industrial Statistics database.[11] In most years, the food and beverages sector amounted to between 20 and 30 per cent of manufacturing value added. The relative participation of the food and beverage sector fluctuated between 18.06 per cent (1990) and 30.20 per cent (in 2002). Other manufacturing sub-sectors that accounted for relatively large shares of manufacturing value added were 'coke, refined petroleum products, and nuclear fuel' (ISIC division 23), whose manufacturing value added share peaked at 19.87 per cent in 1990 before dropping to 6.26 per cent by 2002. The manufacturing value added share of chemicals and chemical products (ISIC division 24) increased from 11.05 per cent of manufacturing value added in 1984 to 16.08 per cent in 2002.

Considering the macroeconomic structure of Argentina's national output, as well as its international trade profile, the country's economy appears to have successfully modernized. This macro-structural profile stands in marked contrast to the sustained volatility of growth performance and the prolonged convergence failure vis à vis the United States, as well as relative to Mercosur and other South American partner economies. Relative to per capita income in the US, Argentina's real GDP per capita fell from 23.63 per cent of the US equivalent in 1960 to 11.07 per cent in 2002 before rebounding to 13.75 per cent by 2006 (no data are available for later years). Over the same period, Brazil's per capita GDP level remained around 10 per cent of the US equivalent, but Chile's rose from 16.37 per cent in 2002 to 17.47 per cent in 2006 and further in later years. This development is illustrated in Figure 4.2, which shows the lasting divergence from US per capita GDP with an intermittent drop in the speed of decline during the 1990s. It is further interesting to note that, adjusting for purchasing power parity (PPP), Argentina's real per capita GDP has continually risen over these reference dates from 15.68 per cent in 1960 to 22.24 per cent in 2002 and 25.96 per cent

Figure 4.2 Argentina: real per capita GDP convergence to US equivalent.

in 2006. Later figures are available from the Penn World Tables and these show a further rise to 36.07 per cent in 2011, although PPP adjusted per capita GDP actually declined relative to the US between 1996 (32.95 per cent) and 2002.

What lies at the root of this apparent heterogeneity in developments is the qualitative articulation of these trade and development flows. The development potential of industrialization and of manufacturing trade clearly depends not only on the magnitude of flows but also their interaction with the encompassing host economy. The experience with import substitution may well play a key role here. At one extreme is Singer's observation expressed in his critique of structurally isolated foreign direct investment (Singer 1950). On the other hand, the sustainability and incentive problems inherent in import substitution approaches to industrialization and development posit a complementary angle on the qualitative properties of industrialization. It is one criticism of import substitution based industrialization strategies that the resultant industrial structures are often not internationally competitive and therefore depend on compensating state intervention and exchange rate manipulation.

Experiences of periodic national liberalization efforts as well as integration into the local Mercosur trade bloc have in their turn had an impact on the evolution of Argentina's economic and trade structure. Trade blocs of this kind bear an inherent danger of trade diversion, although for the case of Argentina Bustos (2011) argues that progressive integration into Mercosur has promoted technological upgrading. Thus Argentina's trade profile shows evidence of modernization and potentially improved competitiveness in the secondary sector. The primary sector remains an important component of the export sector, though. Primary commodity exports continued to account for 64.97 per cent, and food exports accounted for 55.22 per cent

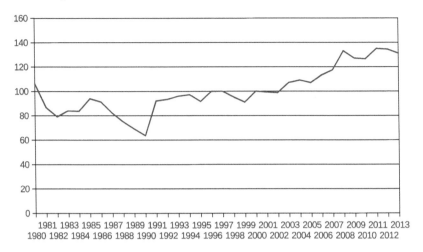

Figure 4.3 Argentina: net barter terms of trade.

Source: World Bank World Development Indicators.
Note: Net barter terms of trade index, 2000 = 100.

of total merchandise exports in 2013. This continued primary sector orientation is not in itself an economic or structural problem – it is entirely rational to export in one's area of comparative advantage and to specialize in the primary sector if this is where this advantage lies. The continued attractiveness of the country's primary sector specialization is further borne out by the sustained strengthening of the net barter terms of trade (NBTT) following a period of moderate decay during the 1980s (see Figure 4.3). The increase in the NBTT index during the final years of the sample may simply be a reflection of the early twenty-first century commodity boom. The terms of trade index remained stable in the preceding years, however, and shows no sign of sustained decline over the period for which data are available. The challenge associated with this primary sector specialization is how to insure the domestic economy against the risks of a narrow commodity orientation and how to facilitate the sustainable development of complementary sectors.

The overall performance problems observed in the Argentinian economy are likely to be substantively rooted in questions of policy orientation and institutional design rather than trade specialization per se. In-depth discussion of these topics is beyond the scope of the present study. Argentina's performance can, however, be placed in the context of other Latin American country experiences. To this end, the discussion will turn to Brazil, one of the Latin American economies noted for its recent economic success and one which has been routinely grouped with India and China as an example of a successful emerging economy.

4.3 Brazil

Brazil differs from its neighbouring Latin American countries in so far as its origins lie in independence from Portugal rather than emancipation from the Spanish

Empire, a difference which matters in so far as its role has historically been less marginal than that of the Spanish colonies (Reyes and Sawyer 2011), so much so that at some point (1808–1821) Brazil was home to the Portuguese capital before gaining independence in 1822 (Pendle 1990, pp. 120–3). In more recent times, Brazil has shared some characteristics of neighbouring Latin American economies like Argentina. Brazil has substantively modernized, and has become a largely urbanized society with an urban population of 84.62 per cent of the total in 2011, compared to 51.04 per cent in 1965. The economy is dominated by the service sector, whose value added share accounted for 67.01 per cent of GDP in 2011and has near parity in female non-agricultural labour force participation (47.1 per cent in 2011).

Like Argentina, Brazil has experienced periods of hyperinflation and volatile growth, with the former leading to rapid depreciations and repeated currency reforms (see Tullio and Ronci 1996 for an account of Brazil's experience with high inflation and hyperinflation up to 1993). Brazilian inflation had been high throughout the 1960s and eventually accelerated to an annual average rate of 2735.49 per cent in 1990, with the currency depreciating by a comparatively modest 318.23 per cent over the year on average. Further hyperinflation episodes followed in 1993, with an average annual inflation rate of 2001.35 per cent, and 1994, with an average annual inflation rate of 2251.70 per cent. Average annual depreciation rates for these two years were 297.55 per cent (1993) and 285.45 per cent (1994). Both hyperinflation episodes were followed by a currency reform, with the most recent introducing the current Brazilian currency.

The country experienced high growth during the 1960s and 1970s, with deep recessions in 1981, 1983, and 1990. Brazil's purchasing power parity adjusted level of real GDP per capita in 2011 was 22.92 per cent of the equivalent value in the USA. Real GDP without purchasing power parity adjustment was a mere 12.90 per cent of the US equivalent value. It is worth noting, moreover, that this achievement in real income convergence is not the end point of a smooth convergence process. Rather, Brazil's real per capita GDP as a percentage of US real per capita GDP had previously reached 16.19 per cent in 1980, shortly before the onset of the debt crisis. From this point, relative real per capita GDP fell to 10.58 per cent of the US equivalent value in 2003 and did not recover a value beyond 12 per cent of US per capita GDP before 2009. This process is illustrated in Figure 4.4.

Also, like Argentina, Brazil has been a member of Mercosur, the regional trade bloc, from its founding in 1991. It has seen the relative importance of its manufacturing value added decline from values around 26–30 per cent of GDP during the 1960s and 1970s to below 20 per cent from 1995. Manufactured export participation in total merchandise exports in the meantime increased from 7.74 per cent in 1965 to a peak value of 58.96 per cent in 1993. The proportion of merchandise exports remained at values above 50 per cent until 2006 and then dropped to 34.12 per cent by 2011 before recovering to 36.37 per cent in 2013. The net barter terms of trade, meanwhile, stagnated briefly between 2000 and 2005 but

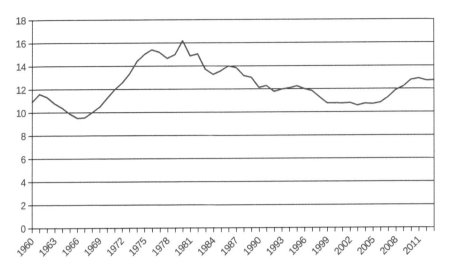

Figure 4.4 Brazil: real per capita GDP convergence to US equivalent.

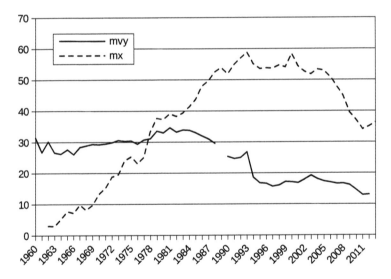

Figure 4.5 Brazil manufacturing share in national value added and exports.

Note: mv/y: manufacturing sector share in value added; m/x: manufacturing export share.

have largely tended to improve over the 1980–2013 interval for which data are available.

The development of manufacturing value added and the manufacturing share of exports are shown in Figure 4.5, where both series tend to decline in the early twenty-first century. The simultaneous strengthening of the net barter terms of trade over this period is shown in Figure 4.6.

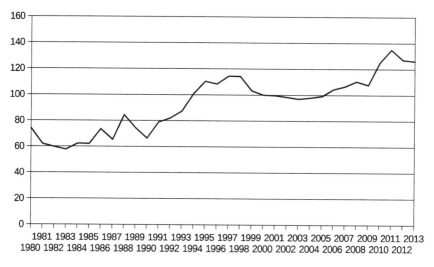

Figure 4.6 Brazil: net barter terms of trade.

Note: Net barter terms of trade index, 2000 = 100.

Table 4.4 Brazil: export shares and concentrations

Year	Food	Raw Mat.	Minerals	Fuel	Total	NHHI
1965	67.34	15.23	11.76	0.00	94.34	0.39
1975	54.08	3.89	14.34	2.32	74.63	0.17
1982	39.63	3.20	15.46	7.16	65.44	0.10
1990	27.70	3.44	24.96	2.16	58.26	0.09
2000	23.39	4.76	16.49	1.64	46.28	0.09
2011	30.50	3.53	24.21	10.54	68.79	0.09

Shares are in per cent. Raw Mat.: agricultural raw materials; Minerals: minerals and metals; Fuel: mineral fuels; Total: total commodity exports; NHHI: normalized Hirschman–Herfindahl index.

The composition and evolution of Brazil's commodity exports point to a shift away from a narrowly defined primary sector orientation. The percentage share of primary commodity exports in the value of total exports has fallen significantly from 94.34 per cent in 1965 to 46.28 per cent in 2000 before recovering to 68.79 per cent in 2011, as shown in Table 4.4.

Within the overall primary commodity aggregate, food exports played a predominant role, with 67.34 per cent of the total export value in 1965 attributable to food exports. This, in fact, was a relatively low value for the early 1960s, given that the comparable figure for 1962 was 71.15 per cent and that food exports accounted for more than 68 per cent of the total export value for most years in the 1962–1968 interval. From the 1970s onwards, however, the relative importance of food exports started to decline, falling to 54.08 per cent in 1975 and

39.63 per cent in 1982. From 1988 onwards, the percentage share of food exports in the total value of exports fluctuated between 20 and 30 per cent, as illustrated by the food export shares of 27.70 per cent for 1990 and 23.39 per cent for 2000. From 2009 the share of food exports recovered somewhat, taking values above 30 per cent as illustrated by the 30.50 per cent export share in 2011.

Agricultural raw materials accounted for 15.23 per cent of exports in 1965 but had fallen to 3.89 per cent by 1975. This new lower value is fairly representative of their subsequent incidence, with agricultural raw materials accounting for 3.20 per cent and 3.44 per cent of exports in 1982 and 1990 respectively, recovering slightly to 4.76 per cent in 2000 and falling back to 3.53 per cent in 2011. Mineral fuels have a low export participation throughout, with export percentage shares listed in Table 4.4 taking values from 0.00 per cent in 1965 to 7.16 per cent in 1982. These figures describe the value range for the export participation of mineral fuels fairly well, although the value of exports in this category increased notably after 2007, with the 10.54 per cent value for 2011 close to the peak value of 11.03 per cent reached in 2012.

Mineral and metal exports have for some time held a relatively large export share, although their 1965 value of 11.76 per cent is higher than for the remaining years of this decade. Exports in this category have subsequently strengthened, though, reaching 14.34 per cent in 1975 and fluctuating between 15–20 per cent during most years in the 1982–2013 interval. Minerals and metals have thus become a strong second primary commodity export category in terms of export value share and even surpassed food exports in 1991 when their participation peaked at 27.36 per cent.

Primary commodity exports have thus become more diversified. The same can be said about Brazil's exports generally. Normalized Hirschman–Herfindahl index values defined over all SITC categories took relatively high values in the beginning of the sample period, with an index value of 0.39 in 1965 which had fallen to 0.17 by 1975. The normalized Hirschman–Herfindahl index decayed at a mean rate of −2.92 per cent over the whole of the sample period, although this global rate can be subdivided into an initial period of fast decline, during which the concentration index changed at a rate of −7.30 per cent per annum on average between 1962 and 1981, whereas its value remained largely stagnant at values close to 0.1 thereafter.

The overall export profile, then, is characterized by a long term shift away from a strong sectoral concentration on commodity exports in general and food exports in particular. Instead, Brazil's export profile has shifted towards a more balanced distribution in the commodity sector and towards a stronger participation of manufacturing exports. In recent years, traditional commodity export sectors have strengthened again – a change that can be interpreted with regards to a change in the geographical distribution of trading activity such as the increasing importance of China as a trading partner. It is further worth noting that the decline in the overall share of commodity exports appears to have been a rather steady process until the possible trend reversal at the turn of the twenty-first century. There are no apparent discontinuities linked to the debt crisis or changes in trade policy orientation during this period.

Table 4.5 Brazil: import shares and concentrations

Year	Food	Raw Mat.	Minerals	Fuel	Total	NHHI
1965	19.82	1.74	11.70	20.55	53.82	0.08
1975	6.16	1.50	13.96	26.15	47.77	0.13
1982	8.46	0.93	4.69	53.54	67.61	0.26
1990	9.40	2.57	5.85	26.96	44.78	0.11
2000	6.56	1.96	4.30	14.90	27.72	0.16
2011	4.53	1.46	5.73	18.54	30.26	0.15

Shares are in per cent. Raw Mat.: agricultural raw materials; Minerals: minerals and metals; Fuel: mineral fuels; Total: total commodity imports; NHHI: normalized Hirschman–Herfindahl index.

While Brazil's exports have shown a relatively consistent tendency towards diversification coupled with a reduced role of the commodity sector, developments on the import side are somewhat more complex, with the overall incidence of primary commodity imports showing a less stable tendency towards decay over time.

The relative importance of commodity imports initially decreased during the early sample period: Table 4.5 shows a decrease of primary commodities as a percentage of total import values from 53.82 per cent in 1965 to 47.77 per cent in 1975. However, commodity imports subsequently rose, reaching a peak of 67.98 per cent in 1984 (the 1982 value reported in Table 4.5 is somewhat lower but still representative of this development). The relative incidence of commodity imports fell subsequently, dropping to levels around 30 per cent from the mid 1990s. (Commodity imports accounted for 29.69 per cent of total imports in 1995, and Table 4.5 shows values of 27.72 per cent and 30.26 per cent for 2000 and 2011 respectively.)

The main driver behind the temporary rise in the value share of commodity imports and their subsequent persistence at a relatively elevated level is the mineral fuel category. Import shares in all three of the other four broad primary commodity aggregates (food, agricultural raw materials, and minerals and metals) have gradually but steadily declined or remained stagnant over the sample period. The share of mineral fuel imports, by contrast, increased from 26.15 per cent in 1975 to 53.54 per cent in 1982 before falling to a range of approximately 10–20 per cent of total imports from 1993.

With the intermittent exception of imports in the mineral fuel category, then, primary commodity imports to Brazil are of very limited importance. Import shares in the different non-fuel sectors appear stable and balanced. The sectoral composition of imports more generally can be assessed in terms of formally computed concentration indices and their development over time.

The overall concentration of imports has likewise increased compared to the beginning of the sample period. The normalized Hirschman–Herfindahl index for one-digit SITC aggregates rose from 0.08 in 1965 to a value of 0.27 in 1983 before falling to a fluctuation range of 0.09–0.15 from 1986 onwards, although normalized Hirschman–Herfindahl index values temporarily rose to values of 0.17–0.18 between 1998 and 2001.

The development of Hirschman–Herfindahl index ratios of SITC two-digit to one-digit aggregations shows a falling export index ratio series in the early part of the sample. This development is indicative of a faster decline in export concentration in the two-digit level SITC series than in the higher level of aggregation. The period of declining concentration ratios is followed by a brief period of increase during the early twenty-first century commodity boom, a development consistent with export consolidation in high performing commodity sectors in response to a rise in foreign demand. Concentration index ratios for imports, on the other hand, largely reflect the changing value of mineral fuel imports, with a sharp rise in the concentration index ratio illustrating the concentration of the import value increase in a narrowly defined fuel category (SITC 33: petroleum and petroleum products) up to 1981, with a notable decline from 1983.

Brazil's trade and production profiles then seem consistent with a modernizing emerging economy, albeit with an incomplete transition to an internationally competitive industrial structure. Like other countries in the region, Brazil has experienced periods of hyperinflation and currency crises in the past, but there has been no recent recurrence of these problems. Against the background scenario of a stabilizing emerging market, the recent resurgence in the relative importance of commodity exports and the continued decline in manufacturing value added as a proportion of GDP stand out.

One possible explanation for this development is Brazil's intensifying interaction with China. Whalley and Medianu (2013) point out that trade and foreign direct investment (FDI) flows between Brazil and China intensified at the turn of the century. As a consequence, Brazil faced increased competition in its traditional developed country export markets while simultaneously availing itself of new trade opportunities in the Chinese market. This development manifested itself in a partial contraction of the Brazilian manufacturing sector and a resurgence in commodity exports (Whalley and Medianu 2013).

These observations appear consistent with China's general impact on world commodity markets and its emergence as a manufacturing centre. They would also point to the emergence of a bilateral trade pattern between the two countries that is strongly reminiscent of the trade embedded division of sectoral participation that was commonly hypothesized in traditional dependency theory. This possibility could be of pivotal importance for Brazil not least because, as Whalley and Medianu (2013) also point out, China has become a more important trading partner for Brazil than Brazil for China.

The observations of Whalley and Medianu (2013) can be juxtaposed with more recent trade data from the Comtrade database. The overall share of commodity exports in Brazil's total exports has indeed increased from 46.28 per cent in 2000 to 68.79 per cent in 2011 before dropping somewhat to 65.21 per cent in 2013. Exports to China have increased from a mere 1.98 per cent in 2000 to 17.47 per cent in 2011 before rising further to 19.22 per cent in 2013. Across all four commodity categories, primary commodity exports to China have increased

Table 4.6 Brazil: trade with China – percentage shares

Year	Food	Raw Mat.	Minerals	Fuel	Total
Exports					
1993	0.20	0.72	8.23	0.00	2.02
2000	3.44	3.43	3.59	4.03	1.98
2011	18.07	22.02	34.60	18.26	17.47
2013	24.60	22.29	37.33	22.67	19.22
Imports					
1993	0.81	1.87	0.05	0.67	0.58
2000	0.41	0.89	1.19	0.90	2.19
2011	5.33	4.34	12.88	0.97	14.49
2013	6.55	6.51	14.57	0.24	15.57

Shares are in per cent. Raw Mat.: agricultural raw materials; Minerals: minerals and metals; Fuel: mineral fuels; Total: total commodity imports.

ahead of general exports to China: mineral and metal exports to China accounted for 34.60 per cent of all exports in this category in 2011, rising further to 37.33 per cent in 2013. The shift to China was somewhat less pronounced for agricultural raw materials, where 22.02 per cent of all exports in this sub-category were directed to China in 2011. The corresponding figures for food and mineral fuels are 18.07 per cent and 18.26 per cent respectively, a magnitude which is close to China's overall incidence in Brazil's exports.

These values and those for imports are illustrated in Table 4.6, which lists percentage trade shares of China in Brazilian exports and imports for 1993, the year in which China officially recognized Brazil as a strategic partner (Jenkins 2012), as well as for the years 2000, 2011, and 2013. Export and import shares have been computed for the four commodity aggregates discussed above and for total trade flows.

On the import side, China's relative importance also increased but the qualitative composition of trade flows is largely the opposite of the export flow. Total import participation increased from 2.19 per cent in 2000 to 14.49 per cent in 2011 and further to 15.57 per cent in 2013. The share of commodity imports from China is generally lower: mineral and metal imports again have the highest percentage share with 12.88 per cent in 2011 and 14.57 per cent in 2013, up from a mere 1.19 per cent in 2000. China's share in other commodity imports remains low, though, with only 5.33 per cent of food imports, 4.34 per cent of agricultural raw material imports, and 0.97 per cent of mineral fuel imports by Brazil being sourced from China. The figures for 2013 are similarly low (see Table 4.6). The pattern in recent years, then, is clearly consistent with the analysis in Whalley and Medianu (2013) and points to a conventional commodity export versus manufacturing goods import relationship in Brazilian Chinese trade relations.

The intensified interaction between the Brazilian and Chinese economies seems consistent with the notion of a BRIC group of emerging economies. It is remarkable, then, that within this group, a major and generally modernizing economy like Brazil should begin to specialize in supplying another emerging market with raw materials. This is not to say that such a trade orientation should be avoided, though it is worth recalling that sustained benefits may depend on securing long term investments from the earnings accruing during the limited time of a commodity boom.

On the other hand, noting the qualitative stratification of Brazilian Chinese trade relations should not distract from the overall magnitude of its impact on the Brazilian economy. The Brazilian economy remains dominated by the service sector, as discussed above, and overall industrial employment has remained fairly stable in the early twenty-first century with employment in the industrial sector accounting for 20.00 per cent of total employment in 2001[12] and 21.90 per cent in 2011. Service sector employment increased slightly from 59.40 per cent in 2001 to 62.70 per cent in 2011, while agricultural sector employment as a percentage of total employment fell more noticeably from 20.60 per cent in 2001 to 15.30 per cent in 2011. The overall pattern in employment then points to a gradual sectoral shift from agriculture to the secondary and tertiary sectors.

This development is even more pronounced in the distribution of value added between broad economic sectors. The agricultural sector's value added accounted for a mere 5.46 per cent of GDP in 2011 and 5.97 per cent in 2001. The value added share for the industrial sector, by contrast, increased slightly from 26.92 per cent in 2001 to 27.53 per cent in 2011, while the service sector's value added accounted for 67.01 per cent of GDP in 2011 compared to 67.10 per cent in 2001.

The combination of diminishing manufacturing sector activity as a proportion of trade and value added coupled with a stable incidence of the overall industrial sector in the labour market and value added can be seen in the context of disaggregated manufacturing sector data. Brazil's largest manufacturing sub-sector is the food and beverages sector (ISIC 15 in the UNIDO Industrial Statistics database), which accounted for values in the range of 15–20 per cent of manufacturing value added in the period 2000–2010 while the sector's employment participation fell in the range of 18–22 per cent over the same time period. The overall distribution of manufacturing activity across sub-sectors remained generally stable in terms of both value added and employment participation over the time period considered. This is true even for the textile sector,[13] where imports from China have increased substantially vis à vis other trading partners from 20.82 per cent in 2000 to 51.27 per cent in 2010.

The evolution of the bilateral trading relationship between Brazil and China is clearly noteworthy in its qualitative characteristics as well as its magnitude. One should take care not to overstate its impact, however. The impact of Chinese competition has made itself felt in the manufacturing sector but appears to materialize as an influence pushing for structural change rather than precipitating sectoral collapse. The international integration of the Brazilian economy, moreover, crucially depends on trade and investment relations within Mercosur. This is the case with regards to its legacy of existing economic relations and networks, as well as with regards to institutional constraints. Mercosur's status as a customs union inherently limits the scope of bilateral trade deals with third parties and may necessitate multilateral negotiations for further international agreements on trade or investment. This position in turn can limit the possible speed and depth of institutional integration with other external trading blocs or individual partners.

Brazil thus stands as one example of an emerging economy developing a modern productive structure from the basis of a commodity-dominated economy. In recent years, this transformative process has coexisted with a relatively open trade policy stance compared to earlier periods that were characterized by the pursuit of import substitution based strategies. It has taken place against a background of improving terms of trade.

4.4 Chile

Chile, one of the smaller South American countries in terms of population, looks back on a protracted history of commodity dependence. During the nineteenth century, Chilean exports were dominated by guano for fertilizer use (Radetzki 2010) and later nitrate (Villalobos 1992) until synthetic substitutes for both commodities were found. The country's large latitudinal extent, coupled with a relatively low population density, provided a rationale and an incentive for early infrastructure investment. The fact that export tax receipts on nitrate provided a large proportion of the state's budget meant that the means for infrastructure investment became available while the commodity boom lasted. Villalobos (1992) argues that this opportunity was indeed seized as the temporary nature of commodity earnings was anticipated. The nitrate boom came to an end with the great depression in 1929 and the increased availability of synthetic nitrate following the First World War, with copper playing an increasing role as a commodity export from the early twentieth century (Aylwin *et al.* 1992).

The status of a small commodity-dependent economy largely determined Chile's economic performance throughout the twentieth century. As a result, its economy was affected by international events like the two World Wars or the Great Depression mainly through their impact on demand for commodities. Real GDP grew at an average rate of 2.6 per cent between 1879 and 1929, a rate which fell to 2.1 per cent for the 1930–1950 interval that included the Great Depression (Gregorio 2004). After the Second World War, Chile maintained a relatively steady growth performance until the period of political turmoil and hyperinflation in the wake of the Allende government and the subsequent coup in 1973, the World Development Indicators supply real GDP figures indicating a geometric mean growth rate of 3.57 per cent over the 1960–1989 interval, although growth rates collapsed to −5.07 per cent in 1973 and −12.06 per cent in 1975 against a background of hyperinflation. A further contraction occurred with the onset of the international debt crisis, with real GDP falling by 10.89 per cent in 1982 and 3.86 per cent in 1983.

Military rule ended in 1990 and growth rates accelerated to an average of 6.61 per cent over the period 1990–1999 while inflation figures (based on the GDP deflator) fell from 22.45 per cent in 1990 to more moderate levels at or below 10 per cent. This continued record of economic stability reflects on a background of institutional stability and political moderation without a tendency to return to the radicalism of the 1970s that had preceded the original coup. By the advent of the twenty-first century, the growth process had slowed, however, levelling out at an average of 4.03 per cent over the 2000–2011 interval, which also coincides with a pronounced commodity price boom.

Manufacturing value added as a share of GDP remains rather low, remaining at 11.48 per cent in 2013, although it reached 20.29 per cent as recently as 1992 and prior to the onset of the recent commodity price boom. The female employment share outside the agricultural sector reached 38.50 per cent in 2012, the latest datum available from the World Development Indicators at the time of writing, but has increased somewhat from earlier values of around 32–33 per cent.

The agricultural sector still accounted for 10.30 per cent of employment and 3.58 per cent of value added in 2011. This marks a slight decline over the decade from 2001 when the corresponding values were 13.60 per cent for employment and 5.16 per cent for the share of the sector's value added in GDP respectively. The industrial sector's employment share amounted to 23.40 per cent in 2011 with a value added share of 38.70 per cent, which is close to the 23.90 per cent employment share in 2001 with a slight increase over that year's value added share of 32.75 per cent. The service sector finally had an employment share of 66.40 per cent (compared to 62.50 per cent in 2001) with a value added share of 57.72 per cent of GDP which marks a slight decline from the 2001 value of 62.09 per cent. The dominant role of the service sector in the distribution of economic activity would commonly be associated with a mature developed economy. It can be placed into the context of the economy's international export specialization.

Chile's exports have been consistently dominated by primary commodities. The commodity export share has fallen somewhat from levels of 96.07 per cent in 1965 to 81.96 per cent in the year 2000 before rising somewhat to around 87.15 per cent by 2011.[14] The rise in the commodity export participation during the first decade of the twenty-first century is likely a reflection of the primary commodity price boom at the beginning of the century. While commodity exports have continued to dominate this structural property of the trade profile, the trajectory of the net barter terms of trade has been less consistent over time. The World Bank's World Development Indicators give data for Chile's net barter terms of trade from 1980 onwards. This terms of trade series has declined almost consistently until the turn of the century before recovering during the twenty-first century commodity price boom (the evolution of the net barter terms of trade is illustrated in Figure 4.7). The net barter terms of trade reduction has not translated into a sustained reduction of export earnings, though. Against a background of growing GDP, net exports as a proportion of national income remained in the value range of 0–5 per cent of GDP for most of the 1990s, except for transitory trade deficits of −2.00 per cent of GDP in 1993 and a deficit growing from −1.69 per cent to −3.27 per cent of GDP over the years 1996–1998.

From the year 2000 onwards, the improvement in the barter terms of trade has coincided with an increasing incidence of net exports in GDP rising from a near balanced position (0.33 per cent) in 2001 to a peak value of 12.92 per cent in

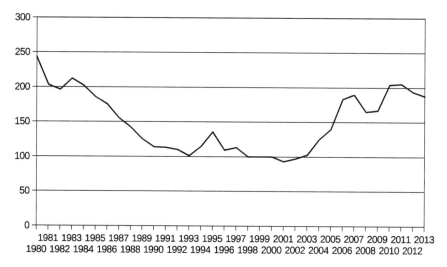

Figure 4.7 Chile: net barter terms of trade.

Note: Net barter terms of trade index, 2000 = 100.

2006 before gradually declining to a deficit of 0.34 per cent of GDP by 2013. This sustained trade surplus materialized not only in the face of increasing barter terms of trade but also against a background of sustained GDP growth – a detail that matters in so far as the incidence of the trade balance has been expressed relative to GDP in the preceding discussion.

Given the persistent export dominance of the primary sector, it seems natural to ask how export competing sectors have developed over time and how the distribution of activity across the constituent sub-sectors of the overall commodity sector has developed or how its development has been constrained by the dominant area of trade advantage. Chile has followed a policy of investing a substantial component of publicly held commodity trade revenue abroad in sovereign wealth funds (Ebert and La Menza 2015), an approach that has the immediate advantage of limiting the extent to which a commodity price boom temporarily increases demand for the domestic currency. Periods of dramatically increased demand for domestic currency can reduce the external competitiveness of export competing sectors and thus constrain the emerging economy's potential for sectoral diversification. This phenomenon is commonly known as 'Dutch disease' and can be substantially ameliorated through the use of extraterritorial sovereign wealth funds: while the increased public revenue from the commodity boom is retained for the benefit of the domestic economy, the impact on the value of the domestic currency is limited by diverting the funds to a holding location denominated in a different currency.

This stabilizing policy is mirrored in the development of the Chilean exchange rate, which in the second half of the twentieth century has consistently depreciated, the price of a US dollar having risen from 4.91 pesos in 1975 to a peak value of

Table 4.7 Chile: export shares and concentrations

Year	Food	Raw Mat.	Minerals	Fuel	Total	NHHI
1965	5.22	1.82	89.02	0.01	96.07	0.48
1975	10.32	6.80	73.77	0.87	91.75	0.42
1982	19.76	9.25	62.85	1.99	93.86	0.24
1990	23.69	8.53	55.47	0.52	88.21	0.25
2000	24.68	10.27	45.87	1.14	81.96	0.16
2011	17.83	5.19	63.10	1.03	87.15	0.22

Shares are in per cent. Raw Mat.: agricultural raw materials; Minerals: minerals and metals; Fuel: mineral fuels; Total: total commodity exports; NHHI: normalized Hirschman–Herfindahl index.

691.40 pesos in 2003 according to official exchange rate data from the World Development Indicators.[15] Since then, the exchange rate has fluctuated with rates of change of the average annual value contained in a ±10 per cent range. The pronounced appreciation, which could otherwise have been expected from the increase in the price of copper (the dominant export commodity), thus appears to have been successfully contained. The containment of Dutch disease effects is likewise reflected in the lasting differentiation of primary commodity sub-sectors.

Columns 1–4 in Table 4.7 give the percentage shares of broad commodity sub-sectors in total exports based on broad aggregates of SITC classified export data following Radetzki (2010). At the beginning of the period covered, Chile's export profile was dominated by the mining sector. This fact is illustrated by the close to 90 per cent export share in the minerals category. Over time, the incidence of minerals in exports fell, reaching 45.87 per cent in 2000 before rising to 63.10 per cent in 2011 during the recent primary commodity boom. Even as of 2013, Chile continued to supply one-third of the world's copper and the mining sector had a larger incidence in exports than in GDP at large, pointing to an activity of sustained comparative advantage (OECD 2013a).

Much of the shift in the structure of the export sector is due to an increased participation of food exports. An increasingly prominent export commodity is wine, which is included in the food category. Chile has become the fourth largest wine exporter in the world market (OECD 2013a), although this sector's quantitative significance is modest with the overall value of beverage exports (SITC 1) remaining below 5 per cent. Another commodity category with increased export participation is agricultural raw materials, whose value rose from 1.82 per cent in 1965 to 10.27 per cent in 2000, before declining during the commodity boom.

Copper thus remains the country's dominant export commodity, but the sustained diversification of commodity exports in the face of a large and protracted commodity price boom is consistent with a successful containment of Dutch disease effects, as discussed previously. The diversification of primary commodity sub-sectors is reflected in the intertemporal evolution of the normalized Hirschman–Herfindahl index (NHHI) across one-digit SITC categories. The NHHI value drops from a value of 0.48 in 1965 to 0.16 by 2000. The increased dependence on the dominant commodity sector is then shown by a recovery of the index value to 0.22 in 2011. Over the 1962–2013 sample period as a whole, the NHHI index decayed at a mean rate of 1.73 per cent per annum following a pattern of almost continuous decline, except for periods of protracted increases in the sub-period up to 1973. The consistent decline in export sector concentration confirms the falling, though still relevant, reliance on a dominant export commodity and thus points to a decreasing vulnerability to fluctuations in one particular market.

During the early sample years, characterized by near exclusive dependence on copper exports, the ratio of Hirschman–Herfindahl indices for two- and one-digit SITC aggregations stayed close to one. The ratio of two to one digit concentration ratios then dropped after 1974 against the background of a fall in copper exports. (In the case of Chile, this particular development coincides with a domestic crisis as well as the general impact of the oil price shock.) Over most of the 1970s and the 1980s, the concentration index ratio tends to decline, showing a somewhat faster decay in trade concentration at a higher level of disaggregation. From 1990 until the onset of the commodity price boom in 2004, export concentration indices at one- and two-digit levels decayed at similar rates, maintaining a concentration index ratio close to 0.7. The index ratio series then recovered to levels of around 0.9 under the influence of high copper prices. These developments are consistent with a general tendency towards internationally competitive diversification of export activity, although its manifestation in the sectoral distribution of export flows will not be robust to the impact large and protracted swings in the price of the dominant export commodity have on the recorded distribution of export values.

Chile's export profile then remains dominated by primary commodity exports, although these have recently diversified over a number of sub-sectors. There are also indications that the challenges inherent in fluctuating commodity earnings have largely been well managed. A topic that remains to be addressed is the status of the prevailing import structure in relation to the economy's overall sectoral stratification and export specialization.

The structure of commodity imports is summarized in Table 4.8. Overall commodity imports fluctuate mostly between 30 and 40 per cent of total imports, although they reached a high point of 57.32 per cent in 1974 and fell to levels as low as 22 per cent during the 1990s, with the lowest recorded primary commodity

Table 4.8 Chile: import shares and concentrations

Year	Food	Raw Mat.	Minerals	Fuel	Total	NHHI
1965	20.07	6.70	5.53	5.75	38.06	0.11
1975	18.53	2.52	5.72	19.78	46.56	0.11
1982	16.21	1.35	2.93	18.54	39.04	0.09
1990	4.38	2.17	4.86	15.68	27.10	0.17
2000	7.38	1.16	3.38	18.18	30.10	0.12
2011	7.32	0.61	4.82	23.95	36.70	0.13

Shares are in per cent. Raw Mat.: agricultural raw materials; Minerals: minerals and metals; Fuel: mineral fuels; Total: total commodity exports; NHHI: normalized Hirschman–Herfindahl index.

import share during the sample period taking a value of 21.98 per cent for the year 1998. Imports generally have not been strongly concentrated, with normalized Hirschman–Herfindahl indices fluctuating around values close to 0.1 over the sample period.

There has, however, been a shift in the qualitative composition of commodity imports. The shares of agricultural raw materials imports has decreased at a moderate pace over the sample period, while the share of minerals and metals in total commodity imports has fluctuated around a share of approximately 5 per cent of commodity imports without any clear intertemporal trend. There has also been a sustained decline in the share of food imports in overall primary commodity imports, while the participation of fuel imports has shown a pronounced increase. Indeed, it was a sharp increase in the percentage of fuel imports in overall commodity imports (from 7.31 per cent to 14.29 per cent) in 1974 coupled with a modest increase in the share of food imports (from 25.82 per cent to 32.66 per cent) which produced the peak value of 57.32 per cent for the share of primary commodity imports in overall imports. The latter component of this development is likely indicative of the first oil price shock but also illustrates the tightening external constraint affecting the Chilean economy in the immediate aftermath of the *Unidad Popular* government.

Looking beyond primary commodities, the manufacturing sector has tended to decline in relative importance since the 1960s. Manufacturing value added as a percentage of GDP has fallen from 24.04 per cent in 1965 to 16.89 per cent in 2000 before dropping further to a value of 11.93 per cent in 2011. The value of manufacturing exports as a percentage of total exports, by contrast, has increased from 3.92 per cent in 1965 to 16.24 per cent in 2000 before dropping slightly to 13.77 per cent in 2011 (see Figure 4.8 for an illustration). The drop in the value of the manufacturing sector's relative export participation is to be expected against the background of a commodity price boom and in the context of the export profile of a commodity-dependent economy. What is worth noting, though, is the coincidence of a declining domestic incidence of manufacturing sector production with a consistently increasing participation in exports. The latter observation points to the expansion of an internationally competitive manufacturing sector so that the combined observation of decreasing relative importance in the domestic economy with increased relative trade participation can at least be seen as consistent with a process of consolidation of an internationally competitive manufacturing orientation.

Within the manufacturing sector, activity related to basic metals has traditionally played a relatively important role. Its share of value added in the manufacturing sector rose from 9.02 per cent in 1965 to 24.73 per cent in 1975.[16] The series subsequently remains volatile, with values fluctuating for example between 22.84 per cent in 1990 and 12.42 per cent in 1994. The overall data series for the manufacturing sector is incomplete after 1994, although a value of 52.89 per cent can be inferred for the 2008 datum. Investment in this sector (as proxied by the gross fixed capital formation) rose from 13.99 per cent in 1965 to a peak of 79.23 per cent in 1975 before falling to 9.52 per cent in 1990.

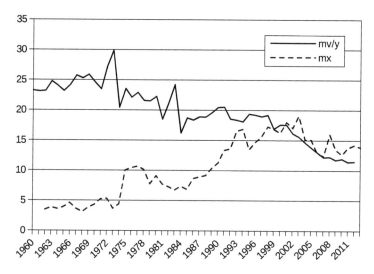

Figure 4.8 Chile: manufacturing share in national value added and exports.

Note: mv/y: manufacturing sector share in value added; m/x: manufacturing export share.

Another sector with a consistently prominent contribution to value added is the food and beverages sector, which accounted for 20.62 per cent of manufacturing value added in 1965, 18.80 per cent in 1975, and 21.88 per cent in 1990. The data reported for the 2005–2008 interval are lower, indicating a contribution to manufacturing value added between 13.39 per cent (2008) and 16.64 per cent (2005).

Investment in different manufacturing sub-sectors is much harder to evaluate. UNIDO data on the gross fixed capital formation are not consistently complete, and relative investment shares are liable to be strongly influenced by individual large scale projects in a relatively small economy like Chile's. During the 1960s and 1970s, manufacturing investment appears to be dominated by the basic metal minerals sector, whose share in the gross fixed capital formation peaked at 79.23 per cent of manufacturing gross fixed capital formation in 1975, as discussed previously.

Investment in the non-metallic mineral products sector reached temporarily high levels peaking at 27.41 per cent in 1983, while the relative incidence of investment in paper and paper products temporarily increased in the early 1980s and again in the 1990s, when it reached a peak value of 57.26 per cent of the manufacturing sector gross fixed capital formation. Investment in food and beverages almost consistently remained within a range of 10–40 per cent of the manufacturing sector gross fixed capital formation, peaking at 39.50 per cent in 1979. What is evident across these sub-sectors is the substantial volatility in their relative incidence. To some extent this should be expected in the context of a moderately sized domestic manufacturing sector in which activities like mining are likely to involve relatively large investment projects at particular time intervals leading to a sudden redistribution of relative sub-sectoral shares of investment activities.

The distribution of investment activities across industrial sub-sectors thus does not point to any clear transformative trends but appears broadly consistent with the diversified export prevalence of commodity-based activities. A detailed analysis of transformative investment activities in manufacturing would go beyond the remit of the present work and require a more detailed analysis of investment flows in various categories beyond manufacturing. A recent study by Fernandes and Paunov (2012) concentrates on the impact of FDI in the context of firm level data and finds that productivity tends to improve with service sector FDI penetration. Fernandes and Paunov (2012) also argue that FDI serves to promote the modernization of less innovative firms, an observation that contrasts with the foreign investment pessimism traditionally associated with foreign investment in commodity-dependent economies with dominant mining sectors.

The Chilean economy, then, presents a picture that defies optimistic expectations of rapid convergence as well as anticipations of a commodity curse leading to a poverty trap. Rather, this economy has benefitted from stability in its institutional as well as economic dimensions. Gregorio (2004) elaborates on the role of a liberal and transparent regulatory regime and stresses the fact of policy continuity following the transition from military rule to democracy after 1990. Structural stability is also reflected in the evolution of the country's macroeconomic framework itself. With a trade and activity profile that, while still dominated by primary commodity sectors, has become less dominated by mining over time, this development has been complemented by intertemporal smoothing of public revenue receipts via the economic and social stabilization funds (ESSF) as well as by the use of overseas investment vehicles to limit the extent of trade related exchange rate fluctuations – see Ebert and La Menza (2015) for a summary account.

Against this background, Chile's economy has grown, not spectacularly but consistently. Gregorio (2004) argues that growth up to 1985 was mainly marked by a recovery from the 1982 debt crisis, and that subsequent growth during the 1980s was mainly attributable to increased employment while growth during the 1990s was mainly driven by capital accumulation prior to a slowdown during the late 1990s. Chile's more recent growth performance has, of course, coincided with the early twenty-first century commodity price boom and the country's PPP adjusted per capita GDP has converged to 37.57 per cent of the corresponding figure for the USA by 2011, although the corresponding figure without purchasing power parity adjustment is a mere 20.36 per cent.

Chile's longer term convergence performance is illustrated in Figure 4.9. Following a period of gradual decline in the earlier part of the sample, Chile's GDP per capita began a process of convergence compared to the US level of per capita income from the mid 1980s. The observed per capita income convergence to 20.6 per cent of the US equivalent level occurred from an initial level of 15.70 per cent in 1960, at the beginning of the sample, and compensated an intermittent decline to 10.85 per cent of US per capita GDP in 1984. What remains to be seen is how the Chilean economy's relative performance is set to develop if commodity

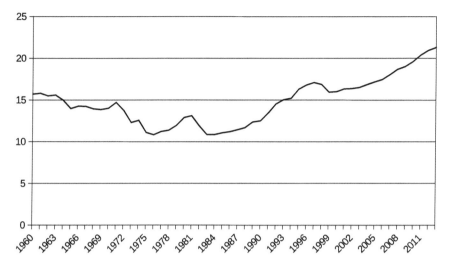

Figure 4.9 Chile: real per capita GDP convergence to US equivalent.

prices generally and copper prices in particular return to more modest levels in the future.

4.5 Botswana

Botswana, the previous protectorate of Bechuanaland within the British Empire, gained independence in 1966 while maintaining close economic relations to neighbouring South Africa. At the time of independence, Botswana's economy was dominated by cattle farming, with mining operations and mainly diamond exports playing an increasing role in later years (Leith 2005).

From independence, Botswana's real per capita GDP grew from US$468.83 in 1966 to US$6476.05 in 2011 (and further to US$7027.25 in 2013).[17] This increase in real per capita income corresponds to a rise from 2.36 per cent of US per capita GDP in 1966 to 14.60 per cent of US per capita GDP in 2011, a level close to that of middle income economies like Chile. Adjusting for purchasing power parity, this corresponds to 34.26 per cent of per capita income in the United States in 2011. Botswana's growth performance has been attributed to a tradition-driven, consensus-focused approach by the post-colonial government (Leith 2005). Hillbom (2011), on the other hand, argues that Botswana, far from proactively promoting development, has consistently acted to protect the position and interests of the existing elites, even though this approach has been accompanied by a sustained record of income convergence.

In spite of differing views on the extent of Botswana's democratic status or constitutional orientation, authors tend not to disagree on the basic empirical facts of institutional and economic stability correlating with an intertemporally consistent measure of economic success. This overall record can be seen against a

wider background of macroeconomic stability and the observed extent of structural transformation in the local economy. Botswana converged consistently over
the years since independence in that there were no protracted periods of stagnation
or decay in real GDP. Year on year growth rates were volatile, though with some
large booms during the early post-independence period in particular, and some
sharp recessions around the turn of the millennium and following the 2008 crisis.
These cyclical fluctuations occurred around a mean growth rate of 8.39 per cent
for the 1960–2013 interval.[18]

Botswana's rapid growth during the early post-independence period was hardly
surprising given the need for basic infrastructure and settlement construction and
the associated high percentage increments resulting from a given addition to a
low existing income base – see Leith (2005) for a background discussion. What is
more remarkable is the country's subsequent experience of relatively rapid growth
and its sustained record of per capita GDP convergence to the US comparative
level. While growth has become more volatile in recent years, there has been no
perceptible break in the general trend towards convergence (see Figure 4.10).

Figure 4.10 shows GDP per capita for Botswana as a percentage of GDP per
capita for the United States of America expressed in constant US dollars. Per
capita income levels began to converge rapidly shortly after independence until
the convergence process slows down from 1990–2005, whereafter there is some
renewed acceleration. It is crucial to note that convergence implies faster growth of
per capita income in Botswana than in the comparator country (the USA), so that
when average incomes in both economies grow at the same pace then the convergence process stagnates. In other words, stagnating convergence need not imply
income growth stagnation in the converging economy in either total or per capita
terms. Botswana's average real income level has simply grown at the same pace

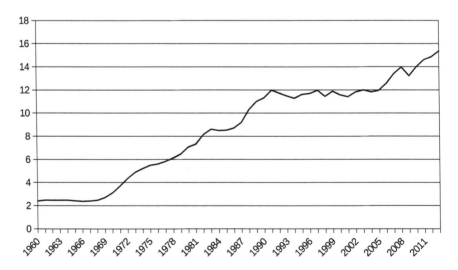

Figure 4.10 Botswana: real per capita GDP convergence to US equivalent.

as that of the advanced economy, while it grew more quickly before and after the 1990–2005 hiatus interval. The role of commodities in Botswana's export profile is one variable meriting consideration when interpreting these recent developments in convergence.

Before considering commodity exports in more detail, a general overview of macroeconomic conditions and macroeconomic stability is worth considering. Botswana did not establish an independent currency (the Pula) and central bank until 1976, a decade after independence (Leith 2005). Botswana's inflation rate has been volatile, reaching peak values above 20 per cent in 1979 and during the 1980s.[19] The inflation rate did not consistently remain at such elevated levels, however, averaging 8.77 per cent over the full 1960–2013 sample interval available.

The mean inflation rate over the sample period is above that for the US dollar, and the Pula has accordingly depreciated over time at a mean rate of 4.76 per cent, around 0.5 per cent below the 5.28 per cent inflation rate differential between Botswana and the USA. The depreciation rate accelerated somewhat later than the inflation rate during the 1980s and has averaged 6.77 per cent after 1990. Leith (2005) reports that Botswana's monetary exchange rate policy targetted the South African rand after the US dollar peg inherited from the Bretton Woods system became unsustainable, and maintained at least some form of capital account control until 1999.

Net exports were negative until 1984, with a trade deficit of 39.89 per cent in 1968 and smaller but substantial trade deficits during much of the early post-independence years. Subsequent trade surpluses peaked at 26.68 per cent of GDP in 1987, although net exports in excess of 10 per cent of GDP were registered for many years during the 1984–2007 interval, whereafter successive trade deficits resurfaced. These trade data are consistent with a small, very open economy which maintained a strong export performance for prolonged periods of time but remains susceptible to external shocks.

Data from the World Bank's World Development Indicators show manufacturing value added to remain consistently below 10 per cent per year. Data on the share of manufactured products in total merchandise exports are only reported from 2000, but consistently remain between 70 and 91 per cent. These data on export and GDP participation do not appear readily compatible: focusing on the year 2006 as an example, we see that net exports reached a relatively high value of 18.17 per cent with exports not net of imports amounting to 52.25 per cent of GDP. These trade data are unlikely to be consistent with a manufacturing value added share of 5.82 per cent of GDP for the same year even in the case of a preponderance of low value added sub-sectors.

Trade data from the Comtrade database show a similar pattern, although higher level SITC disaggregation of these data also helps to explain the apparent inconsistency. If trade data are aggregated into four product groups following Radetzki (2010) as above, minerals and metals exports take values ranging from 4.97 to 23.42 per cent with total commodity exports accounting for between 8.85 and 26.66 per cent during the 2000–2012 interval for which data were reported. The remaining exports would then have to be accounted for almost exclusively by manufactured goods exports.

In the above aggregation of primary commodities, the minerals and metals sector is composed of SITC categories 27, 28, 67, and 68. This aggregate includes industrial diamonds (SITC 2751), which are included in SITC class 27, but excludes non-industrial diamonds (SITC 6672), which happen to be Botswana's main export and are commonly regarded as a commodity export in the context of applied economics discussions. If SITC 6672 (diamonds, not industrial, not set or strung) is added to mining sector exports, the distribution of commodity exports changes. Botswana now appears unambiguously commodity export dependent over the short period for which data are available, and these commodity exports are dominated by non-industrial diamonds.

A similar classification discrepancy appears to be at the heart of the World Bank data: the share of manufacturing exports in merchandise exports is based on SITC data where non-industrial diamonds are included as a basic manufacturing category; data for manufacturing value added as a percentage of GDP are based on ISIC data, where the mining of gemstones, as opposed to their further processing, is classed as separate from manufacturing activities.[20]

Table 4.9 shows mineral exports including non-industrial diamonds to account for almost all of the country's exports, with mining exports consistently above 80 per cent. In fact, exports in SITC category 6672 alone account for between 62.72 and 83.80 per cent of total exports over the 2000–2012 period. This strong dominance of one narrowly defined sector is reflected in the values of the normalized Hirschman–Herfindahl index, which fluctuate between 0.41 and 0.67 but show no clear tendency towards increase or decline. The short period covered clearly limits the explanatory potential of these trade data. They do, however appear consistent with the narrative generally encountered in analyses of the Botswanan economy.[21]

Data for imports, like those for exports, are only available for the 2000–2012 interval. During this time, total commodity imports accounted for between 24.23 per cent of all imports (in the year 2000) and 31.05 per cent of imports in 2011. Food imports fell somewhat from 14.25 per cent in 2000 to

Table 4.9 Botswana: export shares and concentrations

Year	Food	Raw Mat.	Minerals	Fuel	Total	NHHI
2000	2.79	0.34	89.12	0.08	92.32	0.67
2003	2.36	0.12	88.44	0.04	90.96	0.60
2006	2.70	0.15	89.91	0.13	92.90	0.53
2008	2.90	0.29	83.86	0.30	87.36	0.42
2009	5.15	0.17	80.31	0.32	85.94	0.41
2011	2.24	0.18	84.97	0.40	87.80	0.57

Shares are in per cent. Raw Mat.: agricultural raw materials; Minerals: minerals and metals, including diamonds (SITC 6672); Fuel: mineral fuels; Total: total commodity exports; NHHI: normalized Hirschman–Herfindahl index.

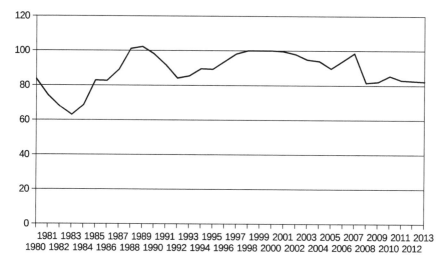

Figure 4.11 Botswana: net barter terms of trade.

Note: Net barter terms of trade index, 2000 = 100.

10.45 per cent in 2011, while fuel imports increased from 4.75 per cent in 2000 to 16.39 per cent in 2011, after reaching a value of 17.17 per cent in 2006. There are, however, no clear trends in import composition over the short period for which data are available.

Botswana thus combines earnings concentrated in a high value product niche and successful economic convergence, at least by the standards of conditional convergence. Moreover, Botswana's net barter terms of trade do not appear to have followed a pronounced decline. The World Development Indicator's NBTT series shows moderate fluctuations of the NBTT between 1980 and 2013, but the decline from the index base-value around the year 2000 is rather modest and appears to level out towards the end of the sample period (see Figure 4.11 for an illustration).

The geometric mean growth rate of the NBTT series between 1980 and 2000 implies an increase of 0.91 per cent per annum, followed by a decline of 1.49 per cent per annum for the 2000–2013 interval. Given the length of the sample, and the likely presence of serial correlation, these in-sample descriptive statistics seem more appropriate than formal trend estimates.[22] In any case, the available data do not appear to show a dramatic decline or a particularly pronounced volatility in the terms of trade.

The extent to which the overall structure of Botswana's economy, and particularly its non-traded components, have developed alongside this specialized trade profile is a question that remains to be addressed. Leith (2005) and Hillbom (2011) point to cattle farming as a traditionally important industry in terms of domestic economic status and power, and Leith (2005) points to the importance of this sector during the operation of the Lomé treaty, which gave preferential access to European Community markets to some developing countries and thus allowed these countries to capture some of the associated rents from trading in protected markets.

While manufacturing value added remained at relatively low levels (as discussed above), female labour force participation outside the agricultural sector rose from 33.5 per cent in 1990 to values consistently above 40 per cent with a non-agricultural female labour force participation of 41.4 per cent in 2010, the latest year for which data are available. Few disaggregated data for the manufacturing sector are available from the UNIDO Industrial Statistics database. Moreover, gaps in the available data are not uniform across different manufacturing sub-sectors, and there are substantive discrepancies in data availability between, for example, value added and output data at different points in time and across different data types. Such discontinuities are much more likely to arise from irregular reporting practice than sudden sectoral shifts and thus should motivate a cautious attitude towards the available manufacturing data. In view of the inconsistent availability of disaggregated manufacturing data and the low overall importance of the manufacturing sector reported in the World Development Indicators, it is probably best to confine one's attention in this particular case to national level aggregate data.

Botswana, then, presents a case of an economy achieving a notable degree of per capita income convergence based on a very narrowly defined commodity export specialization. In spite of this specialization, Botswana has largely avoided Dutch disease type problems (Scott 2010), an achievement that was probably aided by the establishment of the country's sovereign wealth fund in 1993 (Kern 2007). In addition, the country has successfully contained the danger of commodity rents being captured by an isolated elite or the equally damaging alternative of building government support on unsustainable expenditure commitments: Leith (2005) points out that sustainability was assured by limiting government spending commitments to levels below the constraint defined by earnings flows.

Hillbom (2011) criticizes the Botswanan state for its lack of proactive development promotion and its perpetuation of existing hegemonic structures, but concedes that the existing institutional structures have at least viable levels of stability and inclusion to economic benefits from the commodity-based economy. The case of Botswana, then, does in some measure represent an economic and institutional success story, even in the eyes of its critics, and against the background of persistent dependency on export earnings from a single commodity sector. On the one hand, the flow of export earnings from this source has been well managed (Leith 2005; Scott 2010), but on the other hand the persistence of this 'monoeconomy' (Radetzki 2010) condition burdens Botswana with a lasting and structurally pivotal economic risk.

While Botswana illustrates a case of pronounced and lasting commodity export dependence, its past record of income performance sets it apart from many other African countries. Dependence on and access to commodity export earnings has been less unambiguously beneficial in other cases. Two of these will be covered in the following discussion, which will address the case of Nigeria before turning to the example of Zambia.

4.6 Nigeria

Nigeria gained independence from Britain in 1960, giving rise to the emergence of a multi-ethnic, culturally fragmented entity. So much so that the later prime minister Abubakar Tafawa Ablewa, as quoted in Meredith (2013), dismissed Nigerian unity as no more than a British invention. The profound, and geographically stratified, ethnic fragmentation of the country did indeed underpin internal conflict after independence (Meredith 2013). However, following periods of military rule, Nigeria's political structure stabilized with the constitution of 1999 that guarantees a federal structure and has provided a framework for regular elections and peaceful transfers of power (World Bank 2013a). Internal strife, in addition to episodes of military rule, have been threats to the basic stability of the Nigerian state over time, and internal conflict is ongoing at the time of writing.

Regional military conflict in Nigeria (and to some extent affecting neighbouring countries) is currently dominated by the activities of Boko Haram.[23] This destabilizing factor is not only a threat to the domestic constitutional order but has international implications in the region. The latter are ambiguous in so far as the common enemy has motivated the organization of a concerted defence effort. It is possible, therefore, that the current threat has an at least partially stabilizing impact in the region in so far as it produces a lasting security infrastructure. A comprehensive discussion of this conflict dimension is beyond the scope of the present book, but a more detailed discussion can be found in Comolli (2015).

These general considerations of political stability and conflict are crucial for an appreciation of the institutional underpinnings of the country's economic performance. Nigeria's growth experience has been one of highly volatile GDP growth rates and frequent recessions for the period between the demise of the Bretton Woods system and the end of the cold war. The real GDP growth rate between 1960 and 1989 was 2.38 per cent compared to a real GDP growth rate of 5.26 per cent for the 1990–2013 interval. The latter mean growth rate is not greatly affected by the international economic crisis after 2008: mean real GDP growth for the 1990–2008 interval takes a slightly lower value of 5.09 per cent.

With regards to convergence, Nigeria's real GDP per capita initially fell from a peak value of 3.76 per cent of the US equivalent figure in 1974 to 1.35 per cent in 2000. Relative real per capita GDP then stagnated and eventually began to recover, reaching 2.29 per cent in 2011 and 2.31 per cent of the US equivalent figure in 2013, the latest year for which data are available. This process of income divergence and the subsequent resumption of convergence are illustrated in Figure 4.12. Adjusting for purchasing power parity, the relative 2011 value is 6.89 per cent of US real per capita GDP, compared to 1.29 per cent in 1990. This resumption of growth convergence should be interpreted against a background of other complementary macroeconomic indicators.

Inflation, as measured by the GDP deflator, has been high for prolonged periods, taking values in excess of 20 per cent during most years between 1987 and 1996, with a peak rate of 113.08 per cent in 1995 and a low value of 9.29 per cent in 1990. In the post-1997 period, inflation remained highly volatile, though generally

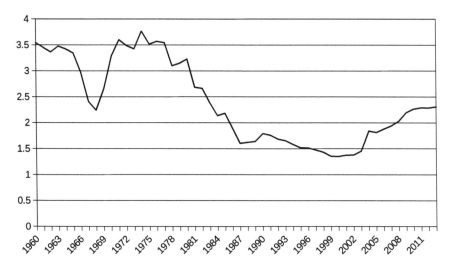

Figure 4.12 Nigeria: real per capita GDP convergence to US equivalent.

within a lower value range for the inflation rate. A number of years experienced deflation, with the lowest inflation rate of −5.67 per cent recorded in 1998, while annual inflation rates could still reach high values in other years, such as the 39.90 per cent inflation rate recorded for 2002 or the post-1997 peak rate of 103.82 per cent in 2010.

The responsiveness of the exchange rate to these inflationary episodes differs. The exchange rate tended to depreciate at varying rates during the 1982–1993 interval. From 1994 to 1998, the exchange rate was maintained at a stable value before depreciating dramatically by 143.96 per cent in 1999. The depreciation rate then moderated gradually, from 9.65 per cent in 2000 to −5.95 per cent in 2008. In fact, the exchange rate appreciated on average over the full 2005–2008 interval before depreciating rapidly at 22.80 per cent in 2009 and returning to moderate rates of change during subsequent years.

Against the background of general macroeconomic stability characteristics, it is interesting to note that economic growth has recently been dominated by the non-oil sector (IMF 2015; World Bank 2013a). Manufacturing value added as a proportion of GDP has increased sharply from 2.47 per cent in 2009 to 7.19 per cent in 2011 and further to 9.03 per cent in 2013, thus recovering shares of national income similar to those which had been recorded during the early 1980s. Manufacturing participation in exports, however, has been less strong and less consistent in its development, rising from 3.59 per cent in 2009 to a peak value of 6.69 per cent in 2010 before falling back to 2.55 per cent in 2011. By 2013, the export share of manufactured products had recovered somewhat to 3.39 per cent, yet its trajectory does not mirror the recent, if as yet short-lived, strengthening of manufacturing value added in national income overall from a historically low basis.

Table 4.10 Nigeria: export shares and concentrations

Year	Food	Raw Mat.	Minerals	Fuel	Total	NHHI
1965	54.38	10.92	6.53	25.88	97.71	0.17
1975	5.16	0.58	0.46	93.24	99.45	0.86
1983	3.77	0.08	0.12	94.41	98.37	0.88
1991	1.46	0.56	0.06	96.63	98.71	0.93
2000	0.14	0.01	0.01	99.64	99.79	0.99
2011	1.80	6.13	0.35	89.13	97.40	0.78

Shares are in per cent. Raw Mat.: agricultural raw materials; Minerals: minerals and metals; Fuel: mineral fuels; Total: total commodity exports; NHHI: normalized Hirschman–Herfindahl index. No data are available for 1982 and 1990.

Service sector participation in GDP initially fell from 33.66 per cent in 1983 to 20.35 per cent in 1996 before growing to 28.74 per cent in 2009 and then to 52.90 per cent in 2011 and further to 57.01 per cent in 2013. These recent increments in non-primary sector activity cannot yet be characterized as a lasting transformation: the change in output composition is simply too recent to allow any such verdict. In the present context, it is also necessary to assess these observations against the background of trading activity and the development of Nigeria's trade specialization.

Nigeria's export profile has been consistently dominated by primary commodities. From 1962 onwards, commodity exports accounted for over 90 per cent of total exports, and from 1969 the main export has been mineral fuels. In 1965, food exports still accounted for 54.38 per cent compared to 25.88 per cent for fuel exports (see Table 4.10). By 1969, food exports accounted for 41.67 per cent of total exports compared to 42.72 per cent for fuels. Food exports then fell to consistently low percentages of total export revenue, registering 5.16 per cent in 1975, 3.77 per cent in 1983, 1.46 per cent in 1991, and 0.14 per cent in 2000. By 2011 this share had recovered somewhat to 1.80 per cent. Fuel exports, by contrast, had risen to 93.24 per cent of total exports by 1975, reached a share of 99.64 per cent of total exports in 2000, before dropping somewhat to 89.13 per cent in 2011.

Exports in the agricultural raw materials and minerals and metals categories have consistently played a very minor role. Agricultural raw material exports contracted from 10.92 per cent in 1965 to 0.58 per cent in 1975 and stayed below 1 per cent for the remainder of the century[24] (see Table 4.10). By 2011, exports in this category had recovered to 6.13 per cent of total exports. Mineral exports dropped from 6.53 per cent in 1965 to 0.46 per cent in 1975 and remained below 1 per cent of total exports for most of the following years.[25]

The concentration of exports across SITC categories has remained largely unaltered. Table 4.10 shows the normalized Hirschman–Herfindahl index increasing from 0.17 in 1965 to a peak value of 0.99 in 2000 followed by a subsequent decline to 0.78 in 2011. Overall, the normalized concentration index has grown at a mean rate of 3.10 per cent per year over the sample period, marking a lasting and substantive increase in the sectoral concentration of export activity. Since

Nigeria's export niche is narrowly located in SITC category 33 (petroleum and petroleum products), export concentrations differ little across one- and two-digit aggregations, with export concentration ratios converging to values close to 1 by 1970.

Specialization in the mineral fuel sector implies high export earnings dependence on a highly fungible commodity with geographically dispersed demand. The relative importance of exports to China has not dramatically increased during the recent commodity price boom. China's incidence in Nigeria's total exports increased from almost 0 per cent for most of the twentieth and twenty-first centuries to 1.62 per cent in 2007, just before the onset of the international financial crisis; then, after a brief contraction in 2008, it recovered to 2.01 per cent in 2011 and 5.62 per cent in 2012. China's overall importance as an export destination for Nigeria thus remains modest.

One sub-category in which China's relative importance has increased notably is in mineral and metal exports where China's share of export receipts had risen to 17.67 per cent by 2012. Another category in which exports to China rose above the total average in recent years was agricultural raw materials, where the share of exports to China amounted to 10.12 per cent in 2012. Both export categories have a limited overall importance in Nigeria's export profile, with a 2012 export share of 0.45 per cent for minerals and metals and 7.27 per cent for agricultural raw materials in 2012. China's incidence, moreover, was substantively lower in earlier years.

In spite of the non-oil sector's growth performance, oil exports remain the main source of government revenue, and part of these export earnings is redistributed among federal state units according to a predetermined formula (World Bank 2013a). Export earnings thus define a financial constraint on public spending that is only partly alleviated by domestically raised public revenue. Even though domestic industrial activity and consumption can generally be expected to require some imported inputs, these need to be financed by export earnings or foreign investment in national accounting terms.

Commodities have traditionally had a limited incidence in Nigerian imports, with the participation of primary commodity imports remaining below 30 per cent in the early years of the sample period. Table 4.11 shows an incidence of 25.43 per cent and 24.85 per cent for total commodity imports to Nigeria in 1965 and 1975 respectively. A commodity import share of more than 30 per cent is first shown in 1983, although it is not easy to assess the overall development of the import composition given the presence of data gaps during the 1980s and 1990s.

The primary commodity import share then fluctuated more strongly with a commodity import share of 17.61 per cent recorded for 1991, 31.13 per cent in 2000, a mere 16.04 per cent in 2010, and 48.38 per cent in 2011. It is worth noting that these fluctuations in the total commodity import share are largely driven by the incidence of food imports, which, for example, rose to 30.56 per cent in 2011 compared to 6.36 per cent in 1991.

Imports in the remaining three commodity categories remained low, although it is remarkable that fuel imports still accounted for 9.95 per cent of total imports in

Table 4.11 Nigeria: import shares and concentrations

Year	Food	Raw Mat.	Minerals	Fuel	Total	NHHI
1965	9.14	0.87	9.12	6.31	25.43	0.16
1975	9.38	1.03	11.75	2.69	24.85	0.19
1983	21.55	1.13	7.68	0.81	31.18	0.15
1991	6.36	0.74	10.01	0.49	17.61	0.13
2000	19.92	0.92	8.57	1.72	31.13	0.14
2011	30.56	4.20	3.66	9.95	48.38	0.13

Shares are in per cent. Raw Mat.: agricultural raw materials; Minerals: minerals and metals; Fuel: mineral fuels; Total: total commodity exports; NHHI: normalized Hirschman–Herfindahl index. No data are available for 1982 and 1990.

2011. The concentration of import activity is not very strongly biased towards one sector and has not shown any clear developments over time, with the normalized Hirschman–Herfindahl index taking values between 0.10 and 0.25 throughout.

In spite of the non-oil sector's strong growth performance, oil revenues retain a crucial role in Nigeria's economy. World Bank (2013a) points out that non-oil sector activities are heavily concentrated geographically, while oil export revenue is in some measure distributed throughout the federation. Even though the impact of oil price fluctuations on the economy is not always apparent in the short term, the value of the currency is actively defended in international markets so that oil price fluctuations tend to impact on reserve holdings rather than having an immediate impact on the exchange rate.

Part of the oil export revenues is invested in the excess crude account, but the various pressures on the public finances have prevented a systematic build up of buffer funds: in addition to interregional transfers, and foreign exchange market intervention, pressure on public spending has been maintained by fuel price subsidies (IMF 2015; World Bank 2013a). This institutional background scenario makes Nigeria dependent on oil export earnings and to some extent on high oil prices. At the time of writing, low prices have forced some adjustments, including foreign exchange rationing by the central bank.[26]

Given its narrow commodity export specialization and the close correspondence between oil price movements and the country's net barter terms of trade (see Figure 4.13), Nigeria does indeed display the symptoms of an underdeveloped economy dependent on export earnings from a volatile, if not consistently downwards trending, commodity niche market. The persistence of this commodity exposure is not exclusively given by the nature of the relevant market, though, but can be linked to deficiencies in the design of institutions and a failure to complete subsidy reforms (IMF 2015). These shortcomings in governance in their turn need to be analysed in the context of the country's history and current experience of internal conflict and tension – a task beyond the scope of the present study but of direct relevance to the more immediately apparent economic problems.

The case of Nigeria illustrates the situation of a developing economy dependent on highly specialized export earnings. In this particular case, the export

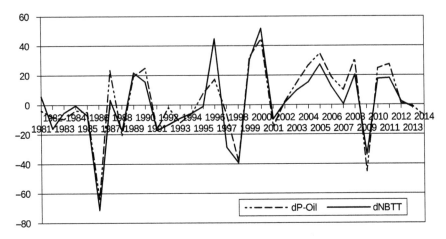

Figure 4.13 Nigeria: changes in NBTT and oil price index.

Note: dNBTT: changes in net barter terms of trade; dP-Oil: changes in oil price index; 2000 = 100.

commodity in question (oil) forms part of a market characterized by highly influential cartel action, with Nigeria itself being a member of OPEC. The following case study concentrates on an economy almost as highly dependent on copper, for which there is no comparable degree of politically driven intervention on a global scale.

4.7 Zambia

Zambia's economy was dominated by copper production and export prior to independence in 1964. Following independence, Kaunda's government consciously intervened to promote rapid economic development. In the course of these developments, mining industries were nationalized, and eventually the political regime moved to a one-party state. If there was one internal force articulating a competing claim to power in some measure, it was the unions organizing workers in the copper belt region (Larmer 2010).

Copper prices remained low for most years of this interventionist policy stance, when export earnings strongly affected the domestic economy. So much so that wage demands in the copper sector were directly influenced by the prevailing world copper price (Larmer 2010). Adam and Simpasa (2010) further point out that the transient nature of copper price rises was often not anticipated by the authorities during this period. Thus low prices, relatively high extraction costs, and the role of copper exports as the main source of export earnings led to a situation in which the management of the nationalized copper sector ceased to be commercially viable.

It was against this background, as well as the recent context of radical political and economic liberalization during the early 1990s, that privatization of copper production had to be negotiated, leading to a privatization arrangement that generated little revenue for the Zambian state (Adam and Simpasa 2010; Larmer 2010).

It is no exaggeration to say that Kaunda's development strategy was no unmitigated success. Zambia's level of GDP per capita stood at 5.29 per cent of US per capita GDP at independence in 1964. From there, it fell in real terms to 1.49 per cent of its US equivalent in 2000, although the pace of decline appears to slow during the 1990s. A recovery of real per capita GDP can be observed during the early twenty-first century with real per capita GDP rising to 2.30 per cent of the corresponding US income level by 2013. To put this development into context, Zambia's per capita GDP in 2013 had recovered its 1986 level in relative terms, a level which itself had materialized following a prolonged period of sustained relative income decline (see Figure 4.14 for an illustration of this process). When adjusting for purchasing power parity, Zambia's per capita income relative to the US does appear higher and has initially risen from 17.90 per cent in 1964 to a peak value of 21.39 per cent in 1967. From this point onwards, purchasing power parity adjusted real per capita GDP in Zambia has tended to decline, reaching a low point of 2.16 per cent of the US equivalent value in 1994 before recovering somewhat, reaching a value of 5.89 per cent in 2011.

Real GDP growth likewise reflects this development. Over the sample period, real GDP growth figures have been volatile with frequent recessions. There is a notable difference between the earlier and the later part of the sample, with growth rates appearing higher on average in later than in earlier sample years. The geometric mean growth rate for real GDP per capita over the 1961–1989 interval, comprising the transition to independence as well as the remaining

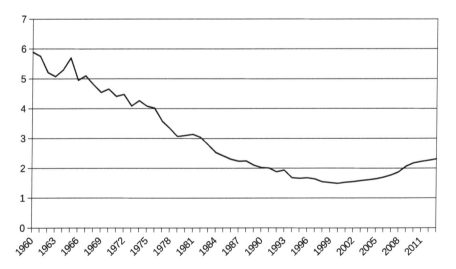

Figure 4.14 Zambia: real per capita GDP convergence to US equivalent.

cold war period, is −1.03 per cent compared to a positive mean growth rate of 2.01 per cent for the 1990–2013 period.

The economy's structure remains dominated by the primary sector, which surfaces in a large industrial participation. In an economy with a strong mining sector this comes as no surprise: industrial value added as a share of GDP rose from 58.78 per cent after independence in 1965 to a peak value of 68.15 per cent in 1969 before decaying gradually to 41.89 per cent in 1993. The share of the industrial sector in value added contracted further to 25.78 per cent in 1999 before recovering to 35.94 per cent of GDP in 2011 and 33.85 per cent in 2013.

The service sector contribution to GDP rose from 25.59 per cent in 1965 to 46.06 per cent in 1982, from where the value added share decreased to 24.01 per cent in 1993 before recovering to 56.50 per cent by 2013. The agricultural sector's share in value added was 15.63 per cent in 1965 and fluctuated within a 10–20 per cent range for most years, although its value added share rose to 34.10 per cent in 1993 before falling back into its previous value range and dropping to 9.64 per cent in 2013. Although the industrial sector overall consistently accounted for a high share of GDP, the evolution of the manufacturing sub-sector differs markedly. The manufacturing value added share in GDP rose from 6.92 per cent in 1965 to a peak value of 37.16 per cent in 1992 before dropping to 27.94 per cent in the following year and then to 10.42 per cent in 1994. After stabilizing at a share of around 12 per cent of GDP during the late 1990s, the manufacturing value added share then declined further, reaching a value of 8.18 per cent in 2013. Rakner (2004) points to the removal of external protection coupled with a continued implementation of import duties on raw material imports as a trigger for the rapid contraction of the manufacturing sector in 1993/94. Among these drivers, the removal of external protection of the manufacturing sector was driven by the intention to move to a more liberal economic regime, while the persistence of import tariffs on raw material imports can be explained by a revenue motive (Rakner 2004, p. 91).

It was then an unintended consequence that these distinct policy motives produced a common effect: while the removal of external protection for the manufacturing sector exposed it to increased competitive pressure, the persistence of tariffs on raw material imports had the effect of increasing at least some of the input costs faced by the manufacturing sector. It therefore seems likely that the dramatic yet transient increase of agricultural sector participation in 1993 can be at least partly attributed to the rapid contraction of the manufacturing sector as a complementary constituent of overall national product.

There are comparatively few data on the employment share of the industrial sector, with the latest datum (for 2005) giving a value of 7.10 per cent. The complementary sectoral data (also for 2005 only) are 72.20 per cent for agriculture and 20.60 per cent for services. Data for female labour market participation outside the agricultural sector are only available for 1990 and 2000 and show an increase from 16.6 per cent to a still modest value of 22 per cent. This sectoral distribution seems consistent with a dualist macroeconomic structure and the presence of a surplus labour supply in a subsistence agricultural sector. For conceptually related reasons, these data should be interpreted with some caution, though. The small number of data points as well as the background scenario of a substantive informal sector further suggest that formally recorded data may only capture a partial picture of the underlying economic process.

On a more aggregate level, inflation rates in the early years of Zambia's independence show pronounced volatility, giving way to hyperinflation from at least 1986 (with an inflation rate of 81.99 per cent) culminating in an inflation rate of 165 per cent in 1992. Inflationary pressures were eventually brought under control following liberalizing reforms with inflation rates decaying gradually from the mid 1990s until reaching an inflation rate of 11.58 per cent in 2011 and 5.65 per cent in 2013.

The sharp acceleration in inflation was not reflected in exchange rate movements during the pre-liberalization period, while a currency peg was maintained. This regime came under increasing pressure, and the auctioning of foreign exchange in 1985 produced substantive exchange rate depreciations (Rakner 2004, p. 58). Further large and sustained currency depreciations were observed during the 1990s, following liberalization when average annual depreciation rates peaked at 97.99 per cent in 1992.[27]

Zambia's exchange rate then was not primarily determined by the international market process for a large part of the available sample period. While an externally managed currency will not mirror market conditions, the world market price of the economy's main export and the country's terms of trade are not so constrained. These variables are key determinants of external pressures on the market value of the currency and therefore merit some attention for this reason as well as with regards to their conventional role as a determinant of the balance of payments constraint. The net barter terms of trade series, however is available since 1980, and changes in the NBTT correlate closely with changes in the copper price index over the available data period (see Figure 4.15). This general development is to be expected given the known dominant position of Zambia's copper sector. This dependence on one particular sector also correlates with a high degree of commodity dependence overall, although the country's trade specialization has recently experienced some limited changes.

While the incidence of commodity exports in Zambia's trade balance has remained high, it has fallen somewhat from the near complete levels of commodity export dependence in earlier years. Table 4.12 shows commodity export shares of 99.29 per cent and 98.66 per cent for 1966 and 1975 respectively. These very high concentrations of primary commodity export shares are characteristic for the early sample years, preceding the gap in trade data from 1980 to 1992. In more recent years this near complete dominance of the commodity sector diminished only slightly to 95.41 per cent in 1993, 89.14 per cent in 2000, and 90.59 per cent in 2011. There were some fluctuations in the total commodity export share. The lowest value in the available data set was obtained for 1999, when total primary commodity exports accounted for 82.94 per cent of total exports.

Given the key role of the copper sector in the Zambian economy, the dominant position of primary commodity exports in the minerals and metal category should

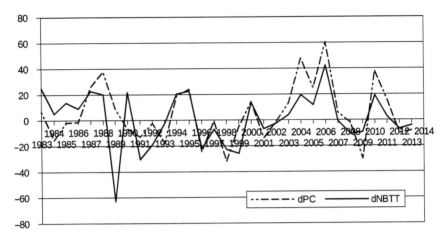

Figure 4.15 Zambia: changes in the NBTT and copper price index.

Note: dNBTT: changes in net barter terms of trade; dPC: changes in copper price index; 2000 = 100.

Table 4.12 Zambia: export shares and concentrations

Year	Food	Raw Mat.	Minerals	Fuel	Total	NHHI
1966	1.57	0.36	97.34	0.02	99.29	0.94
1975	1.41	0.06	96.88	0.32	98.66	0.91
1982	–	–	–	–	–	–
1993	3.91	0.95	88.85	1.70	95.41	0.83
2000	9.39	4.40	74.26	1.09	89.14	0.59
2011	6.89	1.88	81.37	0.45	90.59	0.62

Shares are in per cent. Raw Mat.: agricultural raw materials; Minerals: minerals and metals; Fuel: mineral fuels; Total: total commodity exports; NHHI: normalized Hirschman–Herfindahl index. No data are available for 1966, 1982, and 1990.

not come as a surprise. In the early years of the sample period, the incidence of mineral exports differs little from the incidence of total primary commodities in total exports. The minerals and metals export share for 1966 is shown in Table 4.12 to be 97.34 per cent, while the share for 1975 is 96.88 per cent. This share has fallen somewhat in the later years of the sample with an incidence of 88.85 per cent in 1993, 74.26 per cent in 2000, and 81.37 per cent in 2011.

The reduced incidence of mineral and metals exports within the overall category of primary commodity exports has a counterpart in the increased participation of food exports. World Bank (2014c) comments on the potential of maize exports for export diversification as well as on the prevailing trade barriers. Exports in other primary commodity groups have consistently maintained low export shares. Agricultural raw material exports accounted for less than 1 per cent of export shares during the early years of the sample period and merely accounted for

4.40 per cent of total exports in 2000 and 1.88 per cent in 2011; the highest recorded export share for this primary commodity category was 10.03 per cent in 1999. Mineral fuel exports had a consistently low incidence with 0.02 per cent in 1966 and 0.32 per cent in 1975. In the later years of the sample, this share rose very slightly to 1.70 per cent in 1993, and 1.09 per cent in 2000 before falling again to 0.45 per cent in 2011. Zambia's normalized Hirschman–Herfindahl index in the export sector accordingly dropped from values of close to one in the early years of the sample to values within the range 0.4–0.8 in later years (see Table 4.12). Two- to one-digit SITC concentration ratios stay close to one for the early part of the series and then drop, following a gap in the data record, after the 1994 contraction. This decline is followed by an increase in the concentration ratio with the onset of the recent commodity price boom. The development of the export concentration index ratio then mainly mirrors the impact of copper prices. The period of falling and lower export concentration ratios is rather short and one should be cautious in identifying it as a correlate of deeper structural change. Its strong rebound during the commodity boom would be at odds with the lasting economic significance of such a structural transformation in external relations.

Another counterpart of the moderate decrease in the incidence of the primary commodity exports is an increased export participation of manufactured goods. Manufactured goods exports were negligible, with an incidence of under 1.00 per cent, before the liberalization programme of the 1990s, even though the internal value added share of the manufacturing sector was rising during this time. As the internal share of the manufacturing sector collapsed following the removal of protective barriers in 1993 and 1994 (Rakner 2004, p. 91) the export participation of the manufacturing sector increased (see Figure 4.16), rising to a share of 6.95 per cent in 1995 and then fluctuating between 5.85 per cent and 16.79 per cent[28] of total exports.

This transformation of the manufacturing sector appears consistent with a successful sectoral consolidation resulting in the survival of internationally competitive sub-sectors. Biesebroeck (2005) mentions Zambia among the more successful diversification efforts and observes that in sub-Saharan African countries the manufacturing export share often exceeds the share in GDP. This has not consistently been the case in Zambia, though (see Figure 4.16). Zambia's manufacturing share in total value added fluctuated between 8.10 per cent and 12.40 per cent[29] between 1994 and 2013. The manufacturing value added share in GDP has generally been much more stable than the export share, a fact which may well be attributable to the volatility of the copper price affecting the overall value of the country's main export. A detailed study of the manufacturing sector itself is beyond the scope and focus of the present volume, though, while the impact of China's raw material demand is of more immediate interest.

The share of Zambia's exports destined for China increased from values of less than 1 per cent to 1.70 per cent in 2003 and thence to 5.63 per cent in 2008, recovering a bilateral trade share similar in magnitude to those observed during the 1970s. After the onset of the international financial crisis in 2008, China's export share increased further reaching a peak value of 21.64 per cent in 2013.

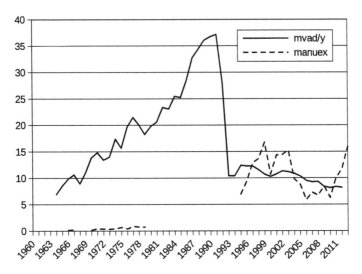

Figure 4.16 Zambia: manufacturing share in value added and exports.

Note: mvad/y: manufacturing value added share as percentage of GDP; manuex: manufacturing share in exports.

It is from 2008 onwards that China's share in the receipt of Zambian exports in the minerals and metals category notably exceeds its share in total exports, with 6.45 per cent of total minerals and metals exports destined for China in 2008 compared to 29.93 per cent in 2013.

On the import side, total commodity imports largely remained within a range of approximately 25–30 per cent of total imports for most of the sample period. This is illustrated in Table 4.13, where the primary commodity share of imports is shown to be 25.04 per cent in 1966 and 29.82 per cent in 1975. No data are available for 1993, although the primary commodity import share remains at 29.43 per cent in 2000. After 2007, the overall import share of primary commodities increases, reaching 39.16 per cent in 2008, peaking at 41.86 per cent in 2010, before falling to 34.86 per cent in 2011 and recovering somewhat to 36.24 per cent in 2013.

What is of some interest is the composition of primary commodity imports over the sample period. Food imports have generally tended to decline, falling from an import share of 10.32 per cent in 1966 to 7.76 per cent in 1975. The share of food imports then recovered to 8.08 per cent in 2000, peaked at 13.09 per cent in 2002, and subsequently fell to 5.09 per cent in 2011. Agricultural raw materials registered a low value throughout, accounting for 1.22 per cent of total imports in 1966 and 1975, rising to 2.82 per cent in 2000 before falling to 0.55 per cent in 2011. The incidence of mineral fuel imports, by contrast, has changed relatively little. Starting from an import share of 7.97 per cent in 1966, the participation of fuel imports rose to 13.57 per cent in 1975 before falling slightly to 12.22 per cent

Table 4.13 Zambia: import shares and concentrations

Year	Food	Raw Mat.	Minerals	Fuel	Total	NHHI
1966	10.32	1.22	5.53	7.97	25.04	0.15
1975	7.76	1.22	7.27	13.57	29.82	0.14
1982	–	–	–	–	–	–
1993	–	–	–	–	–	–
2000	8.08	2.82	6.31	12.22	29.43	0.08
2011	5.09	0.55	21.85	7.37	34.86	0.12

Shares are in per cent. Raw Mat.: agricultural raw materials; Minerals: minerals and metals; Fuel: mineral fuels; Total: total commodity exports; NHHI: normalized Hirschman–Herfindahl index. No data are available for 1966, 1982, and 1990.

in 2000. In 2011, mineral fuel imports accounted for 7.37 per cent of total imports, although this was an atypically low share, which rose to 10.63 per cent by 2013.

The main driver behind the recent increase in the primary commodity import share is the increase in minerals and metals imports. This is also Zambia's main export category, yet minerals and metals imports, which accounted for 5.53 per cent of imports in 1966, 7.27 per cent of total imports in 1975, and 6.31 per cent of imports in 2000, rose to 17.11 per cent of imports in 2008, 21.85 per cent of imports in 2011, and 20.69 per cent in 2013. The most pronounced increase within the overall minerals and metals aggregate can be ascribed to imports within SITC category 2831 ('ores and concentrates of copper, including Matte'). Imports within SITC 2831 accounted for 2.04 per cent of minerals and metals imports in 2003 but then rose to 49.83 per cent in 2008, 52.41 per cent in 2011, and 66.08 per cent in 2013. In all years over this 2003–2013 interval more than 99 per cent of imports in this category came from the Democratic Republic of the Congo.[30]

The increasing importance of copper ore imports from a neighbouring developing economy could be a symptom of a nascent raw material processing sector, building on purely extractive activities and establishing an internationally competitive position. Indeed, this possibility is raised by World Bank (2014c, pp. 19–20), and the increase in copper ore exports over the decade 2003–2013 appears consistent with it.[31]

Zambia thus provides an example of pronounced and lasting commodity dependence coupled with limited success in economic diversification and development. The sectoral concentration of the export sector remained consistently higher than, for example, in Chile, another major copper producer. Adam and Simpasa (2010) point out that the geological properties of Zambia's copper belt region make production relatively costly. This natural starting condition and the legacy of state ownership seem to be compounded by a lack of revenue stabilizing infrastructure such as a sovereign wealth fund. This omission puts Zambia in contrast to more successful commodity-dependent economies like Botswana, whose fiscal restraint facilitated a degree of macroeconomic stability that was missing in the Zambian economy, which found itself persistently constrained by the fluctuating value of current copper prices.

In Zambia's case, then, there is evidence of the kind of incentive cycle identified by Singer (1950) in which resources for diversification are most abundantly available when the incentives for alternative investments are at their weakest. This regularity is likewise commented on by Larmer (2010), although it is worth noting that the transformative processes commonly linked with economic development were not always supported as a matter of policy. Larmer (2010) points to active efforts to counteract rural to urban migration during Kaunda's reign. Concerns about rapid urbanization clearly are understandable in the light of limited labour absorption in urban centres and experiences with mass urban poverty in a number of developing countries. On the other hand, such urbanization is a common counterpart of surplus labour absorption. World Bank (2014c) reports that it is mainly large scale farm units that are internationally competitive. To the extent that this pattern also points to more modernized agri-enterprises, one should expect their production to be less labour intensive. In Zambia, as in other developing economies, it is unlikely that surplus labour will be absorbed by the primary sector alone.

Regional trade offers one possible opportunity for advancing economic development and furthering the international integration of the national economy. In this context, World Bank (2014c) points to Zambia's potential as a trading hub with a central geographical location on the continent, as well as highlighting existing trade impediments arising from lengthy border procedures and complex administrative requirements.

Another source of resource access is international investment, and Zambia has received some inflow of direct investment and expertise from China. This experience is discussed in Alden (2007), who also points out that Chinese investors in Zambia were criticized for extracting resources without contributing to local economic development. This is, in fact, the very criticism at the heart of Singer (1950), who argued that the gains from investment in developing countries were skewed towards the investing developed countries.

In many ways, then, Zambia corresponds to the commodity dependence cum persistent underdevelopment scenario outlined by Prebisch and Singer in the middle of the twentieth century. The national economy is heavily dependent on commodity export earnings and these are dominated by a single primary commodity (copper), while imports are primarily outside the primary commodity sector. Inward investment in turn is concentrated in extractive industries and makes a limited contribution to local economic development. The direct dependence on copper export earnings is further illustrated by the direct effect that fluctuations in copper prices have on the nation's fiscal position or even short term sectoral wage settings.

In spite of all these similarities, there are reasons to see the case of Zambia as more than a case of constrained export earnings. The very criticism of Chinese foreign investment's insularity points to the fact that the volume of available funds in itself does not provide a sufficient explanation for the observed extent of economic transformation to date. The observation of World Bank (2014c) to the effect that procedural reform of customs checks is likely to have a more substantive impact than investment in border facilities also points in the direction of institutional deficiency. In addition to the need for domestic institutional reform, the impact of the dominant commodity sector does, however, highlight the need for an institutionally guaranteed mechanism for smoothing the fluctuations from export earnings.

The preceding discussion covered a number of country cases which combined an ongoing development process with a substantial degree of commodity export dependence. The country cases discussed differ in the extent to which they successfully converged in income terms, or failed to do so, and in the extent to which they diversified out of the primary sector or into different primary sub-sectors. What all these examples have in common is that they have not fully transitioned beyond the point of commodity dependence, even though a significant degree of modernization has taken place in some cases. The remaining two examples address the cases of China and Vietnam, where the process of industrial transformation is much more pronounced and a full transition in the near future is likely.

4.8 China

China has shown a prolonged and successful tendency towards convergence and has received a commensurate amount of attention in the ensuing policy debate. The present discussion does not attempt to add to the general debate of China's development success but will focus exclusively on its implications for international commodity markets and commodity export dependent developing countries. Given the prominence of China's example, the general discussion of the underlying economic conditions is intentionally kept as brief as possible and the focus on commodity trade is emphasized even more strongly than in the other country case studies.

China has shown convergence relative to the US from the 1980s onwards. Some caution appears to be in order when interpreting these early data: Lardy (2002) explicitly raises concerns regarding the quality of Chinese data recorded prior to 1990. Yet, by 2011, China's per capita GDP had reached 7.04 per cent of the US level (20.36 per cent when adjusting for purchasing power parity), after real GDP per capita had grown 9.31 per cent per year on average during the 1990–2013 interval. Accompanying this growth process, there has been some inflationary pressure, with inflation peaking at 20.63 per cent in 1994, but there were no hyperinflation episodes, suggesting that inflationary tendencies have been largely kept under control during this part of the convergence process.

The most remarkable macroeconomic phenomenon, however, is China's structural transformation. China's manufacturing sector value added amounted to 30–33 per cent of GDP from 1990, with a minimum value of 31.42 per cent in 2002 and a maximum value of 33.97 per cent in 1993. The manufacturing export share, by contrast, has increased from 71.58 per cent in 1990 to 93.30 per cent in 2011, and further to 94.02 per cent in 2013. These developments at the aggregate level seem consistent with a consolidation process, establishing the manufacturing sector in internationally competitive areas.

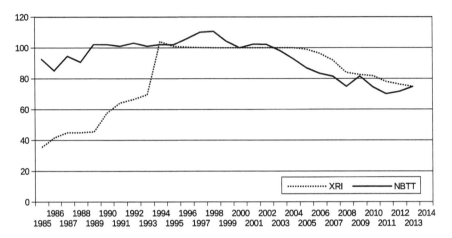

Figure 4.17 China: NBTT and exchange rate index.

Note: NBTT: net barter terms of trade; XI: exchange rate index; 2000 = 100.

China's net barter terms of trade, meanwhile, started to decay gradually from 2002 after remaining largely stagnant in the preceding period (see Figure 4.17). This development in the net barter terms of trade has been largely unresponsive to a large (40.27 per cent) depreciation in 1994 followed by a period of stable exchange rate values from 1996 to 2004 ceding to a gradual and controlled appreciating tendency from 2005 onwards. The management and realignment of China's currency has itself been the object of extensive dedicated discussion (see Goldstein and Weatherstone 2005; Hufbauer, Wong, and Sheth 2006). What is of interest here is primarily the lack of repercussion on the barter terms of trade as well as the intertemporal correlation between weakening terms of trade and sustained income convergence in the presence of increasing export participation. This latter combination of symptoms would be expected if an economy specializes in competitive manufacturing export sectors with reasonably elastic demand.

Such a case would correspond to a situation in which a terms of trade deterioration is primarily a symptom of international competitiveness. In terms of the Thirlwall model discussed in Chapter 3, this mechanism is illustrated in a loosening of the balance of payments constrained growth rate through the relative price term in the general formulation of the constraint. With specific reference to mature, developed economies, a positive feedback loop between falling terms of trade and accelerating growth is discussed in Gandolfo (2002, Chapter 14), although this scenario would categorically differ from the one in which the interdependence of underdevelopment and commodity dependence is a plausible problem.

Moreover, the net barter terms of trade deterioration illustrated in Figure 4.17 coincides with an almost consistently positive trade balance. China's trade balance stayed in surplus during most years after 1990 except for a deficit of −1.92 per cent of GDP in 1993. This trade surplus peaked at 8.82 per cent of

Table 4.14 China: export shares and concentrations

Year	Food	Raw Mat.	Minerals	Fuel	Total	NHHI
1965	–	–	–	–	–	–
1975	–	–	–	–	–	–
1984	15.27	5.71	2.70	23.02	46.70	0.06
1990	12.65	3.49	4.15	8.31	28.60	0.09
2000	5.44	1.09	3.88	3.14	13.54	0.18
2011	2.85	0.53	4.35	1.69	9.43	0.24

Shares are in per cent. Raw Mat.: agricultural raw materials; Minerals: minerals and metals; Fuel: mineral fuels; Total: total commodity exports; NHHI: normalized Hirschman–Herfindahl index. No data are available for 1965, 1975, and 1982.

GDP in 2007 but fluctuated in the value range of 2–3 per cent of GDP for most of the remaining years. While the coincidence of a positive trade balance with falling net barter terms of trade is another phenomenon consistent with a sustained competitive export orientation, the implications for international commodity markets become clearer when the composition of commodity trade flows is considered.

Primary commodity exports from China have fallen dramatically over time – as should be expected given the observed increase in the overall export participation of manufactured goods. Table 4.14 shows a commodity export share of 46.70 per cent for 1984, the earliest year for which data are available. This share is close to the peak value of 53.86 per cent recorded in 1985. Thereafter, total commodity exports fell to 28.60 per cent of total exports in 1990, further to 13.54 per cent in 2000, and finally to 9.43 per cent in 2011. The latest datum available gives a yet lower value of 8.30 per cent of total exports in 2013.

In the early parts of the data series, mineral fuel exports appear to dominate the commodity export profile, with a value of 23.02 per cent reported for 1984, as shown in Table 4.14. This is reported to rise to 30.75 per cent in 1985 before falling to 8.31 per cent of total exports in 1990, to 3.14 per cent in 2000, and 1.69 per cent by 2011. The second most prominent export category was food exports, which is reported to account for 15.27 per cent of total exports in 1984, 12.65 per cent in 1990, before falling to 5.44 per cent in 2000 and 2.85 per cent in 2011. Agricultural raw material exports fell from a lower proportion of 5.71 per cent in 1984 to 3.49 per cent in 1990, 1.09 per cent in 2000, and eventually to 0.53 per cent in 2011. Mineral and metal exports, by contrast, fluctuated around low participation values but did not appear to consistently decline. The export share reported for 1984 is 2.70 per cent compared to 4.15 per cent in 1990, 3.88 per cent in 2000, and 4.35 per cent in 2011.

Even allowing for doubts about the reliability of early data points, there appears to be a clear pattern of decreasing relative importance of commodity exports with pronounced declines in the contribution of fuel and food exports. Concentration in the export sector as measured by the normalized Hirschman–Herfindahl index has increased at an average rate of 4.76 per cent per year, rising from a value of 0.06 in 1984 to 0.24 from 2011. This development seems to be driven by sectoral consolidation in the manufacturing sector, which has consistently increased its export participation over much of the sample period. The ratio of export concentration indices initially falls dramatically in the early 1980s, as export concentrations at the SITC two-digit aggregation level drop while SITC 1 level concentrations rise. In later years, SITC 2 level concentrations recovered leading to a near stabilization of trade index concentration index ratios in later periods. Given the level of abstraction and concerns over data quality in earlier periods, one should be cautious with further interpretations, however. A more detailed look into the evolving incidence of different export categories should give some further insights.

Exports in SITC category 8 (miscellaneous manufactured articles) increased initially from 18.00 per cent of total exports in 1984 to a peak value of 42.53 per cent in 1993 before declining to 25.27 per cent in 2011 (whence they recovered somewhat to 27.23 per cent in 2013). SITC 8 includes diverse manufacturing activities such as scientific and control instruments in sub-category 86, as well as clothing in sub-category 84, although textiles, at a more basic level, are included in SITC 6 (manufactured goods chiefly classified by material).[32] The incidence of exports in SITC 6 has been relatively stable, rising from 19.30 per cent in 1984 to a peak value of 22.39 per cent in 1988 and falling thence to 16.39 per cent in 2013. Exports in SITC category 7 (machinery and transport equipment) rose almost consistently from 5.74 per cent of total exports in 1984 to a peak value of 48.07 per cent in 2010, from where it descended to 46.07 per cent of total exports in 2013. The high level trade categories covered here are rather broad, but provide a concise impression of the consolidation process in a maturing manufacturing sector. The increasing share of SITC 8 is particularly ambiguous since it contains basic and advanced manufacturing categories such as sub-categories 86 and 84, where the share of the former has increased while the latter has fallen (to 3.23 per cent and 8.05 per cent in 2011 respectively). Sub-category SITC 89 (miscellaneous manufactured articles not elsewhere specified) has likewise increased to 7.43 per cent in 2011, contributing to the ambiguity of the recorded developments. Overall, however, the shift towards exports in SITC 7 and away from the textile sub-sector in SITC 6 can be seen as evidence of a general move towards more advanced product niches and away from basic manufacturing activities. This general development should be seen in conjunction with the structural transformation of the import profile.

While the incidence of primary commodity exports has been steadily declining, the role of primary commodities in China's import profile is somewhat more complex. The overall incidence of primary commodity imports initially dropped rapidly from 38.54 per cent in 1984 to 25.02 per cent in 1990 before reaching a nadir of 23.20 per cent in 1998. From this point, commodity import shares recovered, rising to 27.74 per cent in 2000 and further to 39.18 per cent in 2011, before dropping slightly to 37.21 per cent in 2013. These developments are illustrated in Table 4.15, which also provides some information on the structural composition of commodity imports.

Minerals and metals imports initially declined rapidly from 21.28 per cent of imports in 1984 to 7.92 per cent in 1990 before recovering to 9.89 per cent in

Table 4.15 China: import shares and concentrations

Year	Food	Raw Mat.	Minerals	Fuel	Total	NHHI
1965	–	–	–	–	–	–
1975	–	–	–	–	–	–
1984	9.03	7.72	21.28	0.51	38.54	0.10
1990	8.66	6.07	7.92	2.38	25.02	0.16
2000	4.00	4.66	9.89	9.17	27.74	0.15
2011	4.33	3.90	15.35	15.61	39.18	0.12

Shares are in per cent. Raw Mat.: agricultural raw materials; Minerals: minerals and metals; Fuel: mineral fuels; Total: total commodity exports; NHHI: normalized Hirschman–Herfindahl index. No data are available for 1965, 1975, and 1982.

2000 and rising further to 15.35 per cent in 2011. Food and agricultural raw materials imports declined more gradually from 9.03 per cent in 1984 to 4.33 per cent in 2011 in the case of food imports and from 7.72 per cent in 1984 to 3.90 per cent in 2011 in the case of agricultural raw materials. A more pronounced and continuous change has been observed in mineral fuel imports, which increased from 0.51 per cent in 1984 to 2.38 per cent in 1990, 9.17 per cent in 2000, and 15.61 per cent in 2011. The share of fuel imports strengthened further to 16.99 per cent in 2012 before moderating somewhat to 16.00 per cent in 2013.

Throughout this time, the overall concentration of imports by SITC 1 category did not change much. The normalized Hirschman–Herfindahl index rose gradually at an average annual rate of 0.39 per cent per year from 0.10 in 1984 to 0.11 in 2013, peaking at a value of 0.19 in 1993/94 as well as in 2002/2003. The general evolution of China's import profile, then, is what would be expected in a maturing economy with substantive and sustained industrial and infrastructure investment. While this general observation does not rule out internal disequilibria or malinvestments, the general qualitative transformation of the trade profile is largely what one would expect from a modernizing, export-oriented economy: the qualitative shift in the composition of imports is not only characterized by recent increases in fuel and minerals and metals imports; there has also been a substantial shift of export shares within the broad category of machinery and transport equipment – imports of non-electric machinery gradually declined from 19.47 per cent of total imports in 1990 to 17.47 per cent of total imports in 1997 while imports of electric machinery rose from 10.31 per cent of total imports in 1990 to 14.71 per cent in 1997. From 1998 onwards, electric machinery imports took the larger share, accounting for 18.18 per cent of total imports compared to 17.82 per cent of total imports in the non-electric machinery category. In subsequent years, non-electric machinery imports declined further to 15.37 per cent in 2000 and 11.45 per cent in 2011. Imports of non-electric machinery rose further to 21.93 per cent in 2000 and 19.88 per cent in 2011.

The overall structure of industrial production, as inferred from value added data in the UNIDO Industrial Statistics database, appears well diversified. Data on manufacturing value added are available for 1980–2007. Among the more notable developments is a decline in the incidence of value added in the textile sector from 15.14 per cent of the total manufacturing value added data reported in 1980 to 5.23 per cent in 2007, the last datum available. There are also shifts in the relative importance of different machinery-producing sectors,[33] although the normalized Hirschman–Herfindahl concentration index mostly returns values between 0.02 and 0.03 across the reported categories in the manufacturing sector.

China's economy continued to grow at a rapid pace after the onset of the global economic crisis in 2008, although OECD (2013b) notes that this growth process has become more dependent on domestic consumption. While China has experienced an intense process of structural transformation and industrialization, it is worth noting that there remains a rural surplus labour pool that can support further growth (OECD 2013b). The proportion of the labour force employed in the agricultural sector has declined from 68.70 per cent in 1980 to 34.80 per cent in 2011, but remains relatively high compared to more fully industrialized middle income countries. Industrial employment was reported to be 29.50 per cent in 2011 (with the remaining 35.70 per cent in the service sector).

The possibility of continued industrial expansion matters internationally, not least because it raises the prospect of an extension of the ongoing economic transformation process that has generated extensive demand for raw material inputs. In the trade balance, this process becomes apparent in the shift towards mineral and energy imports coupled with the declining overall commodity share on the export side. It is the sheer size of the Chinese economy in conjunction with the resource intensive stage of the ongoing transformation process that has generated such far-reaching spillover effects for commodity-exporting developing countries. Against this background, one should expect either an overall slowdown or a shift away from primary commodity intensive activities to adversely affect the economic growth prospects of a number of developing countries.

More precisely, a slowdown in China's derived demand for commodity inputs would weaken the stimulus to commodity exporting developing countries vis à vis the counterfactual level of demand for a higher growth rate. This effect will in some measure be ameliorated by the permanent increase in the level of Chinese demand as a function of the Chinese economy's given size as opposed to its rate of change.

The existence of surplus labour in the agricultural sector points to at least a necessary condition for ongoing growth-related commodity demand from China. The eventual advent of either a slower equilibrium growth rate or a qualitative reorientation, or both, is widely expected, however. The extent to which commodity-exporting developing countries can adjust to such an eventuality is likely to depend on their potential for reorientation and their ability to move into export and production niches opened up by maturing emerging market economies.

4.9 Vietnam

In the case of Vietnam, the transition from a planned economy commenced prior to what is normally regarded as the end of the cold war, so the a priori assumption of regime change around 1989/90 should be treated with some care. The official introduction of the market-oriented Doi Moi reforms is usually put at 1986 (see Dinh 2013, Chapter 1, although Massina (2006) argues that informal administrative changes had prepared conditions for a formal change in policy stance from an earlier date. Data for Vietnam from the World Development Indicators tend to commence in 1985, or later in some cases. Based on these data, real GDP growth accelerated from 3.74 per cent in 1985 to rates above 5 per cent by 1988.[34] Real income growth rates in this first growth cycle peaked at 9.11 per cent in 1995 before dropping to 5.60 per cent in 1998 and further to 4.66 per cent for 1999 in the wake of the Asian financial crisis.

This initial growth cycle was followed by a recovery of annual growth rates to values between 6 and 7.3 per cent from 2000 to 2008, ranging from a 6.01 per cent growth rate in 2001 to a peak value of 7.28 per cent in 2005. In the wake of the 2008 international financial crisis, annual real GDP growth rates fell to 5.26 per cent in 2009 before recovering to a value of 6.23 per cent in 2010 and dropping to growth rates of 5.11 per cent (in 2012) and 5.28 per cent (in 2013). The weak recovery following the post-2008 downturn has been noted by Dinh (2013). In so far as the short data series available indicates a pattern, it seems to show boom cycles with declining peak values following short downturns. One should be reluctant, though, to infer a regular pattern on the basis of such a limited empirical basis. The data series, aside from charting only one indicator variable, is simply too short to justify general conclusions on an inductive basis. When commenting on the slowing post-2008 growth performance, Dinh (2013) places this observation in the context of Vietnam's trading relations.

The periods of high growth have led to some tendency towards convergence, although Vietnam remains a relatively poor country in GDP per capita terms. Real per capita GDP rose from 0.89 per cent of the equivalent value for the USA in 1986 to 0.91 per cent in 1990 and 2.14 per cent in 2011, rising further to 2.25 per cent by 2013 (see Figure 4.18). Data for purchasing power parity adjusted per capita GDP show an increase from 3.55 per cent of the US equivalent level in 1986 to 8.80 per cent by 2011. By both measures, the relative per capita income level remains low, although the direction of the convergence process remains encouraging.

During the 1980s, Vietnam experienced hyperinflation with correspondingly high depreciation rates: annual inflation rates peaked at 411.04 per cent in 1988 and then tended to fall over the following decade, reaching a single-digit value (8.70 per cent) by 1996. The currency depreciated at an average annual rate of 204.73 per cent during the peak inflation year 1988 and then stabilized as the inflation rate fell. In 1992, the annual depreciation rate had dropped to 10.98 per cent; in 1993, the currency appreciated by 5.14 per cent. Even in 1998, against the background of the Asian financial crisis, the average annual depreciation rate rose no further than 12.72 per cent. For the remaining years of the sample, the average annual depreciation rate has remained at single-digit levels. Inflation rates, likewise, did not return to hyperinflationary levels, although annual inflation rates accelerated to 22.67 per cent in 2008 and again to 21.26 per cent in

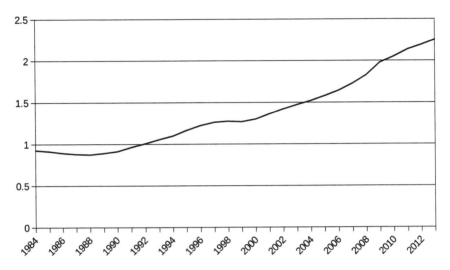

Figure 4.18 Vietnam: real per capita GDP convergence to US equivalent.

2011. Sustained and successful efforts at macroeconomic stabilization have been repeatedly noted in the literature, though (World Bank 2014b).

Vietnam's manufacturing value added as a percentage of GDP initially fell from 22.37 per cent in 1986 to 12.26 per cent in 1990 after the official introduction of liberalizing reforms. It subsequently recovered, converging to a range between 17 and 19.5 per cent of GDP (see, for example, the values of 17.15 per cent in 1998 and 19.38 per cent in 2006). Manufactured goods as a percentage of exports, by contrast, start at a relatively high level of 44.13 per cent in 1997 (the earliest point in the given data series) and then increase to a value of 64.98 per cent in 2011 and further to 74.74 per cent in 2013. This pattern appears consistent with the preponderance of manufacturing sector outward processing trade and often relatively low value added in the relevant activities (see Dinh 2013).

The overall trade balance remained negative until 2011, when the trade deficit narrowed from −8.21 per cent of GDP in 2010 to −4.13 per cent of GDP in 2011, before yielding a trade surplus of 3.50 per cent of GDP in 2012. This surplus strengthened further to 4.09 per cent of GDP in 2013. These data only cover a short period at a high level of aggregation and can therefore not support any conclusions on economic development on their own, although one may note at this stage that an initial trade deficit period followed by a transition to a trade surplus position is consistent with a foreign investment based transformation of the domestic economy's structure. Indeed, in so far as twin deficits are ruled out in the external balance, it is a necessary corollary of such a process.

Primary commodity exports overall accounted for 51.74 per cent of total exports in 1997 and slightly increased their participation to 54.40 per cent in 2000 (Table 4.16). Thereafter, the overall incidence of commodity exports dropped

Table 4.16 Vietnam: export shares and concentrations

Year	Food	Raw Mat.	Minerals	Fuel	Total	NHHI
1965	–	–	–	–	–	–
1975	–	–	–	–	–	–
1982	–	–	–	–	–	–
1997	30.23	2.95	0.60	17.96	51.74	0.14
2000	25.31	1.92	0.72	26.45	54.40	0.13
2011	18.59	3.64	3.17	11.37	36.78	0.11

Shares are in per cent. Raw Mat.: agricultural raw materials; Minerals: minerals and metals; Fuel: mineral fuels; Total: total commodity exports; NHHI: normalized Hirschman–Herfindahl index. No data are available before 1997.

steadily, reaching a value of 36.78 per cent in 2011 and dropping further to 32.40 per cent in 2012. This decline in the incidence of commodity exports is mainly driven by exports in the food category, which accounted for 30.23 per cent in 1997, then dropped to 25.31 per cent in 2000 and further to 18.59 per cent in 2011. The second largest commodity export category, mineral fuels, has been more volatile, showing temporary upswings producing local peak values of 26.45 per cent (in 2000) and 25.77 per cent (in 2005) for its incidence in overall exports. The overall tendency over the short sample period covered shows a declining relative participation, though, with the export share of mineral fuels dropping to 11.37 per cent in 2011.

Agricultural raw material exports have remained relatively stable, with a low export participation fluctuating within a value range of 1–4 per cent of overall exports. The share of mineral and metal exports has remained low, while increasing from 0.60 per cent in 1997 to 3.17 per cent of overall exports in 2011. The overall sectoral concentration of exports has remained relatively stable, showing only a slight decline in the normalized Hirschman–Herfindahl index over the period covered. The index defined over all one-digit SITC categories declined from 0.14 in 1997 to 0.11 in 2011. This modest decline, moreover, masks a temporary uptick to a peak value of 0.15 in 2003. Concentration index ratios fall towards the end of the period as the two-digit level concentration index declines faster than the index for the one-digit aggregation level. It is worth emphasizing, though, that the period available is rather short so one should beware of interpreting these short term developments as symptoms of a structural transformation based on the data pattern alone.

The relative incidence of primary commodities in imports has increased somewhat over the period covered (see Table 4.17). The share of commodity imports increased from 23.94 per cent in 1997 to 29.67 per cent in 2000, and further to 35.84 per cent in 2011. A major commodity category among primary commodity imports is mineral fuels, which accounted for 10.33 per cent of total imports in 1997, 13.63 per cent in 2000, and 11.98 per cent in 2011. In fact, the import share of mineral fuels rose to yet higher levels between 2000 and 2011, peaking at 15.82 per cent in 2008.

Table 4.17 Vietnam: import shares and concentrations

Year	Food	Raw Mat.	Minerals	Fuel	Total	NHHI
1965	–	–	–	–	–	–
1975	–	–	–	–	–	–
1982	–	–	–	–	–	–
1997	4.96	2.40	6.25	10.33	23.94	0.09
2000	5.21	2.91	7.92	13.63	29.67	0.10
2011	8.64	3.95	11.28	11.98	35.84	0.11

Shares are in per cent. Raw Mat.: agricultural raw materials; Minerals: minerals and metals; Fuel: mineral fuels; Total: total commodity exports; NHHI: normalized Hirschman–Herfindahl index. No data are available before 1997.

Another commodity category with a significant import share is minerals and metals, whose participation increased from 6.25 per cent of imports in 1997 to 7.92 per cent in 2000 and further to 11.28 per cent in 2011. Imports in this category, too, peaked around 2008, reaching a share of 13.72 per cent in 2007 and maintaining an almost identical share of 13.71 per cent in 2008. Food imports remained at a relatively modest level but increased from 4.96 per cent of imports in 1997 to 5.21 per cent in 2000 and then to 8.64 per cent in 2011. The import share of agricultural raw materials imports, finally, increased slightly from 2.40 per cent in 1997 to 3.95 per cent in 2011.

Considering import concentrations generally, the normalized Hirschman–Herfindahl index increased somewhat from 0.09 in 1997 to 0.10 in 2000, 0.11 in 2011, and to 0.12 in 2012 subsequently. The index, which had briefly peaked with a value of 0.13 in 2003, thus shows an increase in overall import concentration relative to the 1997 datum over the short sample period available, although the recorded concentration index values mostly fluctuate within the range 0.10–0.12 after 2000, rather than following a consistent upwards trend.

The combination of persistent trade deficit, strengthening commodity import participation, and weakening commodity export share observed in the case of Vietnam implies that the impact of primary commodity price fluctuations on export earnings can be expected to differ from the conventional prediction for developing country trade relations. Other things being equal, an increase in relative commodity prices could in such a case tend to decrease real export earnings. It would unambiguously tend to lower the unit value in the emerging manufacturing export sector and could depress the real value of exports overall, depending on the relative incidence of trade in either category and depending on the extent to which trade quantities react to relative price changes, that is, depending on trade elasticities.

Commodity price changes do not, of course, normally occur under *ceteris paribus* conditions. Vietnam's net barter terms of trade have fallen from the base value of 100 in 2000 to a low point of 93.66 in 2007 before recovering their 2000 value in 2012. They subsequently decreased slightly to 98.64 in the following year (see Figure 4.19). The data period available is rather short, as it only begins in

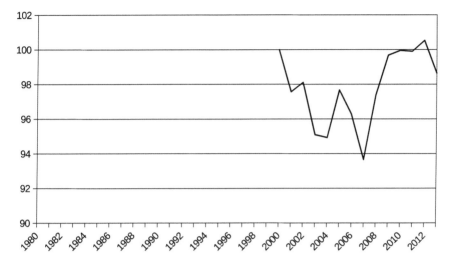

Figure 4.19 Vietnam: net barter terms of trade.

Note: Net barter terms of trade index, 2000 = 100.

the base year (2000), but the period coincident with the early twenty-first century commodity price boom has not seen a consistent barter terms of trade decline. The recent recovery of the net barter terms of trade occurred against a background of persistently strong real primary commodity prices.

The evolution of Vietnam's trade and production pattern is too complex to be captured by a simple comparison of broad commodity and manufacturing sector trade flows or a simple consideration of the terms of trade. As mentioned above, manufacturing export participation has been increasing in most years over the available sample period (see Figure 4.20).[35] The increase in the share of manufacturing sector exports has been maintained over a protracted cycle of net barter terms of trade fluctuations. This development reflects a largely foreign investment driven expansion of manufacturing sector production for the outward processing trade. This process is discussed in Dinh (2013), and suggests that the absorption of local productive resources has been facilitated irrespective of national export earnings on the basis of foreign direct investment, a process commonly associated with industrialization under the 'flying geese' paradigm.

The process of economic modernization is likewise mirrored in changing employment patterns. Industrial employment has increased from 10.60 per cent of total employment in 1996 (the earliest year in this series) to 21.30 per cent in 2011. Over the same interval, service sector employment increased from 19.40 per cent to 30.30 per cent, with agricultural employment concomitantly falling from 70 per cent to 48.40 per cent in 2011. Data for the female employment share outside the agricultural sector are available for 1996 to 2004, with a value of 40.4 per cent for 2004 (this is slightly lower than the values for some earlier years,

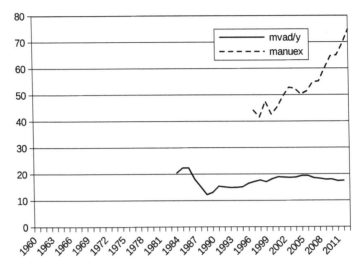

Figure 4.20 Vietnam: manufacturing share in value added and exports.

Note: mvad/y: manufacturing value added share as percentage of GDP; manuex: manufacturing share in exports.

which peaked at 42.2 per cent in 1998). In spite of the apparent transformation at the aggregate level, there are open questions regarding the effectiveness and scope of this transformation process.

It is further instructive to compare these employment figures with contributions to value added as a percentage of GDP. The share of agricultural value added dropped slightly from 27.76 per cent of GDP in 1996 to 20.08 per cent in 2011. The share of industrial value added, by contrast, increased from 29.73 per cent in 1996 to 37.90 per cent in 2011, while the service sector's share remained almost constant with 42.51 per cent in 1996 compared to 42.02 per cent in 2011. The fact that the observed substantial withdrawal of labour resources from the agricultural sector had little impact on this sector's contribution to value added is of course what would be expected in a case where surplus labour resources are mobilized. The coincidence of rising service sector employment with this sector's stagnating output share is, of course, less readily explained.

It has been pointed out by Dinh (2013) that manufacturing activity in Vietnam is heavily concentrated in low-tech and low value added activities. A further problem arises from the particular nature of economic dualism present in Vietnam: both Dinh (2013) and World Bank (2014b) note the pronounced performance difference between domestic and foreign invested firms. While foreign invested firms tend to operate with modern methods and are internationally competitive, local firms often can't compete internationally and supply local protected markets. Given this difference in performance and the lack of integration between local and foreign invested firms, the technology upgrading process underlying the export-oriented development approach followed by other Asian emerging markets has largely failed to materialize.

The observed pattern of manufacturing sector production appears consistent with this analysis. Data from the UNIDO Industrial Statistics database show that the food and beverages sector (ISIC D-15) accounted for a value added share of 20.84 per cent in 2010, the last year for which data are available, while textile-related manufacturing sectors[36] together accounted for 15.35 per cent of total manufacturing value added. The employment share for food and beverage related manufacturers was 12.49 per cent in 2010, while that for the textile-related manufacturing categories mentioned above was 39.76 per cent. Among other manufacturing categories, 'motor vehicles' and 'other transport equipment'[37] jointly account for 8.31 per cent of value added and 4.04 per cent of manufacturing sector employment. Value added from machinery and information and communication equipment[38] accounted for 9.91 per cent of manufacturing value added and 7.33 per cent of manufacturing sector employment.

Precise concordances between trade and production categories are difficult to establish, and sectoral distinctions are not always possible at levels of high aggregation (such as the one- and two-digit codes within the ISIC and SITC systems). The relative importance of food exports was discussed above, and was shown to have declined over time while retaining a non-trivial share of total exports. The remaining manufacturing activities have their trade-related equivalence largely in components of SITC categories 6–8, which in 2010 accounted for 62.70 per cent of total exports. In spite of the manufacturing sector's modest contribution to overall value added, it does play a significant role in exports, and the export-related sectors account for a substantive proportion of manufacturing sector employment. It matters, then, if recent growth in Vietnam is mainly attributed to capital accumulation rather than productivity improvements as argued by Dinh (2013). The country's internal industrial dualism is one of the problems that need to be addressed if further development and convergence beyond the middle income level are to take place. Another element is the successful use of opportunities in the international market.

One opportunity to expand into new trade niches has opened up as China's labour costs have expanded (Dinh 2013). Vietnam's exports to China itself are still characterized by commodity trade: 11.99 per cent of total Vietnamese exports were destined for China in 2011, while China's share as destination of agricultural raw materials exports was 55.60 per cent compared to 25.95 per cent for mineral fuel exports and 10.04 per cent in the case of food exports. In two of the four broad commodity categories considered, China thus attracts a substantively larger share of Vietnam's exports than in average exports overall. The development potential from shifting to higher value added product niches in trade and production need not be based on trade specifically with China, of course. The feasibility of such a strategy is commonly seen to mainly depend on overcoming domestic constraints through further liberalizing reform (World Bank 2014b) or a commitment to human capital upgrading – the focus of the 2014 Vietnam Development Report (World Bank 2013b).

Vietnam's development process, then, does not appear to be primarily constrained by the prevalence of commodity production, nor by constraints on export earnings, but, by all accounts, on institutional factors. Opinions differ as to whether the main precondition for progress is supportive government planning (as argued, for example, by Massina (2006)), in further liberalizing reform (World Bank 2014b), more extensive human capital investment (World Bank 2013b), or a combination of these factors. The ultimate goal of these efforts clearly seems to be an increased integration of domestic, Vietnamese, and foreign invested industry, and thus the option of fully participating and moving up within the global supply chain.

4.10   Summary reflections

The above country case studies illustrate a generalized development in which a number of developing countries initially found themselves in a strongly commodity-dependent position coupled with a low standard of economic development, but subsequently followed a variety of economic trajectories. The country cases discussed show examples of varying developments of commodity export dependence as well as of the overall distribution of the economy's sectoral composition. The structural impact of concentrated commodity earnings depends not only on the possible diversification of export activity but also on the management and administration of export earnings at the aggregate level, as well as its transformative investment within the domestic economy.

Medium term fluctuations in sectorally concentrated commodity export earnings can be managed through the use of sovereign wealth funds, and the external dimensions of Dutch disease effects can be constrained through this mechanism. Chile and Botswana provide examples of two very different economies which have successfully employed this approach. Other economies like Zambia and Nigeria show evidence of the effects of pronounced and sectorally concentrated commodity dependence without similar mitigating institutional safeguards – an omission which left these economies inherently vulnerable to external price fluctuations.

Where government regulation fails to address the issue of export dependence and its collateral implications, two extreme positions of governance failure can be distinguished. The case conventionally considered in the recent development literature is that of excessive intervention and trade restrictions. It is this stance that was commonly associated with the Latin American countries and the onset of the debt crisis of the 1980s, and which ultimately was addressed by the stylized facts underlying the Washington consensus as an emerging market reform paradigm. Within the country case studies considered, the previous and recent policy regimes of Argentina correspond reasonably closely to this traditional interventionist style. Similar basic patterns can be identified for Brazil and Zambia prior to these countries' liberalization efforts. The presence of a prescriptive regulatory policy regime can be expected to correlate with a high degree of internal structural inertia. Internationally competitive and sectorally diversified production structures are historically unlikely to emerge under such circumstances.

The opposite extreme to the excessively interventionist stance would be described by a full or partial loss of internal government control and a failure of basic administrative infrastructure at the national level. Bates (2009) comments on the use of material incentive in the establishment of patronage-based projection of power and later transitions to weakening government and expanding informal sectors in a number of African countries. Perhaps the closest example to this scenario is given by Nigeria, where governance is partly conditioned by sub-national rivalries and central government control is contested in parts of the country subject to the Islamist insurgency (World Bank 2013a; Comolli 2015). The substantial role of the informal sector in the Zambian economy (including in international trade: World Bank 2014c) suggests that the recent experience in this country also is partly reflective of this weakening central governance phenomenon.

Between these extreme positions of government presence, two of the examples covered point to successful middle income convergence: these are the cases of Chile and Botswana noted above for their track record of successful macroeconomic management. This middle income convergence process is often referred to as either the 'middle income trap' or as a conditional convergence equilibrium as anticipated, for example, in Sachs and Warner (1995). The completion of such a conditional convergence process can be seen as the successful materialization of a resource-based comparative advantage potential rather than as a trap, further progression beyond the realization of this given endowment constituting a further prospect and challenge.

Progress from the given base of comparative advantage has clearly been made by China to a point where a central aspect of the present study was the impact of the Chinese take-off on commodity exporting trading partners and demand in commodity markets. Of particular significance is the central role of China's import demand as a pacesetter for commodity-dependent sub-Saharan African economies, a pattern which was particularly obvious in the Zambian case, but less so for Nigeria with its oil-dependent export profile or Botswana with its pronounced focus on non-industrial diamond trade and production. The case of Vietnam is less clear, as the country appears thoroughly embedded in international value chains through its outward processing role, but the extent and momentum of its progress in terms of sectoral transformation is less evident.

China's sustained take-off and its strong demand for primary commodities have supported the primary commodity boom during the early years of the twenty-first century. Strong demand for commodities has in turn led to a protracted boom in developing countries, a growth experience that has withstood the impact of the 2008 financial crisis over the medium term. The immediate effect of a commodity price boom should be reflected in a country's barter terms of trade. Over the 2004–2013 interval, the net barter terms of trade for the countries discussed in this chapter increased by a mean rate of 2.04 per cent for Argentina, 2.67 per cent for Brazil, and 6.20 per cent for Chile. Among the African country cases, the increase was at a mean rate of -1.41 per cent for Botswana, 8.11 per cent for Nigeria, and 6.46 per cent for Zambia.

Vietnam's net barter terms of trade stagnated with a mean growth rate of 0.37 per cent over this interval, while the NBTT of China itself tended to decline with a mean growth rate of −2.68 over the 2004–2013 commodity boom period. This pattern in terms of trade developments during a primary commodity boom is largely reflective of what should be expected in view of the given economies' patterns of specialization and maturity: Chinese demand for primary commodity is readily explained by the predominance of the country's manufacturing sector and the unfolding development of transport and real estate infrastructure. The simultaneous reliance on a low cost export based trading position and competitive labour markets describes a scenario in which declining net barter terms of trade should be expected. This pattern is, of course, the opposite of what was predicted under the Prebisch–Singer prediction of the twentieth century.

Vietnam's terms of trade stasis reflects its stable position in manufacturing value chain integration, while the terms of trade developments in the remaining case study examples tend to mirror the impact of the commodity price boom. In monoeconomies in particular, one should expect fluctuations in the price of the dominant commodity to correlate closely with those in the net barter terms of trade. This tends to be the case for the two copper-dependent exporters in the sample, Chile and Zambia. For Chile, the correlation coefficient between copper price changes and changes in the net barter terms of trade is $\hat{\rho} = 0.0.695$, $t = 5.383$, while for Zambia, the equivalent correlation coefficient is $\hat{\rho} = 0.641$, $t = 4.644$. This correlation is even stronger in the case of Nigeria, the oil-dependent economy in the sample, where the percentage rate of change in the oil price and in the net barter terms of trade have a correlation coefficient of $\hat{\rho} = 0.923$, $t = 13.402$.

The fluctuation of the terms of trade in response to commodity price variations can be expected to directly impact export earnings. How far fluctuations in current export earnings translate into a tightening of the balance of payments constraint and the extent to which further progress in industrial transformation is thereby prevented or slowed down also depends on other factors. Income smoothing measures and the domestic legal infrastructure are among these factors, but tend to be relevant with regards to longer term developments. A compounding element for the impact of short term earnings volatility is the variability of the exchange rate, which in its turn determines domestic import prices and the competitiveness of export competing sectors. For this reason, the degree to which exchange rate fluctuations co-vary with commodity price changes deserves further attention.

Among the three cases of extreme single-sector commodity dependence discussed in the present text, correlations between depreciation rates and the rate of change of the pivotal commodity price are substantially less pronounced than the sample correlations between the net barter terms of trade and the respective commodity prices. The sample correlation coefficients reported subsequently have been computed for the 1980–2013 interval during which exchange rate data are available for all three countries under review, and which corresponds to the time window for which net barter terms of trade data have been obtained. The series could be extended for some country cases, although data during the 1973–1975 interval would be dominated by financial adjustments following the dissolution of the Bretton Woods system as well as by the internal political conflict and the domestic economic crisis in the case of Chile.

The correlation between Nigeria's depreciation rate and the rate of change in the price of oil is $\hat{\rho} = -0.029$, $t = -0.166$, a value which is not surprising if one considers observations such as those made by World Bank (2013a), which note that oil price changes produce fluctuations in foreign exchange reserves rather than the exchange rate, and if one considers further that the oil price is strongly influenced by cartel decisions on the part of OPEC.

There is a much closer correlation between the Chilean and Zambian exchange rates and copper prices. The correlation coefficient for the Chilean exchange rate's rate of depreciation and the rate of change of the copper price is $\hat{\rho} = -0.379$, $t = -2.315$, while the equivalent value for Zambia is $\hat{\rho} = -0.452$, $t = -2.868$. These correlation values are still lower than those between the barter terms of trade and the dominant commodity price, but they are large enough to motivate further investigation of the magnitude and nature of this intertemporal correlation. The formulation of time series models to capture the intertemporal relationship between the price and exchange rate series does itself depend on the stationarity characteristics of the constituent series.

If both the relevant country's depreciation rate and the rate of change of the dominant commodity's price are stationary, it should be possible to simply estimate the relationship between both rate of change series as

$$e_t = \alpha + \beta p_t + v_t, \tag{4.3}$$

where e_t is the depreciation rate, p_t the rate of change of the dominant commodity, α is a constant, and v_t an ARMA residual term. Where the unit root null hypothesis cannot be rejected for the constituent series, the usual spurious correlation problems arise. It is, however, still possible for a linear combination of two non-stationary variables to be stationary such that in

$$e_t - \gamma p_t = u_t \tag{4.4}$$

the residual term u_t is stationary if the series is cointegrated. It is worth noting that a common order of integration for the non-stationary constituent series of the econometric model is a necessary condition for the existence of a cointegrated relationship. The rejection of the unit root null hypothesis for the residual u_t from an estimated model like Equation (4.4) is the sufficient condition.[39]

In the present case, the series of interest are already differenced, since both express rates of change in the variables of interest (the exchange rate, in the case of the depreciation series, and the rate of change of commodity price levels respectively). The unit root null hypothesis can be rejected for the series of the rate of change of the copper price. The test statistic from an augmented Dickey–Fuller test, allowing for a constant and up to four lagged differenced terms, is $\tau = -3.298$, implying a p-value of 0.015. The ADF test fails to reject the unit root null hypothesis for both countries' depreciation rate series, however: the unit

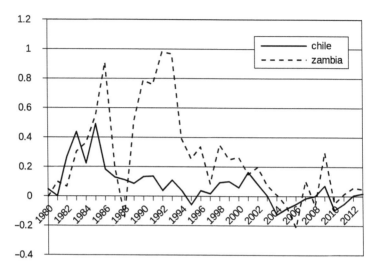

Figure 4.21 Chile and Zambia: depreciation rates 1980–2013.

root test statistic for Chile's depreciation rate is $\tau = -2.189$, implying a p-value of 0.210, while for Zambia, the corresponding value is $\tau = -1.724$, which corresponds to a p-value of 0.419. The gradual decline in Chile's depreciation rate suggests that the result may be different when allowing for a trend in the ADF test, but in this case the unit root test statistic takes a value of $\tau = -2.277$ (which implies a p-value of 0.446). Zambia's depreciation rate shows pronounced volatility in the early part of the sample but stabilizes in later years (see Figure 4.21 for an illustration). A continuous linear trend does not appear to plausibly represent this development.[40]

There is no evidence, then, of a systematic, deterministic relationship of commodity prices on annual average exchange rates even in those countries where commodity dependence is pronounced. This observation does not rule out, of course, that unanticipated short term price swings produce short term exchange rate reactions. The fact, however, that price volatility in the dominant export commodity does not appear to systematically translate into a conditioning factor for depreciation rates over the duration of the pass-through interval in a trade balance context points to a limited importance of commodity dependence as an overwhelmingly destabilizing force.

The case studies in the present text have shown examples of countries that have successfully managed the impact of earnings fluctuations through institutionalized provisions like sovereign wealth funds, have assured sustainability through a sustained fiscally conservative policy stance (as in the case of Botswana), or simply were able to rely on reserve holdings to stabilize the exchange rate, as in the case of Nigeria. Not all of these approaches are equally sustainable in the long term. Reliance on reserve holdings in particular presupposes short-lived external shocks if external realignment is to be avoided, but short run pressure on the exchange rate may well be contained for a limited period and under a number of policy regimes.

The external pressure from a long term decline in export earnings is, of course, not as readily contained through mere management of export earnings or fiscal discipline. Long term reductions in a dominant commodity export are best understood as a cause, and potentially a driver, of structural transformation. Again, the examples of the case studies covered show successful diversification in some but not all country cases covered. A number of highly commodity-dependent economies have successfully and sustainably diversified their export profiles away from the primary sector. Examples in this category include not only China but also two of the Latin American case study examples (Argentina and Brazil). The case of Chile shows how diversification is possible within the broad primary sector.

Likewise, the convergence trajectories of different economies are not always readily mapped onto the extent and nature of their commodity export dependence. Argentina and Brazil have experienced a non-trivial reduction in their overall commodity export concentration but have been outperformed by Chile, in terms of real per capita income convergence to the level of the USA. From their position in 1965, the per capita real income levels of Chile and Brazil were 13.97 per cent and 9.90 per cent of US per capita GDP respectively, compared to 22.16 per cent in the case of Argentina. By 2011, Chile's per capita GDP had risen to 20.36 per cent of the US level, while that of Brazil had risen to 12.90 per cent. The latest available figure for Argentina is for 2006 and gives a per capita GDP level of 13.75 per cent of the level attained in the United States.

These developments did not follow uninterrupted trends. Chilean GDP per capita tended to decline until shortly after the onset of the 1982 debt crisis and then began to rise relative to US per capita GDP. In Argentina's case, GDP per capita tended to decline relative to the equivalent level in the United States until 1990, when the Argentine economy experienced a recovery leading to a convergence period lasting up to 1997. Brazilian per capita GDP initially converged up to 16.19 per cent of the US equivalent level in 1980 before declining in relative terms over the decade following the international debt crisis, before beginning to recover in relative terms from around 2006 following the onset of the commodity price boom.

Comparing these developments to purchasing power parity adjusted data from the Penn World Tables, it becomes clear that developments appear different when taking into account the cost of living. During Argentina's period of divergence, purchasing power parity adjusted real per capita income remained within a range of 10–15 per cent of the US equivalent level. In the case of Brazil, the decline in real per capita GDP from 1980 onwards is more reminiscent of an interval of protracted real per capita income stagnation. Even during this period there is one noticeable increase in 1996, which is likely linked to a pronounced slowdown in domestic inflation after 1995, when hyperinflation came to an end.

What these developments show, then, is a strongly diversified pattern of intertemporal economic trajectories. The economies considered in the case studies are among the more advanced economies – in terms of productive structure – in the southern cone region of Latin America. They are also at the heart of the policy debate from which the original Prebisch–Singer hypothesis emerged. All the countries discussed experienced pronounced commodity dependence in their export earnings at the beginning of the sample period, yet their experiences in terms of growth and convergence differ substantively. A similar conclusion can be reached with regards to the structure of their export profiles. The one economy where the sectoral concentration of export earnings was particularly pronounced (Chile) has been remarkably successful in diversifying the composition of its primary commodity sector while retaining a strong commodity orientation in its export profile. Brazil, on the other hand, had diversified its exports out of the overall primary commodity sector for some time, yet proved particularly susceptible to the impact of the commodity boom at the beginning of the current century.

This observation from the 'historic heartland' of the Prebisch–Singer hypothesis carries over to other examples in the case studies considered. The importance of original and persistent commodity orientations influences developing countries' economic performance but does not inescapably constrain them. While the case of China as a globally influential economy differs from the more general consideration of small developing economies, it is worth noting that a pronounced shift away from a once substantial commodity sector towards internationally competitive industry has its roots in a change in domestic policy orientation.

Among the remaining developing country cases in the preceding discussion, Vietnam provides a case of successful diversification out of the primary commodity sector into the industrial sector. This is mirrored in a shift towards steady income convergence in terms of real per capita GDP towards the US level. Real per capita GDP in Vietnam has increased from 0.89 per cent in 1989 to a still very modest 2.14 per cent in 2011. Adjusting for purchasing power parity, this corresponds to an increase from 3.52 per cent of US real per capita GDP in 1989 to 8.80 per cent in 2011. It has been noted, though, that in this case the sectoral reorientation coincides with a continued separation of the outward-oriented and domestic industrial sectors, thus echoing part of the original critique directed at commodity export dependence and structural dualism in the absence of continued commodity specialization.

Botswana is among the African country cases discussed, and has shown signs of successful convergence coincident with volatile but apparently non-trending terms of trade over the available data period. While retaining a very pronounced and narrowly defined commodity export dependence, this economy has been a consistently successful example in other terms of convergence. The case of Botswana can thus be contrasted with those of Nigeria and Zambia in the same region. Zambia and Nigeria consistently retained a strong dependence on export earnings from a dominant commodity. Their performance with regards to stabilization and convergence of real income and living standards provides a much more mixed picture.

Botswana's real GDP per capita increased from 2.41 per cent of the US equivalent figure in 1965 to 14.60 per cent in 2011. Correcting for purchasing power parity this corresponds to an increase from 2.29 per cent in 1965 to 34.26 per cent in 2011. This dramatic increase compares to a decline from 3.34 per cent in 1965 to 1.37 per cent in 2001 for real per capita GDP in the case of Nigeria. In the case of Nigeria, real per capita GDP relative the US recovered somewhat in the twenty-first century commodity boom, reaching 2.29 per cent in 2011. In purchasing power parity terms the change is from 8.40 per cent in 1965 to 1.29 per cent in 2001 and 6.89 per cent in 2011. For Zambia, the decrease in per capita real GDP relative to the US equivalent level is from 5.69 per cent in 1965 to 1.53 per cent in 2001 before recovering partly to 2.22 per cent during the recent commodity price boom. Adjusting for purchasing power parity, the decline is from 17.21 per cent of the US equivalent level in 1965 to 2.98 per cent in 2001, with a recovery to 5.89 per cent by 2011.

While the patterns of commodity dependence are similar between Zambia, Nigeria, Botswana, and – in some measure – Chile, their economic success and their development over time differ profoundly. Out of the four monoeconomies discussed, two (Chile and Botswana) have track records of sustained income convergence and macroeconomic stability. Both economies increased their real GDP per capita, while in the case of the other two monoeconomies real per capita GDP declined substantially while general macroeconomic conditions showed signs of instability. The difference is particularly stark in a comparison of Chile and Zambia, which both depend strongly on export earnings from copper. Chile's real per capita income has increased by 45.78 per cent relative to the same measure for the United States, while that of Zambia has fallen 60.93 per cent. This difference in convergence correlates with identical price developments for the dominant export commodity, while Chile has been more successful in implementing an ordered economic liberalization and maintaining a sovereign wealth fund to contain the feed-through of international price fluctuations to the domestic economy.

In good logic, neither of these two specific country cases, nor the larger group of case studies in the present volume, can on their own provide a suitable basis for extrapolation to the complex determinants of the convergence and development process in commodity-dependent economies generally. Against the background of the wider applied literature, one can conclude, though, that the country cases discussed in this volume provide a suitable illustration of a simple stylized fact: commodity export dependence generates particular problems and challenges for the affected economies, but it does not spell out their destiny. The extent and the manner in which these challenges can be mastered and contained very much depends on the institutional arrangements and policy choices of the affected economies. It is this political economy dimension rather than the initial trade specialization that drives the subsequent development process.

Notes

1 Indeed, Rostow (1997, pp. 41–50) mentions India, along with China, as cases of a separate, planning based growth and development paradigm.

2 Relative per capita GDP levels have been computed based on expenditure based and purchasing power parity adjusted real GDP and population data from the Penn World Tables (v8.1).

3 These describe oil seeds, nuts, and kernels; crude minerals and fertilizers not elsewhere specified; and metalliferous ores and metal scrap respectively.

4 The latter two identify iron and steel and non-ferrous metals respectively.

5 This formula follows a well-established normalization approach to establish a [0,1] interval between the minimum and maximum values of an index (see Meilak 2008, p. 42).

6 It should likewise be obvious that the non-normalized version of the concentration indices will be used here since ratios cannot be computed if the denominator index series tends towards zero.

7 The UNIDO Industrial Statistics do record International Standard Industrial Classification (ISIC) data from a number of countries, but reporting is often incomplete and the data cover the manufacturing sector only.

8 Available from www.rug.nl/research/ggdc/data/pwt/pwt-8.1 (accessed on 9th May 2016).

9 The UNIDO Industrial Statistics database was accessed through the UK Data Service interface, since no other form of access was available to the author.

10 Data from the World Bank's World Development Indicators. Manufacturing value added is a component of industrial sector value added.

11 Sectorally disaggregated data on the gross fixed capital formation are available for 1993 only, so no analysis of intertemporal developments is possible.

12 No data are reported for the years 2000 and 2010.

13 This is taken to be represented by ISIC 17 and 18 and SITC 84.

14 Calculations based on trade data from the UN Comtrade database.

15 The current Chilean peso dates from 1975 and replaces the escudo, which was in use from 1960 to 1975.

16 Calculations are based on ISIC classified data from the UNIDO Industrial Statistics database.

17 Data source: World Development Indicators.

18 Based on geometric mean growth rate calculations from real GDP data in the World Development Indicators. GDP data are supplied for the 1960–1965 pre-independence period.

19 Inflation figures are based on the GDP deflator as reported in the World Development Indicators.

20 More specifically, the manufacturing export share series is based on SITC categories 5–8, excluding sub-category 68. This aggregate would include sub-category 66, which includes the relevant diamond product. The World Development Indicators use SITC revision 3, while the present calculations are based on SITC revision 1; in the case of sub-category 6672 this implies a further stratification into three sub-categories to 6672 but has no implications at the level of aggregation considered. In the ISIC revision 3 data used for the computation of manufacturing value added, the World Economic Indicators data are based on ISIC divisions 15–37, whereas mining of gemstones is listed under division 14 as class 1429 and would thus be excluded from the WDI series.

21 Export concentration ratios over the available data period take values close to 1 and show no appearance of change, although the sample available is too short for any meaningful attempt at locating the impact of structural change in the trade profile.

22 Furthermore, the relevant diamond market is strongly influenced by one company (de Beers) with which Botswana's government closely cooperates (Leith 2005) and is therefore subject to limited competition, at least for the earlier part of the sample period. It is therefore not clear that the recorded NBTT series should be seen as a manifestation

of a stochastic but constant data-generating process that would form a suitable basis for statistical inference.

23 This organization recently declared allegiance to the terror organization 'Islamic State' and identifies as its African subsidiary (Comolli 2015).
24 With the exception of the year 1996, where the export share was 1.62 per cent.
25 The one exception to this observation is the minerals and metals export share of 1.13 per cent recorded for 2010.
26 *The Economist*, 29th August 2015, p. 61, 'Defending the Naira'.
27 The overall development of Zambia's exchange rate regime during the currency peg period and the subsequent liberalization is a complex matter, whose in-depth discussion is beyond the scope of the present volume. A more comprehensive analysis can be found in Bates and Collier (1993) and Rakner (2004).
28 These export shares are for 2006 and 1999 respectively.
29 These percentage shares are for 2011 and 1996 respectively.
30 Import shares from DRC computed on the basis of Comtrade data round to 0.99 for SITC 2831 in every year over the 2003–2013 interval. Roberts *et al.* (2015, p. 21) likewise comment on copper ore imports from DRC.
31 In this context, data on related manufacturing activities outside the mining sector would be desirable, but no manufacturing sector data for Zambia are available in the UNIDO Industrial Statistics database.
32 SITC 65: Textile yarn, fabrics, made up articles, etc.
33 ISIC categories 29–32; no recent data are reported for the gross fixed capital formation by sector.
34 Annual real GDP growth briefly dropped to 4.98 per cent, and thus just below 5 per cent in 1990.
35 Exceptions to this rule are contractions in the manufacturing export share in 1997–1998, 1999–2000, and 2003–2005.
36 ISIC codes D-17 (textiles), D-18 (wearing apparel, fur), and D-19 (leather, leather products, and footwear).
37 ISIC D categories 34 and 35.
38 ISIC D categories 29–32.
39 This approach follows Engle and Granger (1987); for a textbook discussion see Enders (1995).
40 The ADF test on Zambia's depreciation rate with trend yields $\tau = -3.547$, $p = 0.035$. The cointegrating regression including trend is

$$e_t = \underset{3.784}{0.695} - \underset{-2.620}{0.571} p_t - \underset{-2.309}{0.011} t + u_t;$$

the ADF test result for u_t, however, is $\tau = -2.769$, $p = 0.375$, which fails to reject the unit root null hypothesis for the residual from the cointegrating regression, so that the sufficient condition is not met. It could be argued that this is also the case for the necessary condition since the unit root pretest for the rate of change of copper prices including trend returns $\tau = -3.194$, $p = 0.085$, although this may result from a loss of power after adding the trend term.

References

Adam, C. S. and A. M. Simpasa (2010). 'The Economics of the Copper Price Boom in Zambia'. *Zambia Mining and Neoliberalism*. New York: Palgrave Macmillan. Chap. 3, pp. 59–90.
Alden, C. (2007). *China in Africa*. New York: Zed Books.
Aylwin, M. et al. (1992). *Chile en el siglo XX*. Barcelona: Edicion Planeta.

Bates, R. (2009). *When Things Fell Apart.* Cambridge: Cambridge University Press.

Bates, R. H. and P. Collier (1993). 'The Politics and Economics of Policy Reform in Zambia'. *Politics and Economics Interactions in Economic Policy Reform.* Ed. by R. H. Bates and A. O. Krueger. Oxford: Blackwell, pp. 387–443.

Biesebroeck, J. V. (2005). 'Exporting raises productivity in sub-Saharan African manufacturing firms'. *Journal of International Economics* 67, 373–91.

Bustos, P. (2011). 'Trade liberalisation, exports and technology upgrading evidence on the impact of MERCOSUR on Argentinian firms'. *American Economic Review* 101, 304–40.

Comolli, V. (2015). 'The regional problem of Boko Haram'. *Survival: Global Politics and Strategy* 57.4, 109–17.

Dinh, H. T. (2013). *Light Manufacturing in Vietnam – Creating Jobs and Prosperity in a Middle-Income Economy.* Washington, DC: World Bank.

Ebert, L. and T. La Menza (2015). 'Chile, copper and resource revenue: A holistic approach to assessing commodity dependence'. *Resources Policy* 43, 101–11.

Enders, W. (1995). *Applied Econometric Time Series.* Wiley Series in Probability and Mathematical Statistics. New York: John Wiley & Sons, Inc.

Engle, R. and C. Granger (1987). 'Co-integration and error correction: representation, estimation, and testing'. *Econometrica* 55.2, 251–76.

Fernandes, A. and C. Paunov (2012). 'Foreign direct investment in services and manufacturing productivity: evidence for Chile'. *Journal of Development Economics* 97, 305–21.

Gandolfo, G. (2002). *International Finance and Open-Economy Macroeconomics.* New York: Springer.

Goldstein, M. and D. Weatherstone (2005). 'Renminbi Controversies'. *Conference on Monetary Institutions and Economic Development.* CATO Institute. Washington, DC.

Gregorio, J. D. (2004). *Economic Growth in Chile: Evidence, Sources and Prospects.* Technical report. Santiago: Banco Central de Chile.

Hillbom, E. (2011). 'Botswana: a development-oriented gate-keeping state'. *African Affairs* 111.442, 67–89.

Hirschman, A. O. (1964). 'The paternity of an index'. *American Economic Review* 54.5, 761.

Hufbauer, G. C., Y. Wong, and K. Sheth (2006). *US–China Trade Disputes: Rising Tide, Rising Stakes.* Washington, DC: Institute for International Economics.

IMF (2015). *Staff Report for the 2014 Article IV Consultation.* IMF Country Report 15/84. Washington, DC.

Jenkins, R. (2012). 'China and Brazil: economic impacts of a growing relationship'. *Journal of Current Chinese Affairs* 1, 21–47.

Kern, S. (2007). *Sovereign Wealth Funds – State Investments on the Rise.* Technical report. Frankfurt am Main: Deutsche Bank Research.

Lardy, N. R. (2002). *Integrating China into the Global Economy.* Washington, DC: Brookings Institution Press.

Larmer, M. (2010). 'Historical Perspectives on Zambia's Mining Booms and Busts'. *Zambia Mining and Neoliberalism* New York: Palgrave Macmillan. Chap. 2, pp. 31–58.

Leith, C. (2005). *Why Botswana Prospered.* Montreal: McGill Queen's University Press.

Massina, P. (2006). *Vietnam's Development Strategies.* Abingdon: Routledge.

Meilak, C. (2008). 'Measuring export concentration: the implications for small states'. *Bank of Valetta Review* 37.

Meredith, M. (2013). *The State of Africa: A History of the Continent Since Independence.* New York: Simon and Schuster.

OECD (2013a). *Chile 2013.* OECD Economic Surveys. Paris.

OECD (2013b). *China.* OECD Economic Surveys. Paris.

Pegg, S. (2010). 'Is there a Dutch disease in Botswana?' *Resources Policy* 35.1, 14–19.

Pendle, G. (1990). *A History of Latin America.* London: Penguin Books.

Radetzki, M. (2010). *A Handbook of Primary Commodities in the Global Economy.* Cambridge: Cambridge University Press.

Rakner, L. (2004). *Political and Economic Liberalisation in Zambia 1991–2001.* Uppsala: The Nordic Africa Institute.

Reyes, J. and C. Sawyer (2011). *Latin American Economic Development.* London: Routledge.

Rhoades, S. A. (1993). 'The Herfindahl–Hirschman index'. *Federal Reserve Bulletin,* 188–9.

Roberts, S. et al. (2015). *Growth Promotion through Industrial Strategies: Zambia.* Working paper. London: London School of Economic and Political Science.

Rostow, W. (1997). *The Stages of Economic Growth: A Non-Communist Manifesto.* Cambridge: Cambridge University Press.

Sachs, J. and A. Warner (1995). 'Economic reform and the process of global integration'. *Brookings Papers on Economic Activity* 26.1, 1–118.

Singer, H. (1950). 'U.S. foreign investment in underdeveloped areas – the distribution of gains between investing and borrowing countries'. *American Economic Review* 40.2, 473–85.

Smith, S. C. and M. Todaro (2008). *Economic Development.* 10th edn. Harlow: Addison Wesley.

Tullio, G. and M. Ronci (1996). 'Brazilian inflation from 1980 to 1993: causes, consequences and dynamics'. *Journal of Latin American Studies* 28.3, 635–66.

Villalobos, S. (1992). *Breve Historia de Chile.* Santiago: Editorial Universitaria.

Whalley, J. and D. Medianu (2013). 'The deepening China–Brazil economic relationship'. *American Economic Review* 59.4, 707–30.

World Bank (2013a). *Nigeria Economic Report.* Working paper. Washington, DC: The World Bank.

World Bank (2013b). *Vietnam Development Report 2014.* Annual report. Washington, DC: The World Bank.

World Bank (2014a). *Cameroon Economic Update.* Working paper. Washington, DC: The World Bank.

World Bank (2014b). *Taking Stock – An Update on Vietnam's Recent Economic Developments.* Hanoi: The World Bank in Vietnam.

World Bank (2014c). *Zambia Economic Brief – Promoting Trade and Competitiveness.* 88863. Washington and Lusaka: World Bank.

Young, A. (1995). 'The tyranny of numbers: confronting the statistical realities of the East Asian growth experience'. *The Quarterly Journal of Economics* 110.3, 641–80.

5   Conclusion

Commodity dependence in developing countries – economic destiny or minor complication?

5.1 Introduction

The empirical study of commodity price trends has largely failed to confirm the presence of a pronounced downwards trend across primary commodity categories. By failing to confirm a general common trend per se, this empirical result contradicts a set of strongly pessimistic predictions for price trends which saw commodity prices in either precipitous decline or destined for an inexorable upwards trend. Plausible as initial fears of resource exhaustion and rising prices may have appeared under a given set of assumptions and from a given historical perspective, they were not consistently borne out by subsequent developments. A similar observation holds true for the complementary export pessimist scenario:[1] Prebisch and Singer had understandable reasons for anticipating a secular commodity terms of trade decline, given the price data they had access to and given the pattern of international economic specialization they witnessed at the time (see also Toye and Toye 2003), but actual price developments did not turn out as predicted.

The discussion of empirical developments of real commodity prices showed that the widespread sharp price decline from the late nineteenth century to the mid twentieth century was followed by a tendency towards real price stabilization among commodities in general, with a pronounced lack of comovement among those commodities that did display discernible trends. The early twenty-first century commodity price boom appears to have driven a generalized real commodity price recovery that deviates from the above general observation. It remains to be seen how commodity prices develop once China's economy matures and how commodity prices react to the take-off of other emerging market economies.

While the discussion of commodity prices concentrated on the nature of basic statistical properties of representative price series, the discussion in the preceding chapter has been focused on individual country case studies. These studies suggest that a strong and sustained commodity export orientation is in principle compatible with substantial differences in growth and income convergence, as well as in the quality and nature of the macroeconomic environment in general. The country cases discussed also differ in their diversification experience and in the evolution of their sectoral trade profiles over time. It should be noted, though, that these individual country cases are just that: individual case studies that may or may not be representative of general economic developments.

Even though general regularities cannot be inferred from individual cases, the opposite is more plausible: a limited number of cases that should be incompatible with an initial situation of commodity dependence can serve to refute or at least cast doubt on the prediction of self-reinforcing dependence. The cases of Botswana and Chile cast doubt on the incompatibility of income convergence and commodity dependence, while successful transitions such as those of China call the self-perpetuating nature of commodity dependence directly into question.

The economic development of individual country cases is naturally too complex to be analysed based on no more than a comparison of recorded commodity prices. This is one reason why it is worthwhile to look into detailed country case studies as well as more stylized macroeconomic characteristics and indicators. However, some general predictions can be based on the Prebisch–Singer variant of export pessimism.

Commodity export dependence is predicted to be self-perpetuating, because export earnings fail to provide investable funds when commodity prices are low and diversification incentives are strong, while periods of elevated commodity prices provide incentives for investment in the commodity sector at a time when resources for investment are available, thus deepening the existing structural dependence on dominant commodity exports.

Given that export earnings are not expected to feed into industrialization and that commodity-related FDI is not expected to have a transformative impact on the domestic economy, one should also expect a strong correlation between income convergence and past as well as present export dependence. To the extent that single-sector dependence, or, more generally, a narrowly defined commodity export dependence, accentuates this problem, one should further expect the extent of sectoral export concentration to be related to any correlation between export dependence and convergence failure. The subsequent discussion will address the general evidence for these predictions.

5.2 On the persistence of commodity dependence

The extent and persistence of commodity dependence can, as a first approximation, be related to the proportion of export earnings accounted for by the total export revenue in the four broad primary commodity categories defined in Chapter 4. If dependence on commodity exports is inherently self-perpetuating, then it should be uncommon for commodity-dependent developing countries to diversify out of their commodity-dominated export sector. The proportion of economies for which a strongly dominant commodity sector is observed should accordingly not decline noticeably. The case studies discussed above show that export diversification has occurred in a number of cases. If such successful diversification episodes are common, one should expect their incidence to be reflected in the number of countries retaining a high commodity export share and in its evolution over time.

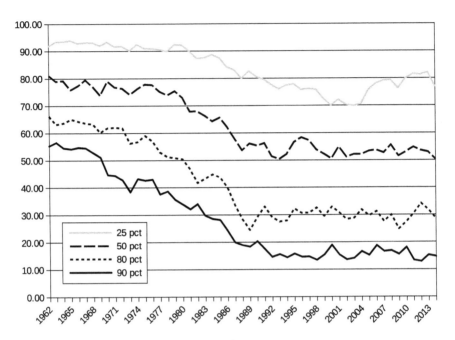

Figure 5.1 Incidence of commodity export shares.

Figure 5.1 shows the percentage of countries reporting trade data to the UN Comtrade database with a primary commodity export share at or above the value shown with the graph. The line labelled '90 pct' thus illustrates the percentage of reporting countries in which 90 per cent or more of export earnings originate in the primary commodity sector (and likewise for the 80, 50, and 25 percentage shares).[2] The values underlying this illustration need to be interpreted with care, given the likely impact of confounding influences. One should recall, for example, that the number of reporting countries over the sample period covered is not constant: events like individual secessions and the break-up of Yugoslavia and the Soviet Union have increased the number of country cases subject to consideration, while events like the German and Yemeni unifications have tended to reduce the overall country count. In addition, data availability from continuously present countries has changed over time, with some countries (like, for example, Vietnam and Cambodia) experiencing gaps in the data record during part of the time horizon. There also appears to be a general improvement in data reporting from developing countries from the turn of the century onwards.

These imperfections in the available data record can be expected to exaggerate the incidence of commodity-dependent countries in recent periods to the extent that more data are made available by commodity-dependent countries, a tendency that itself can be ameliorated to the degree that these developing countries improve their reporting performance at a time when they successfully diversify out of their

Table 5.1 Incidence of developing countries by commodity export share

Commodity share	1965	1990	2000	2011
$X_{com} \geq 90\%$	91.11	66.67	80.65	90.48
$X_{com} \geq 80\%$	88.89	66.67	81.48	79.17
$X_{com} \geq 50\%$	80.95	70.18	79.52	80.23
$X_{com} \geq 25\%$	69.23	66.27	73.91	72.66

X_{com}: Share of primary commodity exports as a percentage of total exports. The table shows the percentage of low and middle income countries in the respective commodity dependence categories.[3]

commodity niche. A priori judgements on the relative magnitude of these influences are difficult to reach, but some insights can be gained from the presence of commodity-dependent low and middle income countries at different points in time. Within the data underlying Figure 5.1 the number of low and middle income countries reporting a commodity export dependence of 90 per cent or higher dropped from 41 in 1965 to 14 in 1990, before recovering to a count of 25 in 2000 and 19 in 2011. The lower and middle income count for 1965 corresponds to a percentage of 91.11 per cent of highly commodity-dependent countries. For subsequent years, the corresponding percentage rates are 66.67 per cent (1990), 80.65 per cent (2000), and 90.48 per cent (2011). This development is consistent with a temporary drop in reported data availability from low and middle income countries, creating the impression of a temporary fall in commodity dependence, as well as with a later increase in the number of countries in this category. The corresponding developments for the remaining commodity export earnings shares discussed are presented in Table 5.1.

It is apparent from the data presented in Table 5.1 that this pattern of a temporary dip in the data reported from low and middle income countries is repeated for lower commodity export shares. The probability of a country being in the low and middle income category, given that its commodity export earnings exceed a given threshold percentage, tends to drop with the magnitude of this percentage;[4] the incidence of low and middle income countries among those reporting commodity export earnings above 90 per cent in 2000, for example, is 80.65 per cent, while it falls to 73.91 per cent for those with commodity export earnings at 25 per cent of total exports or above.

What Figure 5.1 illustrates is a substantial decline in the proportion of reporting countries with commodity export shares of 80 per cent or more between the start of the sample period and the end of the 1980s. While this decline appears to stagnate in the latter half of the sample period, it is worth noting that it has not been reversed by increased reporting from low and middle income countries, an increase in their number, or the impact of the twenty-first century commodity boom. The decline in the incidence of reporting countries with commodity earnings of 50 per cent or more of total export earnings is far less dramatic, while the decrease in the proportion of countries reporting a commodity export participation of 25 per cent or more is modest and does appear to reverse the earlier decline under the influence of the early twenty-first century commodity price boom. Taking account of the above-mentioned concerns over the number of reporting countries, it thus seems that the phenomenon of strong commodity dependence is not generally self-perpetuating, as a matter of empirical fact, but rather appears to be in decline.

The trajectory of broadly defined commodity dependence may of course differ from the development of export specialization in its constituent categories. Few countries ever showed extreme dependence on agricultural raw material exports, and even the proportion of those who depend on it for 25 per cent or more of their export earnings dropped from 22.89 per cent (19 countries) in 1965 to 4.46 per cent (7 country cases) in 2011. These figures are indicative of the sustained decay of the proportion of reporting countries in this group from the historic maximum value of 28.41 per cent in 1969. The proportion of low and middle income countries in this category rose from 78.95 per cent in 1965 to 100 per cent in 2011.

Export dependence on the agricultural raw material sub-sector therefore appears to be of limited extent in a small number of cases. Indeed, the proportion of countries reporting more than 50 per cent of export earnings in this sub-sector has never exceeded 10 per cent over the sample period considered, and has remained below 5 per cent from 1968 onwards. There were no reported cases of export earnings participation in excess of 90 per cent at any point during the 1962–2011 interval, and very few cases, in few years, of export dependence above 80 per cent in this sub-category.

Dependence on food exports for more than 90 per cent of export revenue has been reported by less than 10 per cent of countries in the sample for all years, and this is the case for 80 per cent or more of export revenue in most years. The proportion of reporting countries that depend for 50 per cent or more of their export revenue on food exports has steadily declined over the sample period from a value of 39.76 per cent in 1965 to 14.65 per cent in 2011. The average annual rate of decline is 2.15 per cent if the geometric mean rate of change is inferred from interval end points in 1965 and 2011. The decline in the reporting countries depending for 25 per cent or more of their export earnings on food exports is similar, with a drop from 57.83 per cent of reporting countries in the sample in 1965 to 29.30 per cent in 2011. The geometric mean rate of decline is somewhat lower, with an implied average drop of 1.47 per cent per year between the start and end points of the 1965–2011 interval. The decline in both series slows somewhat during the twenty-first century commodity price boom towards the end of the sample period, but there is no sustained reversal in the incidence of commodity dependence at any point. The incidence of low and middle income countries tends to remain stable at relatively high levels. The percentage of low and middle income countries in the 50 per cent and above export earnings category was 87.88 per cent and 82.61 per cent in 1965 and 2011 respectively. The corresponding low and middle income country shares for the 25 per cent and above category are 79.17 per cent and 89.13 per cent for 1965 and 2011 respectively.

These developments in food export dependence are illustrated in Figure 5.2. What the cases of food and agricultural raw materials illustrate is the limited and

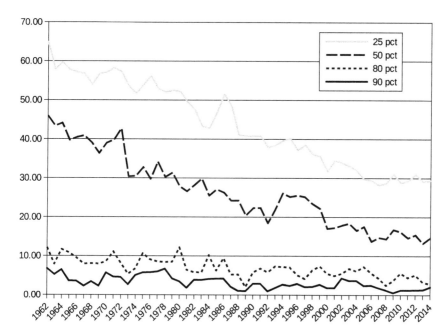

Figure 5.2 Incidence of food commodity export shares.

diminishing role of trade in these categories in the second half of the twentieth and the beginning of the twenty-first centuries. This general tendency is robust to the advent of the upwards pressure in commodity prices observed from 2004 onwards. The present observation on diminishing export revenue dependence in these agriculture-related primary commodity sub-sectors does, of course, not imply that the associated trade flows are qualitatively unimportant. It does show, however, that agriculture-based trade does not appear to be an overwhelming determinant of observed balance of payments constraints and generally appears consistent with the diminishing role of the agricultural sector commonly associated with a process of national or global economic development.

The general characteristics of exports in the agricultural sector differ from the fuel and minerals and metals sectors. A key event in shaping the relative importance of mineral fuel exports was the oil price shock of 1973–1974: the total number of countries with a mineral fuel export share of 90 per cent or more of total export revenue rose from 3 (3.61 per cent) in 1965 to 11 (9.32 per cent) in 1974. By 2011, it had fallen back to 4 (2.55 per cent). The shares of reporting countries in different categories of fuel export earnings are illustrated in Table 5.2. The incidence of countries with 80 per cent or more of export earnings arising from mineral fuel exports is somewhat higher than in the 90 per cent cluster, but the evolution of this export orientation cluster over time is similar. The incidence of countries with 80 per cent or more of export revenue arising form mineral fuel

Table 5.2 Share of mineral fuels in total exports

Commodity share	1965	1974	2000	2011
$X_{fuel} \geq 90\%$	3.61	9.32	3.66	2.55
$X_{fuel} \geq 80\%$	4.82	11.02	7.93	4.46
$X_{fuel} \geq 50\%$	4.82	15.25	12.80	11.46
$X_{fuel} \geq 25\%$	7.23	19.49	18.29	21.66

X_{fuel}: Share of mineral fuel exports as a percentage of total exports. The table shows the percentage of reporting countries with export shares at or beyond the percentage shown in the column headed 'Commodity share'.

exports rose from 4.82 per cent in 1965 to 11.02 per cent in 1974 before dropping to 4.46 per cent in 2011.

While the share of mineral fuel exporting economies with a very high dependence on mineral fuel exports peaked dramatically following the 1973 oil price shock before declining subsequently, the incidence of exporters with intermediate levels of mineral fuel export dependence is much less volatile in its intertemporal pattern. Countries with mineral fuel exports accounting for 50 per cent or more of total export revenues increased their incidence from 4.82 per cent in 1965 to 15.25 per cent in 1974. By 2011, the participation of countries in this category stood at 11.46 per cent, a value close to the 12.80 per cent recorded in 2000. The participation of countries registering a mineral fuel export value of 25 per cent of total exports or above was 7.23 per cent in 1965 and then rose to 19.49 per cent in 1974. By 2011, this value remained at 21.66 per cent, which is also close to the 2000 value of 18.29 per cent.

There is a substantial but not overwhelming presence of low and middle income countries among those with a significant proportion of mineral fuel derived exports. Among those with 90 per cent or more of mineral fuel based export revenue, 66.67 per cent where in the lower and middle income category in 1965, compared to 75 per cent in 2011. At the opposite extreme, 83.33 per cent of countries with 25 per cent or more of their export revenues in the mineral fuel category were classed as low and middle income countries in 1965, compared to 61.76 per cent in 2011. These percentage figures should be treated with some caution, though. One reason for this is the relatively low number of country cases at very high levels of mineral fuel export dependency in particular: the 1965 percentage of low and middle income countries refers to two out of three country cases where mineral fuel exports accounted for 90 per cent or more of total exports. Another reason is the obvious problem of endogeneity: the prolonged period of high oil prices made it likely that highly oil-dependent countries would no longer be classified as belonging to a low income group, in spite of the distinct possibility that the observed rise in income may be disconnected from any underlying substantive development process.

A further peculiarity worth noting is the sharp decline in the number of country cases with intermediate levels of mineral fuel export participation. In 1985,

18.75 per cent of the countries in the sample reported a mineral fuel participation in total exports of 50 per cent or above, while only 8.42 per cent of countries in the sample met this criterion for 1988. This decline in relative participation coincides with a drop in the number of country cases in this category for which data are available from 18 in 1985 to 8 in 1988. For the group of countries with mineral fuel exports at or in excess of 25 per cent of exports a decline from 25.00 per cent to 16.84 per cent between 1985 and 1988 coincides with a drop in the number of country cases reported from 24 to 16. In both percentage categories, the number of country cases and the incidence of countries in the relevant category recovered subsequently. The observed coincidence in the evolution of percentages and the number of reported country cases points to a deterioration in the quality of reported data as a possible confounding influence coincident with the weakening of oil prices over the same period.

Mineral fuel prices are bound to be dependent on crude oil prices and these are known to be substantially dependent on cartel-based manipulation, although the extent of OPEC's influence is seen as limited by some (such as Radetzki 2010). Nevertheless, this background fact needs to be borne in mind when assessing the role and relative importance of mineral fuel exports. With this caveat of cartel influence on price developments, one can nevertheless observe a substantial and sustained impact of mineral fuel export earnings on a substantial proportion of the countries reporting trade data to the UN. In contrast to agriculture-related trade, this influence did not, so far, appear to be in decline, although the number of highly fuel export dependent economies remained limited to a low number of countries.

A similar general impression of continued relevance arises from an analysis of mineral and metals exports. Extreme dependence on mineral and metals exports has historically been rare, with only two countries depending for 90 per cent or more of their export earnings on the metals and minerals sector in 1965, while the corresponding figure for the 80 per cent incidence threshold was 3. By 2011, only one country (Zambia) was dependent for more than 80 per cent of its export earnings on the minerals and metals sector, while none were dependent on it for 90 per cent or more of total exports. The proportion of countries depending for 50 per cent of their exports or more on the minerals and metals sector initially dropped from a value of 7.23 per cent in 1965 to 2.91 per cent in 1990. In this group, the recent commodity price boom did coincide with a recovery in the share of export-dependent countries, though, and a share of 7.01 per cent in this intermediate export dependence category had been recovered by 2011.

The lower intermediate export dependence category of 25 per cent or more for minerals and metals exports also shows a strong decline from the early 1960s to the 1990s. The number of countries reporting an incidence of the sub-sector in this category dropped from 18.07 per cent in 1965 to 6.80 per cent in 1990 before recovering to 14.65 per cent by 2011. Low and middle income countries account for a consistently high percentage of countries in this category, with 73.33 per cent in 1965, 71.43 per cent in 1990, and 78.26 per cent in 2011. The corresponding percentages for the 50 per cent category are 83.33 per cent in 1965, 33.33 per cent (for one out of three country cases) in 1990, and 81.82 per cent in 2011. At the higher commodity dependence clusters in this commodity category, the number of country cases is consistently too low for such percentages to be meaningful. What is generally apparent, though, is the stylized fact of persistent export dependence in the metals and minerals sub-sector at intermediate levels and the extreme rarity of countries, including low income countries, finding themselves in almost exclusive dependence on export earnings in this category.

The pattern of export dependence across commodity sub-categories and the evolution of these patterns over time identify some crude yet crucial stylized facts about developing country commodity dependence. The relative importance of exports from agricultural and agriculture-related commodity sectors has generally been in decline, even though the prices of some agricultural commodities showed temporary recoveries, and in some cases even tended to trend upwards over time (see Chapter 3). The relative importance of export revenue from the mineral fuel and minerals and metals sectors differs systematically from this general characteristic. Even though the value of mineral fuel exports is partially driven by cartel action – in a way that minerals and metals exports are generally not – both have the common property of being functionally tied to industrial activity. The incidence of export revenue in both commodity sub-sectors has also failed to systematically diminish.

A linkage between demand for primary commodities and industrial activity in centre economies is of course at the heart of the original Prebisch–Singer hypothesis, and dependency theory more generally. The recent experience differs in so far as the booms in industrial demand sustaining the relative importance of the commodity trade are now conventionally linked to successful emerging economies. In other words, recent experience points to the continued presence of limited numbers of countries successfully following export-oriented growth strategies and boosting international demand for primary commodities in industry-related sub-sectors as they build their secondary sector industrial infrastructure. To the extent that the establishment of an industrial infrastructure is particularly resource intensive, one should expect this foundational stage in an emerging market's development to give rise to particularly intensive commodity demand. During the recent emerging market development experience, this foundational infrastructure development has of course been particularly pronounced in China. Given the size of this particular emerging economy, the external effect of a protracted international commodity price boom is hardly surprising.

What remains to be addressed is the extent to which this commodity price boom impacted on the growth performance of other developing countries, and to what extent their economic growth and development at the onset of the present millennium has been conditioned by it. The subsequent discussion will therefore look into the recent growth experience of low and middle income countries and how it relates to commodity exposure.

5.3 Economic growth, the terms of trade, and commodities

Recalling the introductory review of dependency theory and of balance of payments constrained growth theory, it is worth returning to the original point of interest in the importance and evolution of commodity prices and commodity export earnings. It is therefore to the relationship between export earnings, the terms of trade, and economic growth that we turn in this section.

The remainder of this section will focus on the recent growth experience of the early twenty-first century. This period is relatively short and it is also atypical in that it is dominated by an extraordinary commodity price boom that is likely to have dominated the developing country experience of the balance of payments constraint's trade component. The period under consideration, then, is somewhat atypical with respect to its commodity price development; it is still attractive as a sample period for two reasons: its relative recency makes it relevant to the analysis of temporally proximate events, not only in the sense of the data used being recent, but crucially because the global economic structure and the nature of international trading relations had time to transition out of the cold war based bloc configuration by this time while the initial disruption of systemic reform in a large number of countries had become a historical fact by the turn of the century. The second reason is simply the empirically observed improvement in general data availability, allowing for a more comprehensive sample of countries and attenuating the potentially confounding influence from a non-random presence of data gaps.

Naturally, the disadvantage of focusing on a recent sample period is the lack of evidence in earlier periods, and this can be a potentially confounding influence, if the observations from the omitted period differ systematically from that of the included period while being produced by the same fundamental economic structure, since in this case the data from the earlier period would provide contemporaneously relevant information. Conversely, including data from the earlier period is likely to be a confounding influence if these data were produced by a data-generating process that differs substantively from that of the later period. This is a distinct possibility here since the trade data recorded are not merely affected by idiosyncratic country policy differences but by structural discrepancies on a global scale. Trading relations within the Soviet bloc developed to a significant extent in parallel to those in the open market, and thus arguably did not form part of an integrated market economy on the international level. The constituent economies of this bloc also tended to be centrally planned economies, that is, not protectionist market economies or economies prone to distortionary intervention but countries whose governments explicitly embraced a centralized and policy-directed regime of planned resource allocation. Growth and investment trajectories in these economies were therefore substantially driven by planning priorities, and reactions to changing economic constraints could at least be deferred over the medium term.

It can be argued that such failures to adjust to a changing market environment are inherently economically inefficient and that the cumulative build-up of such inefficiencies materially contributed to the prolonged stasis and eventual collapse of the planned economies in the Soviet bloc and unaffiliated planned economies.[5] Thus, while the price data of globally traded commodities can be plausibly modelled in a continuous time series, the same is not true of, for example, mean growth rates of economies which collectively and near simultaneously underwent a profound structural shift at a given point in the time sample. This discontinuity, coupled with the lower incidence of data reported by low income economies and former members of the Soviet bloc in the earlier part of the series, motivates a differentiated approach to discussing the data: data for the later part of the sample will be discussed in the context of a basic but formal correlational analysis, while discussion of earlier data will focus on a less formal interpretative account of the observed pattern.

A number of low and lower-middle income countries have experienced very high growth rates in real per capita income at the beginning of the new millennium. A number of former Soviet republics experienced real per capita income growth in excess of 7 per cent per annum on average over the period 2000–2011. Among these, extreme dependence on commodity exports is also common. Turkmenistan, for example, grew at an average rate of 7.08 per cent per annum over the sample period and relied for 91.61 per cent of its export earnings on the primary commodity sector in 2000. Other economies showed similar combinations of high mean growth and high commodity export dependence at the start of the sample period. This combination is illustrated by the recorded mean per capita income growth figures (with commodity export shares in parentheses) for a number of ex-Soviet republics such as Kazakhstan 7.16 per cent (93.83 per cent) and Azerbaijan 12.16 per cent (92.35 per cent). In yet other cases, high growth in ex-Soviet republics coincides with notably lower commodity export shares in the year 2000. Examples of this are Belarus with 7.76 per cent (34.74 per cent) and Armenia with 8.01 per cent (41.99 per cent).

Yet other country cases with relatively high growth rates include African countries like Angola, with per capita real income growth of 6.95 per cent, and Equatorial Guinea (10.46 per cent), for which no detailed data on commodity trade are available in the Comtrade database. Of course China, with its increasing role in manufacturing exports, is among the fastest growing economies. One possible interpretation is that of China's economic take-off driving commodity demand worldwide and improving the growth prospects of commodity-dependent economies via a widespread and sustained commodity price boom. The varied commodity export profiles of fast-growing developing countries suggest that such an interpretation would at best be a simplification.

Even a simplified account may capture the essence of a significant contributory process, though. If the influences identified in the Prebisch–Singer thesis and the basic balance of payments constraint mechanism postulated by Thirlwall are empirically relevant, one should expect their manifestation to be detectable in the impact of a commodity boom on developing country growth performance. A balance of payments constrained growth prediction for commodity-dependent developing economies facing low price elasticities would predict a commodity price boom to directly correlate with accelerated growth in these commodity-dependent exporting economies. Statistically, this relationship should be detectable in a significant partial correlation between the terms of trade (as part of the Thirlwall formulation) and the observed rate of income growth. To the extent that this influence is self-reinforcing, it should also co-vary with increasing concentration of export activity in the booming commodity sector – a pattern that should translate into an overall intensification of export activity concentration in the comparative advantage sectors of commodity-dependent exporters.

One could further expect that starting conditions in terms of initial commodity dependence or trade concentration correlate with the impact of a commodity price boom on the balance of payments constraint in so far as a stronger initial commodity exposure can be expected to correlate with a more substantial balance of payments constraint relaxation from a given positive terms of trade shock. On the other hand, a stronger initial concentration of export activity in a given set of commodity sub-sectors would limit the scope for further concentration of trading activity as a consequence of the commodity price boom.

To investigate the empirical evidence for this relationship formally, mean annual per capita growth rates over the 2000–2011 interval are regressed on identifying variables for the balance of payments constraint and a set of control variables for factor inputs as well as international integration. Standard control variables to account for additions to factor inputs conventionally include population growth, as a proxy for labour force growth, and the gross fixed capital formation as a proxy for investment into physical capital. Following an approach taken by Greenaway, Sapsford, and Pfaffenzeller (2007), these controls are supplemented by an openness indicator, relating trade to GDP, as well as foreign direct investment (FDI) as a percentage of GDP. Part of FDI will of course feed into the capital accumulation process and will therefore correlate with the impact of the gross fixed capital formation. (Parts of FDI may not feed into additions to domestic capital, though, but could, for example, contribute to financial consolidation in domestic firms.) Inclusion of FDI as a proportion of GDP then not only gives an indication of investable resource mobilization from abroad in a quantitative sense but can also serve as an indicator of interaction with the international corporate infrastructure and knowledge base if foreign investment integrates with domestic economic activity.

The interpretation adopted by Greenaway, Sapsford, and Pfaffenzeller (2007) is motivated by the reasoning underlying endogenous growth theory. It therefore differs in fundamental outlook from the balance of payments constrained growth perspective which emphasizes access to a threshold quantity of investable resources and retains a native focus on export earnings rather than foreign investment, the receipt of which is inherently conditional on continued approval on the part of the foreign investor. Export earnings are at least potentially available to the domestic economy irrespective of contingent claims based on a benchmark value specific to an extraneous economy. This latter observation does itself build on implied assumptions of domestic habitat preference. These seem reasonable, to the extent that domestic economy based exporters are predominantly subject to liability defined in domestic legal tender terms, but do not explicitly account for countervailing opportunities to respond to incentives for investment abroad.

A comprehensive discussion of the realism of the various explicitly formulated and implied assumptions underlying alternative theories of international trade and investment and their relevance to the commodity dependence problem could be pursued at great length, and at the cost of distracting from the main topic under discussion. The present discussion will therefore proceed based on two basic econometric model alternatives for assessing the recent growth experience in the early twenty-first century.

For the following correlational analysis, the country cases considered will be limited to low and middle income countries as identified in the World Development Indicators. The general cross-sectional regression model is then

$$\dot{y}_i = \alpha + \beta_1 pop_i + \beta_2 I y_i + \beta_3 f d i_i + \beta_4 x y_i + \beta_5 x v_i + \varepsilon, \tag{5.1}$$

where $\dot{y}_i$ is country i's mean real per capita GDP growth rate over the 2000–2011 interval. α is a constant, pop_i the mean population growth rate for country i serving as a proxy for labour force growth with a given participation rate, and $I y_i$ is the investment to GDP ratio in economy i as measured by the gross fixed capital formation as a percentage of national income. $f d i_i$ represents the total amount of foreign direct investment receipts of country i as a percentage of GDP, while $x y_i$ measures the degree of export orientation in the conventional way via exports as a percentage of GDP. This measure of export orientation relative to domestic income is supplemented by $x v_i$, the geometric mean rate of change of the value of exports of country i in real US dollar terms, deflated to the GDP deflator's 2000 base year value. This last variable is intended to capture a change in the balance of payments constraint over the sample period, given the export orientation of the economy.

The inflow of foreign direct investment relative to domestic income can be seen as an indicator of global corporate networking and exchange as discussed above, or as a mainly quantitative factor contributing to a relaxation of the balance of payments constraint. Under the former interpretation, emphasis is given to the endogenous growth aspects of FDI: foreign investment can help in technology upgrading and may enable the local economy to mobilize firm-specific comparative advantages in given productive sectors. The second interpretation is liable to put the emphasis on the availability of additional investable resources from foreign investment flows, without inviting a specific focus on the associated structural transformations. Naturally, these interpretations are not mutually exclusive, even though they appeal to different theoretical traditions, and both justify the expectation of a positive correlation between investment flows and economic growth.

The export variable $x y_i$ expresses the relative importance of the foreign sector. One would expect this variable to take a higher value for a more open, export-oriented economy. However, there are also reasons to expect a higher level of export intensity for small open economies whose domestic economy is too small for internal specialization. Furthermore, the export to GDP ratio may rise if export demand is mainly dependent on foreign demand and remains unchanged at a time when domestic economic activity contracts: at such a time, domestic GDP could cyclically contract for a given magnitude of exports, producing a higher value for the X/Y ratio. On the other hand, GDP may rise with rising exports during a commodity boom – as would be predicted by the Thirlwall model – in which case the movements in export value and income would tend to balance each other. The expected impact of the export orientation variable is therefore inherently ambiguous from the position of balance of payments constrained growth theory. If export orientation is taken as a structural indicator of an internationally well-integrated market economy with efficient internal resource allocation, then a high constant value of the export to GDP ratio can indeed be expected to correlate positively with export-led economic growth. This structural value should manifest itself across cyclical fluctuations, but its empirical manifestation would require a data series of sufficient length for business cycles to average out over the period for which the export to GDP ratio is measured. There is no inherent reason to expect such a result over a period characterized by a protracted commodity boom.

For the present case then, neither perspective leads to a well-defined expectation for the impact of a high export to GDP ratio. This fact can be seen as a reason for not including the variable in the first place. Since openness indicators are conventionally included in this applied context, it does, however, stand to reason that the variable's potential ambiguity in the present context should be allowed to manifest itself empirically as well rather than being excluded a priori.

The rate of change of the real export value index (xv_i), finally, is intended to capture the impact of an increase in export revenue on economic growth. The Thirlwall model would predict this impact to be positive not only over a the period of a commodity boom but in the longer term if high commodity earnings are not counterbalanced by periodic shortfalls. In this respect, balance of payments constrained growth theory tends to be more optimistic than the Prebisch–Singer theory, which in its original formulation anticipated that favourable earnings fluctuations would coincide with counterproductive incentive fluctuations so that the fulfilment of the necessary condition would not be complemented by the sufficient one. If growth is not seen as constrained by export earnings in the first place, there is no a priori reason to predict an impact of earnings on income growth beyond the direct effect of the export windfall. For the present sample period, which is dominated by a commodity boom, a positive correlation between export earnings and income growth should be expected in any case. It is less clear how significant one should expect this to be when controlling for the miscellaneous variables in the econometric model.

The two control variables – investment and population growth – are expected to have the conventionally anticipated signs. Investment is generally assumed to add to the capital stock and therefore to tend to accelerate growth, unless it rises to unsustainable values – see Romer (2006) for the standard account of classical growth theory. Additions to the labour force, and thence to labour inputs into production, are likewise expected to be correlated positively with output growth. As the dependent variable is expressed in per capita terms in the present case, this would of course imply a negative coefficient estimate for the population growth term.

A variant model to the general model specified in Equation (5.1) seeks to disaggregate some components of the export value component. This alternative specification is given in Equation (5.2):

$$\dot{y}_i = \alpha + \beta_1 pop_i + \beta_2 Iy_i + \beta_3 f di_i + \beta_4 xy_i + \beta_5 tt_i + \beta_6 xc_i + \beta_7 hi_i + \varepsilon, \quad (5.2)$$

where the control variables and the openness indicator are as above, and tt_i stands for the mean rate of change in the net barter terms of trade, xc_i for the proportion of primary commodity export earnings in total export earnings in the year 2000, and hi_i is the mean rate of change in the normalized Hirschman–Herfindahl Index index. The expected correlation of the geometric mean rate of change in the net barter terms of trade and the mean real per capita income growth rate is positive, as was expected for the growth rate of the overall export value index. The commodity export share for 2000 is intended to capture the initial extent of commodity dependence: a given terms of trade rise is liable to produce a relatively larger export earnings impact in a more commodity-dependent economy as a matter of simple arithmetic. It should also be expected to correlate positively with balance of payments constrained growth in a commodity-dependent economy to the extent that commodity dependence is self-reinforcing so that the relative importance of a dominant commodity sector can be expected to increase further during a growth episode produced by a balance of payments constraint relaxation from a commodity price boom.

Self-perpetuating commodity export dependence should also be reflected in the pattern of export concentration as measured in the Hirschman–Herfindahl index. On the other hand, the potential for the concentration index to rise would itself be limited by very high initial levels of commodity dependence, although there may well be potential fur further activity concentration within the broad commodity sector. Positive growth in the Hirschman–Herfindahl index should nevertheless tend to positively correlate with an increase in balance of payments constrained growth driven by a commodity boom. How strongly this tendency manifests itself is ultimately an empirical question.

The results obtained for both models are shown in Table 5.3. Columns one and three report the full econometric model estimates for models one and two; columns two and four show the specific models obtained after sequentially eliminating variables with insignificant coefficient estimates until all remaining coefficient estimates with the exception of the coefficient on the constant appear statistically significant. The coefficient estimates for the control variables (population growth and the gross fixed capital formation) have the expected signs and show reasonably stable values in the general and specific model estimates; both coefficient estimates appear statistically significant based on a standard t-test.

The foreign direct investment variable in Model 1 has a positively signed point estimate, as predicted, but is consistently insignificant. The coefficient on the openness indicator, in the form of the export to GDP ratio, has a very small, negatively signed coefficient point estimate that is very clearly insignificant – again, as anticipated. The coefficient on the growth rate of the real export value index, finally, takes a positive and consistently significant coefficient estimate.

Table 5.3 Correlates of per capita income growth*

Variable	Model 1		Model 2	
α	0.019 0.023	0.009 0.012	1.009 0.849	0.759 0.955
pop_i	−0.664 −3.825	−0.665 −3.995	−0.536 −2.227	−0.538 −2.842
Iy_i	0.088 3.086	0.097 3.638	0.134 3.323	0.130 4.345
fdi_i	0.050 1.101	–	0.095 1.281	–
xy_i	−0.001 −0.068	–	0.001 0.054	–
xv_i	0.174 6.462	0.174 6.516	–	–
tt_i	–	–	0.173 2.137	0.142 2.424
xc_i	–	–	−0.014 −1.300	–
hi_i	–	–	0.038 0.810	–

* t-ratios are given below coefficient estimates.

For the general model, there is no indication of heteroscedacity from the Breusch–Pagan test statistic, which returns a value of BPG = 6.796, corresponding to a p-value of 0.236, and thus fails to reject. There is no indication of multicollinearity from variance inflation factors.[6] Ramsey's RESET test returns a test statistic of RESET = 3.963, $p = 0.022$, however, pointing to a possible misspecification of the general model. These general conclusions supported by the diagnostic statistics are robust to the more restrictive formulation of the specific model: the Breusch–Pagan test still fails to reject (BPG = 4.076, $p = 0.253$) and the RESET test still rejects (RESET = 6.430, $p = 0.002$). The results obtained for Model 1 thus largely correspond to what should be expected on theoretical grounds but show evidence of possible misspecification. A comparison with the second model alternative should therefore be of particular interest.

Columns three and four of Table 5.3 show the results for the general and specific forms of Model 2. The results for the impact of population growth, the gross fixed capital formation, and the participation of FDI in GDP reflect the qualitative conclusions from Model 1 in that their coefficients take the same sign and the inference on their statistical significance is identical. The estimated coefficient for population growth is close in magnitude to the one obtained in Model 1, but the estimated coefficient for the gross fixed capital formation term is now noticeably larger. The point estimate of the coefficient for the foreign direct investment term now also takes a larger value, but remains clearly insignificant. The openness indicator xy_i now takes a very small positive insignificant value, although this result is best interpreted as a confirmation of an insignificant estimate in which the sign of the point estimate does not matter, given its proximity to the zero value of the null hypothesis.

The role of export earnings is now modelled over three components: the mean geometric growth rate of the net barter terms of trade over the sample period (tt_i), the proportion of commodity exports out of total exports at the beginning of the sample period (xc_i), and the geometric mean rate of change of the normalized Hirschman–Herfindahl index (hi_i). Of these, the coefficient estimate for the terms of trade variable appears significant, with the expected sign and a magnitude of the point estimate close to that for the growth rate of the export value index in the general model. The coefficient estimates for the commodity share and the concentration index are clearly insignificant. The diagnostic statistics for Model 2 differ from those for Model 1. The Breusch–Pagan test for the general model now rejects ($BPG = 18.351$, $p = 0.010$). The RESET test now does not indicate misspecification of the general model ($RESET = 0.839$, $p = 0.436$) and there is still no indication of multicollinearity from variance inflation factors.[7]

For the specific model estimate, obtained again by sequentially eliminating insignificant coefficient estimates, the control variables (population growth and the gross fixed capital formation) retain significant coefficient estimates, while only the terms of trade variable among the three export earnings indicators considered remains statistically significant. The coefficient for tt_i, the mean rate of change of the net barter terms of trade, has, moreover, decreased somewhat compared to the general model estimate. The Breusch–Pagan test now fails to reject the homoscedasticity null hypothesis ($BPG = 4.843$, $p = 0.184$), the RESET test also fails to reject ($RESET = 1.392$, $p = 0.253$). Model 2 therefore is consistent with the hypothesized impact of the commodity price boom on low and middle income country growth; it does differ in some respects from the first econometric model specification, though.

For one, the first econometric model incorporates total export earnings, but does not differentiate with regards to its components, whereas the second model does. Moreover, the second model relies on more narrowly defined export measures, only one of which proves to be statistically significant. Model 2, relying on the barter terms of trade index as main export indicator, appears more appropriate in so far as the diagnostic tests employed did not give evidence of misspecification for the specific model. While the terms of trade coefficient in the specific model estimate takes a lower value than in the general model, this appears plausible in so far as the variable in question captures the impact of real commodity prices but not of world growth in demand for primary commodity exports. This aspect may also be reflected in the somewhat higher point estimate for the constant in Model 2 compared to Model 1. With the real per capita income growth rate as dependent variable, the constant should capture the trend growth rate once the explicitly parameterized independent variables have been accounted for. Its higher value when moving from an export value index to a relative price index is therefore plausible. The continued lack of significance of the coefficient estimate for this constant term could be seen as indicative of an insignificant exogenous trend growth rate. On the other hand, the fit of this model is limited, with an adjusted multiple correlation coefficient of $\bar{R}^2 = 0.210$ compared to $\bar{R}^2 = 0.387$ for Model 1. These results highlight the fact that simple correlational models like the ones used here should be interpreted with great care and that their explanatory potential is inherently limited.

With these caveats in mind, the results obtained are consistent with the conclusion that the impact of commodity markets on growth is in some measure dependent on terms of trade movements, and that real commodity prices play a potentially important role. The evidence for the role of export earnings more generally is less solid. This limited evidence for primary commodity exports as a determinant of growth during a period that was largely characterized by a pronounced and lasting commodity price boom is remarkable. This general result, as well as the observed lack of evidence for a significant impact of initial commodity dependence, can be seen as pointing to at most a limited role of primary commodity export earnings as a driver of growth in low and middle income economies. It is also worth noting that this observation does not preclude individual country cases in which the economy is dependent on export earnings and export earnings are near exclusively determinant of economic growth. The recent evidence does not, however, point to this scenario as a generally prevalent pattern.

The World Bank's net barter terms of trade series is available for some countries from 1980 and for a larger sample from 2000. Lower and middle income countries are well represented in the 1980–2000 sub-period, although the number of country cases in the earlier sub-period is only 80 compared to 150 low and middle income countries in 2011. As discussed above, this phenomenon is likely due to a change in the number of reporting countries as well as in reporting performance.

For the study of the earlier sub-period, the barter terms of trade series has been retained as an independent variable. The geometric mean rate of change of the barter terms of trade and of real per capita GDP has then been computed as above. While the quality and availability of data over this period, as well as the change in international economic relations and institutions between the two periods, should caution against reliance on a continuous inferential approach, an informal consideration and discussion of the basic correlational properties between both variables remains a possibility. A simple correlation coefficient for the mean rate of change of the net barter terms of trade and the growth rate of real per capita GDP returns a rather low value of $\rho = 0.186$, with $t = 1.627$, $p = 0.108$ indicating a statistically insignificant and small estimated value. It is an inherent weakness of bivariate correlations that the influence of further potentially relevant variables is not accounted for.

In principle, omitted confounding influences can affect a measured correlation either way, but in the present case the control variables considered above would be expected to weaken the case for a significant relationship further. The sub-period in question was marked by a tendency towards real commodity price decline, while a number of low and middle income countries experienced low or negative real per capita income growth rates for at least part of the sub-sample period. If the specific form of Model 2 obtained for the 2000–2011 interval is re-estimated for the earlier sub-period, the terms of trade term no longer appears statistically significant:

$$y_i = \underset{0.419}{0.513} - \underset{-2.889}{0.955} pop_i + \underset{4.167}{0.130} I y_i + \underset{1.478}{0.122} tt_i + \varepsilon. \qquad (5.3)$$

The result from Equation (5.3) may be taken, at first sight, to provide clear evidence against a significant influence of the barter terms of trade. However, the econometric model, when applied to the earlier sub-sample, appears misspecified based on Ramsey's RESET test (RESET $= 5.535$, $p = 0.005$), although the Breusch–Pagan test fails to reject (BPG $= 0.983$, $p = 0.805$). The best interpretation of this estimate is, then, as evidence of poor model fit. This conclusion is in line with the preceding discussion where it was argued that the data-generating process during the pre 2000 sub-sample cannot be taken to be representative of the same data-generating process for later sample periods. For the 1980–2000 interval in particular, it is worth bearing in mind that the earlier decade in this sample period encompasses the 1982 debt crisis as well as Latin America's 'lost decade'. The latter half of the sample covers an era of transition for former Eastern bloc economies and this is likely to be reflected in the amount and quality of the data reported by these economies.

A robust study of the diverse influences on growth performance during this sub-sample period would therefore have to consider influences such as financial disruption, the debt burden, and regime transitions. While these topics are both relevant and rewarding, they lie outside the scope and subject matter of the present study. Based on the evidence obtained, one can conclude that the observed and estimated correlations between the commodity terms of trade and growth do not clearly contradict notions of balance of payments constrained growth in developing countries, but neither are the observed pattern strong and robust enough to be seen as a confirmation. If there is one concise lesson from the recent history of commodity prices and developing country growth it lies in the complexity of the relationship rather than its reduction to a simple rule. The basic properties of this relationship are probably best analysed by considering the complementary insights gained from the study of commodity price trends, developing country growth, and concrete examples of country experiences.

5.4   Concluding observations

The debate about the role of primary commodities in the process of economic development dates back to the post-Second World War era, while the tradition of basing dramatic predictions on the expected availability of natural resources can be traced back at least to the days of Malthus. The present study considered the predictions of secular price decay and self-perpetuating commodity export dependence, which characterized the early debate on international trade and development. The discussion in Chapter 3 on long run secular trends during the twentieth and early twenty-first centuries showed that the presence of long run trends is uncertain for the majority of commodities, while most estimated trend components are small in size even if statistically significant. Towards the end of the sample period a possible trend reversal has been seen as a possibility, although the most salient characteristic across primary commodities in general is a lack of homogeneity in long run price movements.

The heterogeneity in price trajectories can be juxtaposed with differing country experiences with commodity export earnings. Different economies surveyed in the case studies have managed their commodity export profiles in a variety of ways and have evolved differing internal and external economic activity profiles, with corresponding changes in commodity dependence as well as differing experiences in specialization within the primary sector. The degree to which economies covered in the case studies succeeded in converging towards high income levels does not appear to exclusively depend on their traditional area of comparative advantage in the primary sector. Indeed, the experiences of persistently commodity-dependent economies like Botswana, Chile, and Zambia highlights the role of institutions in managing and mobilizing commodity export earnings for development. Sovereign wealth funds have been shown to successfully contain Dutch disease phenomena during commodity export booms, while a tradition of fiscal discipline has provided an environment of economic and political stability conducive to economic growth in both Botswana and Chile. Zambia and, in some measure, Nigeria, show how economic opportunities and substantial if volatile commodity export earnings can yield at best limited benefits if the stability and institutional infrastructure for successful and productive resource mobilization are insufficiently developed.

Other Latin American countries like Argentina and Brazil have strong manufacturing and service sectors, although in the case of Brazil, trading relations with China still had a decisive impact on the country's export profile. On the other hand, the export profile of China itself shows a clear transition towards manufacturing exports and commodity imports. The importance of the nascent manufacturing sector is also evident in Vietnam – a smaller transition economy – but it is the transformation of China that has substantively added to international demand for primary commodities and was arguably at the heart of the recent commodity price boom. This general fact is often reflected in China's share in commodity exports of developing economies.

The pattern of commodity dependence among low and middle income countries more generally also is at variance with the general assumption of widespread and self-conserving commodity dependence. In agriculture-related sectors, commodity export dependence has generally decreased, and most dramatically so for the share of countries with extreme levels of dependence on the agricultural sector. In the case of mineral fuels and minerals and metals, this decline is far less dramatic and the continued relevance of these commodity sectors is more pronounced. This pattern, too, can be seen as evidence of a general trend towards global industrialization, even if some economies persist in specializing in supplying raw material inputs to this process for at least part of the time.

One conclusion from the present study, then, is this: in spite of commodity markets' remarkable affinity to doomsday predictions – irrespective of the direction in which commodity prices are predicted to move – they have persistently failed to define economic destiny. Where individual economies have failed to prosper because they remained lastingly dependent on narrowly defined and volatile commodity export sectors, the explanation for this experience is more likely found in the design of this country's economic policy and economic institutions than in the raw fact of commodity dependence per se.

There is indeed evidence of economies tending to diversify out of the commodity sector as they develop into labour intensive manufacturing processes. Since a pattern of sequential upgrading from labour intensive to more skill and technology intensive manufacturing sub-sectors takes time and may be limited by the absorptive capacity of the external market, one should not expect more than a limited number of commodity-dependent exporters to successfully transition at any point in time. A concerted entry of all developing economies into a small number of labour intensive manufacturing export sectors, such as textiles, would most likely lead to intensive international wage competition in these sectors and could well have the main effect of producing diminishing terms of trade for the manufacturing sectors concerned. If developing country growth is to lead to a general rise in the standard of living, this would suggest a need for a phased transition into manufacturing. This in turn implies that some commodity-dependent countries would be best placed to maximize the benefits of commodity exports until an opportunity to successfully diversify out of them arises.

While there has been substantial research into the circumstances under which commodity earnings can contribute to domestic instability or corruption, there remains a need to explore the conditions that enable a degree of conditional convergence from a commodity-centred economic position, since this is a trading specialization that a number of developing countries are likely to retain for some time to come. A related area should seek to explore under what conditions international integration into commodity markets can lead to diversification into nascent manufacturing activities and subsequent upgrading.

One can conclude, then, that commodity markets and commodity exports do not spell economic destiny but do remain a pivotal component of opportunities for economic development and diversification. Grasping these opportunities involves the prudent management of commodity earnings as well as activity diversification, product upgrading, and creative positioning within broad commodity sectors. It is this understanding of commodity dependence as both challenge and opportunity, not merely as a problem of which a deeper understanding needs to be developed, that can lead to a variant perspective of the intermediate stages of the economic transition process. Much of the research in this area will have to be undertaken at the level of individual countries or commodity markets, since commodity dependence and the development of commodity-dependent economies are phenomena that are too complex to be appropriately understood in terms of simple broad trends such as declining terms of trade or consistently tightening resource constraints.

Notes

1 The notion of terms of trade focused pessimism in reference to declining terms of trade is found in Gandolfo (2002, p. 86), where it is more precisely referred to as elasticity pessimism, highlighting the assumed causal mechanism in the critical elasticities condition.

2 The percentage share has been computed based on the sum total of commodity categories as defined in Chapter 4 relative to the sum of exports in all SITC categories.
3 Thus, in 1965, 91.11 per cent of countries with 90 per cent or more of export earnings in the commodity sector were classed as low or middle income countries, while the incidence of low and middle income countries among countries depending for at least 25 per cent of their export earnings on the commodity sector was 69.23 per cent.
4 There are occasional exceptions to this overall tendency. One example is given by 80.65 per cent of countries with commodity export shares at or above 90 per cent being in the lower to middle income category in 2000. This share rises slightly to 81.48 per cent for a commodity export share of 80 per cent and above.
5 This is not the place to discuss alternative economic systems. The fundamental case is put concisely in Hayek (1945).
6 The variance inflation factors returned are: pop_i: 1.075, Iy_i: 1.076, fdi_i: 1.083, xy_i: 1.074, and xv_i: 1.049.
7 The variance inflation factors returned are: pop_i: 1.237, Iy_i: 1.442, fdi_i: 1.223, xy_i: 1.102, tt_i: 1.294, $xc_i = 1.502$, and $hi_i = 1.031$.

References

Gandolfo, G. (2002). *International Finance and Open-Economy Macroeconomics*. New York: Springer.

Greenaway, D., D. Sapsford, and S. Pfaffenzeller (2007). 'Foreign direct investment, economic performance and trade liberalisation'. *The World Economy* 30.2, 197–210.

Hayek, F. (1945). 'The use of knowledge in society'. *American Economic Review* 35.4, 519–30.

Radetzki, M. (2010). *A Handbook of Primary Commodities in the Global Economy*. Cambridge: Cambridge University Press.

Romer, D. (2006). *Advanced Macroeconomics*. 3 edn. New York: McGraw-Hill Higher Education.

Toye, J. and R. Toye (2003). 'The origins and interpretation of the Prebisch–Singer thesis'. *History of Political Economy* 35.3, 437–67.

Data sources

Commodity price data

The data for the Grilli and Yang data set were updated as in Pfaffenzeller, Newbold, and Rayner (2007) where possible. Data for jute were updated directly from the Food and Agriculture Organization website from 2004 onwards (F.O.B. Mongla, at sight (Friday closing price)). The series for beef, wool, and hides were obtained as annual averages from monthly IMF commodity data. The series for rubber was continued with the 'Rubber TSA20, nearby futures contract' series from the World Bank data set from 2012 onwards. Wheat data had to be updated from the HGCA International Physical Data for 2012 and 2013. Timber prices were reconstructed from UK Forestry Commission questionnaire data.

Macroeconomic profile data

General data on country characteristics were obtained or computed from the World Bank's World Development Indicators. These variables include the value added and employment shares in the industrial, agricultural, service, and manufacturing sectors, the levels and growth rates of GDP, GDP per capita and the exchange rate, the net barter terms of trade, female employment outside the agricultural sector, and net exports.

PPP adjusted GDP per capita

Data on purchasing power parity adjusted GDP per capita were obtained from the Penn World Tables 8.1 from the series for expenditure-side real GDP at current PPPs (in millions of 2005 US dollars) and population (in millions).

Trade data by SITC

Trade data for trade with China and the rest of the world were retrieved from the United Nation's Comtrade database via the UK Data Service (UKDS).

Manufacturing data by ISIC

Manufacturing data classified by ISIC were obtained from the UNIDO Industrial Statistics database via UKDS: United Nations Industrial Development Organization (2015): INDSTAT2 Industrial Statistics Database (Edition: 2015). UK Data Service. DOI: http://dx.doi.org/10.5257/unido/indstat2/2015 (accessed on 10th May 2016).

Index

For Product Safety Concerns and Information please contact our EU
representative GPSR@taylorandfrancis.com
Taylor & Francis Verlag GmbH, Kaufingerstraße 24, 80331 München, Germany

www.ingramcontent.com/pod-product-compliance
Ingram Content Group UK Ltd.
Pitfield, Milton Keynes, MK11 3LW, UK
UKHW020948180425
457613UK00019B/581